200
FUN THINGS
to Crochet

200 FUN THINGS to Crochet

DECORATIVE FLOWERS, LEAVES, BUGS, BUTTERFLIES, AND MORE!

Edited by Victoria Lyle

St. Martin's Griffin
New York

Library of Congress Cataloging-in-Publication Data available
upon request

ISBN: 978-1-250-11173-9

Our books may be purchased in bulk for promotional,
educational, or business use. Please contact your local
bookseller or the Macmillan Corporate and Premium
Sales Department at (800) 221-7945, extension 5442,
or by e-mail at MacmillanSpecialMarkets@macmillan.com.

First U.S. Edition: January 2017

10 9 8 7 6 5 4 3 2 1

Conceived, designed, and produced by
Quarto Publishing plc
The Old Brewery
6 Blundell Street
London N7 9BH
www.quartoknows.com

QUAR·FNTC

Additional designs: Jan Eaton, Caroline Sullivan
Pattern checkers: Betty Barnden, Lucia Calza, Susan Horan,
Lucille Kazel
Illustrators: Kuo Kang Chen, Coral Mula, John Woodcock
Photographers: Simon Pask, Phil Wilkins
Art director: Caroline Guest
Creative director: Moira Clinch
Publisher: Sam Warrington

Printed by 1010 Printing International Ltd, China

Note

The patterns in this book have previously appeared in:
- *100 Flowers to Knit & Crochet* by Lesley Stanfield
- *75 Birds, Butterflies & Little Beasts to Knit & Crochet*
  by Lesley Stanfield
- *75 Seashells, Fish, Coral & Colorful Marine Life to Knit
  & Crochet* by Jessica Polka
- *50 Sunflowers to Knit, Crochet & Felt* by Kristin Nicholas
- *75 Floral Blocks to Crochet* by Betty Barnden

Caution

Designs that are stiffened with wire, incorporate pins or
hairpins, or are decorated with beads or sequins are not
suitable for babies and young children. When making
items for youngsters, always use top-quality, clean stuffing
marked as suitable for toys, and sew on any small parts
(such as petals) very securely.

CONTENTS

ABOUT THIS BOOK

This book provides a delightful collection of 200 fun things to crochet, from flowers and plants to fish, bugs, and other critters. Each of these gorgeous creations can be used to embellish garments and accessories. There is also a collection of floral blocks for creating afghans or other projects of your own devising. Begin by looking through the pattern selector (pages 7–29), which displays all 200 designs in miniature together, select your design, and then turn to the instructions page to create your chosen piece. At the back of the book you will find some tips on crochet techniques (pages 208–221).

Skill level

Each design is accompanied by a symbol indicating the skill level required.

Basic

Intermediate

Advanced

A crochet hook symbol indicates the skill level required, from 1 to 3.

The type of yarn and any other necessary extras are specified at the beginning of each pattern.

Charts are provided for the majority of the designs to amplify the instructions (a few are not included due to space constraints).

Full written instructions are provided for each design.

Blocks of the same shape are all the same size, for easy mixing and matching.

Mix and match suggestions are shown for a selection of the floral blocks.

Assembly diagrams are provided where helpful.

Chart symbols specific to a design are explained next to the chart. See page 222 for a list of the standard crochet symbols used in this book.

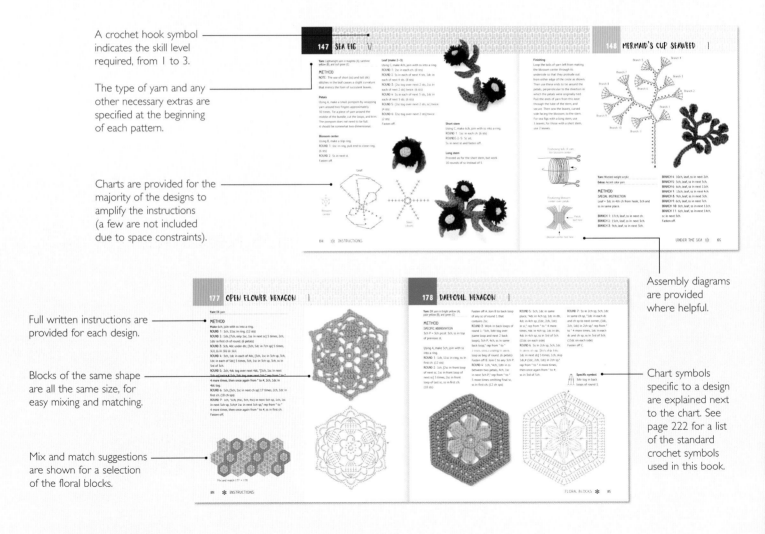

FLOWER GARDEN

HELLEBORE
page 30

MECONOPSIS
page 30

SWEET PEA
page 31

FOXGLOVE
page 32

LAZY DAISY
page 33

CHRYSANTHEMUM
page 33

WILD ROSE
page 34

ASTER
page 34

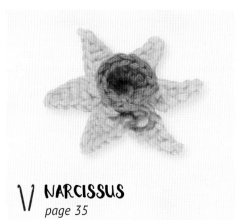

NARCISSUS
page 35

FLOWER GARDEN

PANSY
page 36

BUTTERCUP
page 37

BORAGE
page 37

FUCHSIA
page 38

OLD-FASHIONED PINK
page 38

DIANTHUS
page 39

PRIMULA
page 40

SCABIOUS
page 40

CAMELLIA
page 41

\/ **AURICULA**
page 42

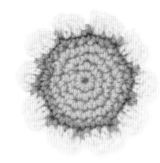

\/ **CHAMOMILE**
page 42

| **MICHAELMAS DAISY**
page 43

\|/ **MARIGOLD**
page 44

| **TRADESCANTIA**
page 45

\/ **PELARGONIUM**
page 45

\/ **HELENIUM**
page 46

\/ **SANTOLINA**
page 46

\/ **LILY OF THE VALLEY**
page 47

FLOWER GARDEN

\|/ **PERIWINKLE**
page 48

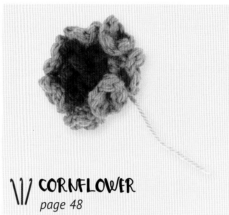

\|\/ **CORNFLOWER**
page 48

\|\/ **VIOLA**
page 49

\|\/ **ROSETTE**
page 50

\|\/ **GERBERA**
page 51

\|/ **GERANIUM**
page 52

\|/ **ZINNIA**
page 52

\|\/ **ORIENTAL POPPY**
page 53

\|/ **BACHELOR'S BUTTON**
page 54

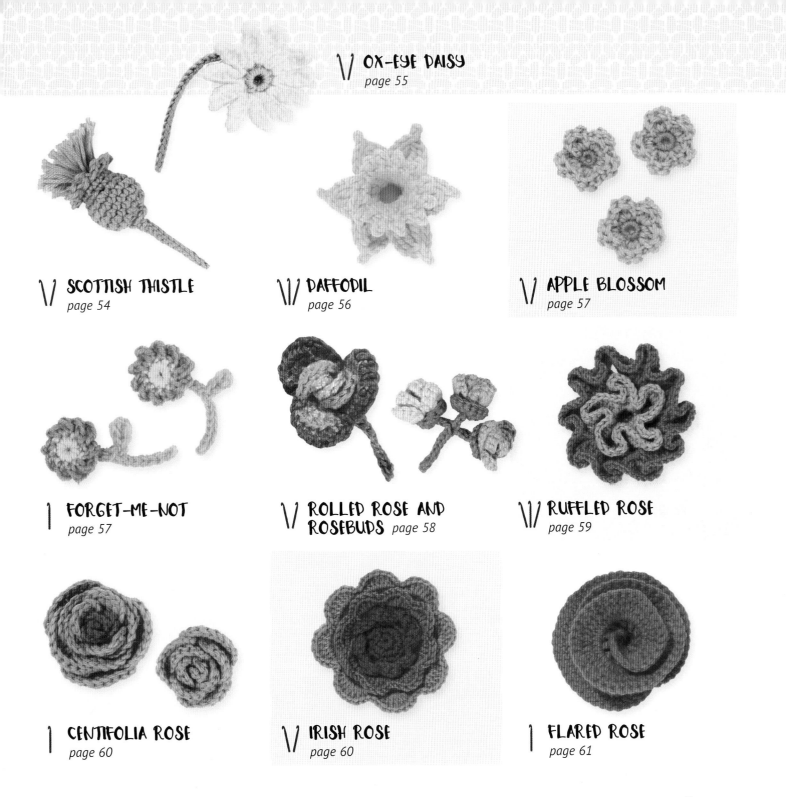

\\/ OX-EYE DAISY
page 55

\\/ SCOTTISH THISTLE
page 54

\\\/ DAFFODIL
page 56

\\/ APPLE BLOSSOM
page 57

| FORGET-ME-NOT
page 57

\\/ ROLLED ROSE AND
ROSEBUDS *page 58*

\\\/ RUFFLED ROSE
page 59

| CENTIFOLIA ROSE
page 60

\\/ IRISH ROSE
page 60

| FLARED ROSE
page 61

SUNFLOWER MEADOW

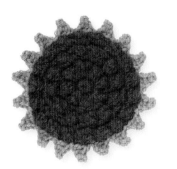

COMMON SUNFLOWER
page 62

STARBURST
page 62

OPENWORK STAR
page 63

SMALL BUD
page 64

LARGE BUD
page 64

PURPLE PASSION
page 65

AZTEC GOLD
page 66

SEA ANEMONE
page 67

BICOLOR GEM
page 68

LACE SUNBEAM
page 69

AUTUMN BEAUTY
page 70

LITTLE GEM
page 71

SUNBRIGHT
page 72

SUNBURST
page 72

RASPBERRY RUFFLE
page 73

SUNFLOWER MEADOW

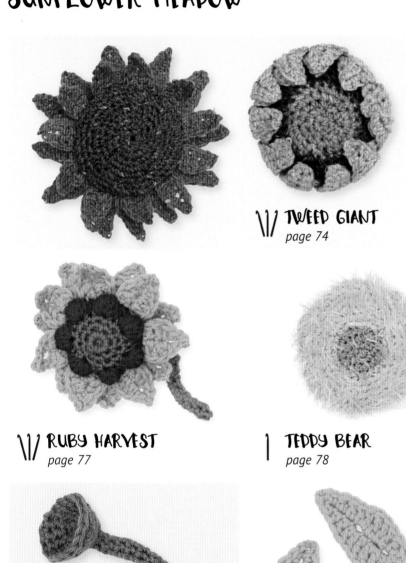

\\// **TWEED GIANT**
page 74

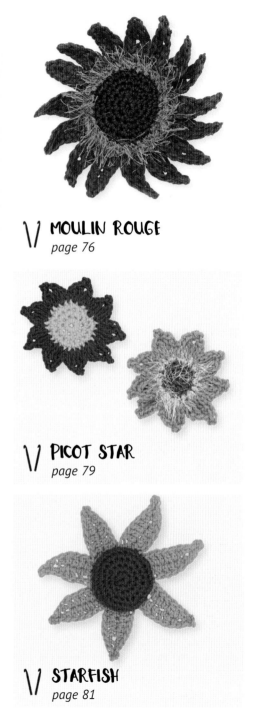

\\/ **MOULIN ROUGE**
page 76

\\// **RUBY HARVEST**
page 77

| **TEDDY BEAR**
page 78

\\/ **PICOT STAR**
page 79

\\/ **FLOWER BACK AND STEM**
page 80

| **SUNFLOWER PETALS**
page 80

\\/ **STARFISH**
page 81

PLANT LIFE

TEARDROP AND TOOTHED LEAVES
page 82

TULIP TREE LEAF
page 83

IRISH LEAF
page 84

IVY LEAF
page 84

FERN LEAF
page 85

GINKGO LEAF
page 86

PLAIN CLOVER LEAF
page 87

VARIEGATED CLOVER LEAF
page 87

PLANT LIFE

\\/ **SPRING OAK LEAF**
page 88

\\/ **AUTUMN OAK LEAF**
page 88

\\|| **ACORN**
page 89

| **NETTLE LEAF**
page 90

| **MISTLETOE**
page 90

\\|| **HOLLY LEAF AND BERRIES** *page 91*

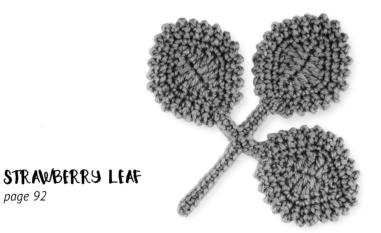

\\/ **STRAWBERRY LEAF**
page 92

| **STRAWBERRY**
page 93

\|/ **FIG**
page 94

\|/ **FIG LEAF**
page 95

\/ **LIME AND LEAF**
page 96

\/ **GRAPES**
page 97

\/ **EAR OF WHEAT**
page 97

\|/ **APPLE**
page 98

\/ **OLIVES**
page 100

\/ **WAXCAP**
page 101

\/ **PORCINI MUSHROOM**
page 102

PLANT LIFE

RADISHES
page 104

CHILI
page 104

PEAPOD
page 105

CORN
page 106

BELL PEPPER
page 107

STRIPED SQUASH
page 108

YELLOW SQUASH
page 109

CUTE CRITTERS

BEETLE
page 110

SLEEPING LADYBUG
page 110

\\/ **FLYING LADYBUG**
page 111

\\/ **BUMBLEBEE**
page 113

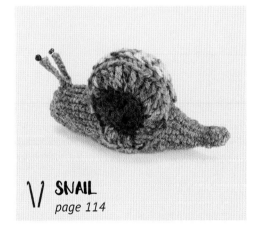

FURRY CATERPILLAR
page 113

\\/ **SNAIL**
page 114

SPIDER
page 115

\\// **MONARCH BUTTERFLY**
page 116

\\/ **GOLDEN HAIRSTREAK**
page 118

\\// **ORANGE TIP**
page 118

CUTE CRITTERS

\/ **RED ADMIRAL**
page 119

\\/ **LARGE WHITE**
page 120

\\/ **CAMBERWELL BEAUTY**
page 122

\/ **BRIMSTONE**
page 123

\/ **CLOUDED YELLOW**
page 124

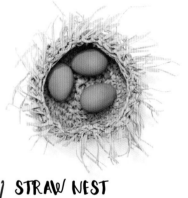

\/ **STRAW NEST**
page 125

| **FEATHERED NEST**
page 126

| **PIGEON FEATHER**
page 126

\/ **HEN'S EGG**
page 127

UNDER THE SEA

GOLDFISH
page 128

HERRING
page 129

SARDINE
page 130

BLUE DAMSELFISH
page 131

GOBY
page 132

BLUE LINE GROUPER
page 133

PURPLE GAMMA
page 134

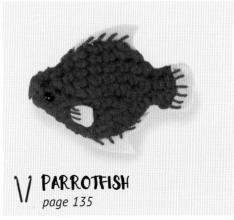

PARROTFISH
page 135

HAMMERHEAD SHARK
page 136

UNDER THE SEA

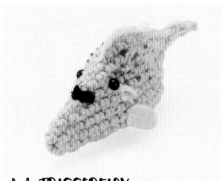

TRIGGERFISH
page 137

ANGLERFISH
page 138

DOLPHIN
page 140

SPERM WHALE
page 141

PYGMY OCTOPUS
page 142

DUMBO OCTOPUS
page 143

SHRIMP
page 144

HERMIT CRAB
page 145

SEAHORSE
page 146

BLUE STARFISH
page 147

ANEMONE
page 148

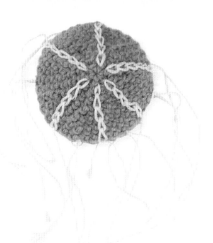

PHOSPHORESCENT JELLYFISH *page 149*

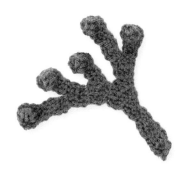

BRANCHING SEAWEED
page 150

SEA URCHIN SHEL
page 151

CAULASTREA POLYPS
page 152

BULLION CORAL
page 153

SEA FIG
page 154

MERMAID'S CUP SEAWEED
page 155

FLORAL BLOCKS

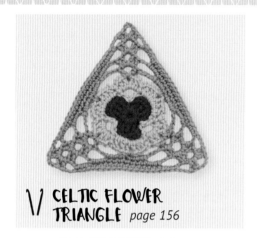

\V CELTIC FLOWER
TRIANGLE *page 156*

\V VIOLET TRIANGLE
page 157

| WINDFLOWER TRIANGLE
page 158

| GERANIUM TRIANGLE
page 159

\\| CENTAURY TRIANGLE
page 160

\\| LILY TRIANGLE
page 161

| MICHAELMAS DAISY
TRIANGLE *page 162*

\/ JONQUIL TRIANGLE
page 163

CELTIC FLOWER SQUARE
page 164

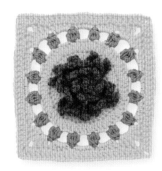

CHRYSANTHEMUM SQUARE
page 165

STAR FLOWER SQUARE
page 166

CORAL TRELLIS SQUARE
page 167

LACY DAISY SQUARE
page 168

SUNFLOWER SQUARE
page 169

IRISH ROSE SQUARE
page 170

POPPY SQUARE
page 171

EMBOSSED FLOWER SQUARE *page 172*

FLORAL BLOCKS

THREE DAISY SQUARE
page 173

TULIP SQUARE
page 174

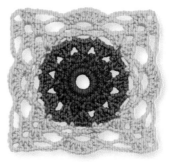

SNEEZEWORT SQUARE
page 175

OFF-CENTER SQUARE
page 176

RUFFLED FLOWER SQUARE *page 177*

DANDELION DIAMOND
page 178

ASTER DIAMOND
page 179

KINGCUP DIAMOND
page 180

IRISH DIAMOND
page 181

CLEMATIS DIAMOND
page 182

FOUR DAISY DIAMOND
page 183

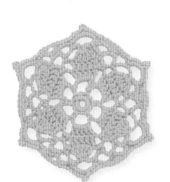

OPEN FLOWER HEXAGON
page 184

DAFFODIL HEXAGON
page 185

OPEN DAHLIA HEXAGON
page 186

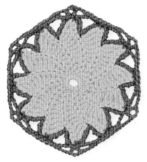

SPINNING DAHLIA HEXAGON *page 187*

SNOWDROP HEXAGON
page 188

SPIRAL WINDFLOWER HEXAGON *page 189*

FLORAL BLOCKS

\/ **DIANTHUS HEXAGON**
page 190

\/ **OLD FRENCH ROSE HEXAGON** *page 191*

\/ **CORNFLOWER HEXAGON**
page 192

\/ **LARGE FLOWER HEXAGON**
page 193

\/ **BUSY LIZZIE HEXAGON**
page 194

\/ **GARLAND HEXAGON**
page 195

\/ **SWIRLING HEXAGON**
page 196

| **SPRING MEADOW HEXAGON** *page 197*

\/ **THISTLE CIRCLE**
page 198

FLORAL CIRCLE
page 199

POPCORN FLOWER CIRCLE
page 200

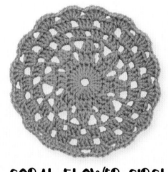

CORAL FLOWER CIRCLE
page 201

\/ **BUTTERFLY CIRCLE**
page 202

\/ **PENNY FLOWER CIRCLE**
page 203

HELENIUM CIRCLE
page 204

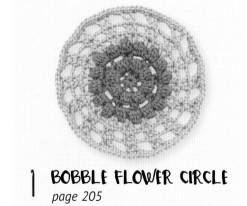

BOBBLE FLOWER CIRCLE
page 205

\/ **DANDELION CIRCLE**
page 206

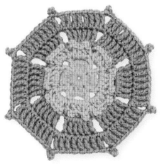

CELTIC FLOWER CIRCLE
page 207

HELLEBORE 1

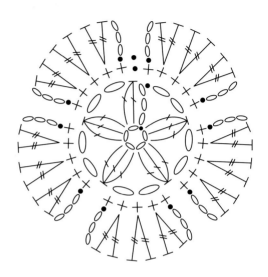

Yarn: Fine cotton in yellow (A), ocher (B), and pale green (C)

METHOD

Center

Using A, make 5ch, join with ss into a ring.

ROUND 1: 3ch, 2dc cluster, 2ch, [3dc cluster, 2ch] 4 times, with B ss in top ch of 3ch. (5 clusters and 5 ch sp)
Continue with B.
ROUND 2: [5sc in ch sp] 5 times, with C ss in first sc. (25 sts)
Continue with C.

ROUND 3: [Ss in next sc, 3ch, 2tr in each of next 3sc, 3ch, ss in next sc] 5 times, ss in first ss.
Fasten off invisibly.

---

2 MECONOPSIS 1

Yarn: DK wool in yellow (A) and blue (B)

METHOD

Using A, make 6ch, join with ss into a ring.
ROUND 1: 1ch, 9sc in ring, with B ss to 1ch. (10 sts)
Continue with B.

ROUND 2: [4ch, 2tr cluster in next sc, 4ch, 1sc in next sc] 5 times, ending ss in 1ch of round 1.
Fasten off invisibly.

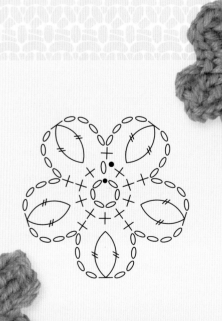

SWEET PEA 1

Yarn: Sport-weight yarn in green (A) and pastel colors (B)

METHOD

Sepals

Using A, make 4ch, join with ss into a ring.

ROUND 1: 4ch, 7tr in ring, RS to the outside, roll into a tube and ss in top ch of 4ch. (8 sts)

ROUND 2: [4ch, skip 3ch, 1sc in next ch, ss in each of next 2 sts] 4 times, ending ss in first ch. (4 sepals)

Fasten off.

Petals

Using B, make 7ch.

ROW 1: Skip 4ch, 1tr in each of next 3 sts. (4 sts)

ROW 2: 2ch, 1sc in st below, 2sc in each of next 2 sts, 2sc in top ch of 4ch. (8 sts)

ROW 3: 2ch, 1hdc in st below, 2dc in next st, 2tr in next st, 2dtr in next st, 1ch, 2dtr in next st, 2tr in next st, 2dc in next st, (1hdc, 1sc) in top ch of 2ch.

Fasten off.

Stem

Using A, make a 6in (15cm) long ch, skip 1ch, ss in each remaining ch. Fasten off.

Finishing

Join ends of rows 1 and 2 of petals, insert this tube in the tube formed by the sepals, and catch together lightly. Attach the stem to the base of the flower.

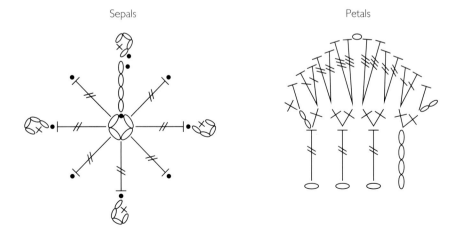

Sepals

Petals

FOXGLOVE \/

Yarn: Sport-weight yarn in pink (A) and green (B)

Extras: Strong wire (e.g. fencing wire)

METHOD

Larger flower (make 7)

Using A, make a slip ring.

ROUND 1: 3ch, 5dc in ring, pull end to close ring, ss in top ch of 3ch. (6 sts)*

ROUND 2: 4ch, 1tr in each of next 5 sts, ss in top ch of 4ch.

ROUND 3: 3ch, 1dc in st below, 2dc in next st, 3ch, ss in same st, ss in next st, 4ch, 1tr in same st, [2tr in next st] twice, 1tr in next st, 4ch, ss in same st. (13 sts) Fasten off.

Smaller flower (make 5)

Work as larger flower to *.

ROUND 2: 3ch, 1dc in each of next 5dc, ss in top ch of 3ch.

ROUND 3: 3ch, 2dc in next dc, 3ch, ss in next dc, 1ch, 2sc in each of next 2dc, ss in next dc. Fasten off.

Calyx (make 5)

Using B, work as larger flower to *.

ROUND 2: 3ch, 1dc in st below, 1dc in next st, 3ch, ss in same st, [ss in next st, 3ch, 1dc in same st, 1dc in next st, 3ch, ss in same st] twice. (12 sts) Fasten off.

Stem

Bend one end of the wire into a small loop. Using B, cover the loop and stem with sc, fastening off securely.

Finishing

Fit each flower into a calyx and close the ends of the remaining three to make buds. Starting at the looped end of the wire, attach the buds, then the smaller flowers, alternating each one. Attach the larger flowers in the same way.

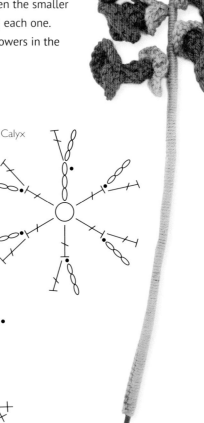

Calyx

Larger flower

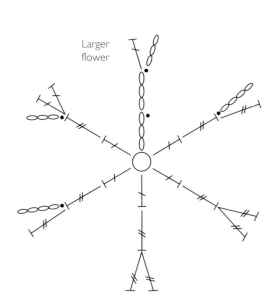

Smaller flower

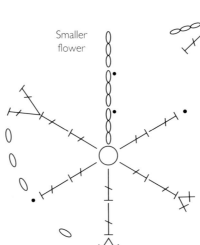

5 LAZY DAISY |

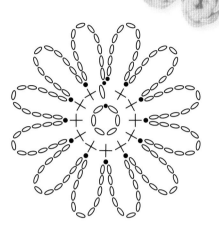

Yarn: DK cotton in yellow (A) and white (B)

METHOD
Center
Using A, make 6ch, join with ss into a ring.
ROUND 1: 1ch, 11sc in ring, using B ss in
1ch. (12 sts)

Petals
Continue with B.
ROUND 2: [11ch, ss in next sc] 12 times,
ending ss in ss of round 1.
Fasten off invisibly.

6 CHRYSANTHEMUM |

Yarn: DK wool

METHOD
Make 4ch.
DOUBLE ROW 1: Skip 2ch, 1sc in
each of next 2ch, 17ch, turn, 1sc in
each of 2sc, 1sc in top ch of 2ch.
DOUBLE ROW 2: 1ch, 1sc in each of
next 2sc, 17ch, turn, 1sc in each of
2sc, 1sc in 1ch.
Repeat double row 2, 34 times.
Fasten off.

Finishing
Pin out loops and press. Coil the
straight edge, stitching as you go.

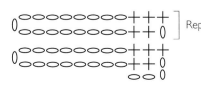

7   WILD ROSE   \/

Yarn: DK wool in yellow (A), white (B), and pink (C)

METHOD

Center

Using A, make a slip ring.

ROUND 1: 2ch, 9sc in ring, pull end to close ring, using B ss in top ch of 2ch. (10 sts)
Continue with B.

ROUND 2: 1ch, [2sc in next sc, 1sc in next sc] 4 times, 2sc in next sc, using C ss in 1ch. (15 sts)
Fasten off. Continue with C.

First petal

ROW 1 (RS): 1ch, 1sc in each of next 2sc. (3 sts)

ROW 2: 1ch, 1sc in next sc, 1sc in 1ch.

ROW 3: 4ch, (1dtr, 1tr) in sc below, 1dc in next sc, (1tr, 1dtr, 1tr) in 1ch. (7 sts)
Fasten off invisibly.

2nd petal (RS)

Join C in next sc of round 2 and then work as first petal. Make 3 more petals as the 2nd petal.

Stamens

Cut 4 lengths of A, each approximately 4¾in (12cm) long. Thread one onto a yarn needle, leaving an end long enough to knot, take it through the edge of the center ring, make a backstitch on the WS, and bring it to the front. Do the same with remaining lengths of A, then knot them and trim.

8   ASTER   \/

Yarn: Fine cotton in dark green (A), pale green (B), and mauve (C)

METHOD

Flower

Leaving a long end, use A to make a slip ring.

ROW 1: 3ch, 4dc in ring, pull end to close ring. (5 sts)

ROW 2: 3ch, 2dc in each of next 3dc, 1dc in top ch of 3ch. (8 sts)
Fasten off.

ROW 3: Join B in front strand of top of last dc, [5ch, ss in front strand of next dc] 6 times, 5ch, ss in front strand of top ch of 3ch. (7 loops)
Fasten off invisibly.

ROW 4: With RS facing, fold loops forward and join C in back strand of end dc of row 2, [8ch, skip 1ch, 1sc in next ch, 1hdc in next ch, 1dc in each of next 3ch, 1hdc in next ch, 1sc in next ch, ss in back strand of next dc] 7 times, ending ss in back strand of top ch of 3ch of row 2.
Fasten off invisibly.

Stem

RS facing, insert hook in slip ring at base and pull long end through. Make 10ch, skip 1ch, ss in each of 9ch. Fasten off invisibly.

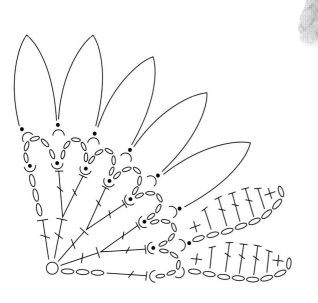

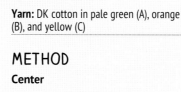

Yarn: DK cotton in pale green (A), orange (B), and yellow (C)

METHOD

Center

Using A, make 4ch, join with ss into a ring.

ROUND 1: 1ch, 5sc in ring, using B ss to 1ch. (6 sts)

Continue with B.

ROUND 2: 3ch, working in the front strand of each st: 1dc in ss below, 2dc in each of next 5sc, ss in top ch of 3ch. (12 sts)

Fasten off invisibly.

Petals

Place left thumb inside the center and, RS facing, work in the back strand of each st of round 1: join C in a sc of round 1, [6ch, skip 1ch, 1sc in next ch, 1hdc in next ch, 1dc in next ch, 1tr in next ch, 1dtr in next ch, ss in next st of round 1] 6 times, ending ss in same st as join.

Fasten off.

Center

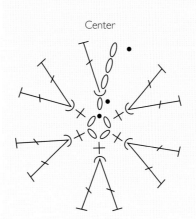

Petals

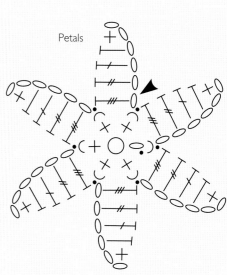

Yarn: DK wool in yellow (A), purple (B), and mauve (C)

METHOD

Center and first petal

Using A, make 6ch, join with ss into a ring.

ROW 1 (RS): 2ch, 2sc in ring, working last wrap with B 1sc in ring. (4 sts)

Continue with B.

ROW 2: 3ch, 1dc in sc below, 2tr in each of next 2sc, 2dc in top ch of 2ch. (8 sts)

Fasten off invisibly.

ROW 3 (RS): Join C in base of post of last dc of previous row, 1ch, 1sc in post of dc, (1sc, 1ch, 1dc) in top of dc, 1ch, (1tr, 1dtr) in next dc, 2tr in each of next 4tr, (1dtr, 1tr) in next dc, 1ch, (1dc, 1ch, 1sc) in top ch of 3ch, 1sc in next ch, ss in next ch.

Fasten off invisibly.

2nd petal

Join B in center ch ring.

ROW 1 (RS): 2ch, 2sc in ring. (3 sts)

ROW 2: 3ch, 1tr in sc below, 1tr in next sc, (1tr, 1dc) in top ch of 2ch. (5 sts)

Fasten off.

ROW 3 (RS): Join C in base of post of last dc of previous row, 1ch, 1sc in post of dc, (1sc, 1ch, 1dc) in top of dc, 1ch, (1tr, 1dtr) in next tr, 1ch, 2tr in next tr, 1ch, (1dtr, 1tr) in next tr, 1ch, (1dc, 1ch, 1sc) in top ch of 3ch, 1sc in next ch, ss in next ch.

Fasten off invisibly.

3rd petal

As 2nd petal. Weave in ends.

4th petal

With RS facing, join C in first sc in A on first petal, working behind center petals make 4ch, 1sc in base of 2ch of row 1 of first petal, turn.

ROW 1 (WS): *4ch, 3tr around ch bar. (4 sts)

ROW 2: 3ch, 1tr in tr below, 2tr in each of next 2tr, (1tr, 1dc) in top ch of 4ch. (8 sts)

Fasten off.

ROW 3: RS facing, rejoin C in base of first tr of row 1, 1ch, 1sc in post of tr, 1sc in top of tr, 1sc in each of first 2ch of row 2, (2sc, 1ch, 1dc) in top ch, 1ch, 2tr in next tr, 1tr in each of next 3tr, 2tr in next tr, 1ch, (1dc, 1ch, 1sc) in next tr, 3sc in post of next dc, 1sc in each of next 2ch, ss in next ch.

Fasten off invisibly.

5th petal

With WS facing, join C in ch bar, then work as 4th petal from *.

Finishing

Press petals separately. Catch together 4th and 5th petals, slightly overlapping rows 1 and 2.

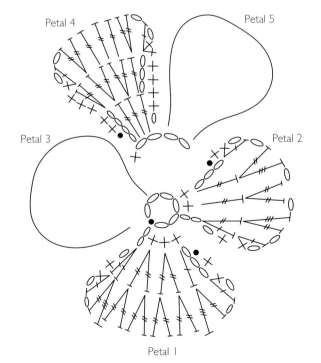

Petal 4

Petal 5

Petal 3

Petal 2

Petal 1

11 BUTTERCUP

Yarn: Fine cotton in green (A), lime (B) and yellow

ROUND 3: [2ch, 2dc...

METHOD

Using A,
into a rin
ROUND 1
ss in 1ch
Continue
ROUND 2
3sc in ea
ss in 1ch
Continue

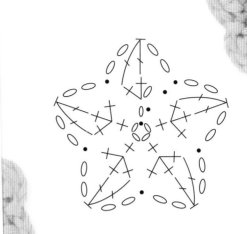

12

Yarn: DK w
pale green (

METHOD

Flower (make 7)

Using A, make 6ch, join with ss
into a ring,
ROUND 1: [2ch, 2dc, 2ch, ss in
ring] 4 times. (4 petals)
Fasten off.
ROUND 2: Using B, join yarn
between petals, [1sc between
petals and into ring, 1ch behind
petal] 4 times, ss in back of first
sc, make 10ch for stem.
Fasten off invisibly.

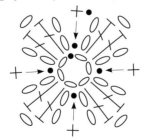

Specific symbol

+ 1sc worked over sc and
↓ ring into center space.

13 FUCHSIA \\\//

Yarn: Fine cotton in pink (A) and purple (B)

METHOD
Outer flower

Using A, make 4ch, join with ss into a ring.

ROUND 1: 3ch, 5dc in ring, ss in top ch of 3ch. (6 sts)

ROUND 2: 2ch, 1sc in st below, 2sc in each of next 5dc, ss in top ch of 2ch. (12 sts)

ROUND 3: 4ch, 1tr in each of next 11sc, ss in top ch of 4ch.

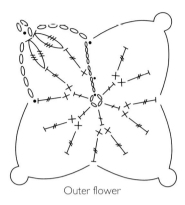

Outer flower

ROUND 4: [5ch, 2dtr cluster in next tr, 3ch, skip 2ch, ss in next ch, 2dtr cluster in next tr, 5ch, ss in next tr] 4 times, ending ss in ss of previous round. Fasten off invisibly.

Bell

Using B, make 6ch, join with ss into a ring.

ROUND 1: 2ch, 8sc in ring, ss in top ch of 2ch. (9 sts)

ROUND 2: 3ch, 1dc in each of next 8sc, ss in top ch of 3ch.

ROUND 3: 5ch, 1dtr in next dc, [2dtr in next dc, 1dtr in each of next 2dc] twice, 2dtr in next dc, ss in top ch of 5ch. (12 sts) Fasten off invisibly.

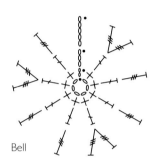

Bell

14 OLD-FASHIONED PINK \\/

Yarn: Fine cotton in pink (A), magenta (B), and white (C)

METHOD
Center

Using A, make a slip ring.

ROUND 1: 3ch, 9dc in ring, pull end to close ring, with B ss in top ch of 3ch. (10 sts)
Continue with B.

ROUND 2: 1ch, 1sc in st below, 2sc in each of next 9dc, with C ss in 1ch. (20 sts)
Continue with C.

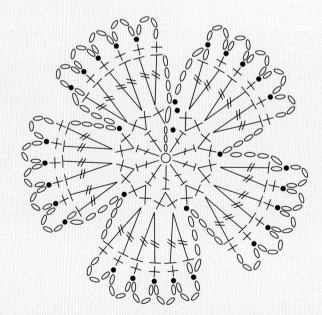

First petal

ROW 1: 4ch, 2tr in each of next 3sc, turn.

ROW 2: 1ch, 1sc in each of next 5tr.

ROW 3: [4ch, ss in next sc] 4 times, 4ch, ss in 1ch, do not turn, 4ch, ss in next sc of round 2.

Without fastening off, work 4 more petals in this way, ending ss in first ch of first petal. Fasten off invisibly.

Stem

Using A, make 15ch, skip 1ch, ss in each of next 14ch. Fasten off.

Stamens

Cut 3 short lengths of A, knot the ends and trim.

Finishing

Sew on stem. Attach bell inside flower, then stamens inside bell.

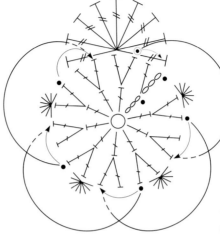

Specific symbols

Take hook behind petal just made (round 3).

Final ss of round 3.

Yarn: Fine cotton in pink (A), magenta (B), and white (C)

METHOD

Center

Using A, make a slip ring.
ROUND 1: 3ch, 9dc in ring, pull end to close ring, with B ss in top ch of 3ch. (10 sts)
Continue with B.
ROUND 2: 3ch, 1dc in st below, 2dc in each of next 9dc, with C ss in top ch of 3ch. (20 sts)
Continue with C.

Petals

ROUND 3: Skip 2dc, *9tr in next dc, skip 2dc, ss in next dc, take hook behind petal just made and insert from front to back in first dc after petal center, yo and pull yarn through dc and loop on hook;** making next 9-st petal in dc immediately after ss of previous petal, repeat from * to ** 4 times, ending 5th petal with ss in the dc before the center of first petal, then take hook behind petal just made and ss in top of first tr of first petal. Fasten off.
ROUND 4: Join B in first tr of a petal, 1ch, [1sc in next tr, 1ch] 8 times, 1sc in ss.
Fasten off invisibly.
Edge each petal in this way.

16 PRIMULA \/

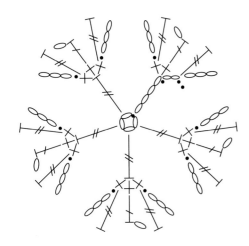

Yarn: DK yarn (split into 2 strands) in green (A), yellow (B), and pale yellow (C)

METHOD

Flower

Using A and leaving a long end, make 4ch, join with ss into a ring.

ROUND 1: 4ch, 4tr in ring, with B ss in top ch of 4ch. (5 sts)

This forms a tube with WS of sts to the outside. Now, using B, work around top of tube.

ROUND 2 (RS): 2ch, 2sc in ss, 3sc in each of next 4tr, with C ss in top ch of 2ch. (15 sts)

Continue with C.

ROUND 3: *3ch, 1tr in ss, 1dc in next sc, 1ch, 1tr in next sc, 3ch, ss in same sc as tr, ss in next sc; repeat from * 4 times, working last ss in ss of round 2.

Stem

Insert hook in base of first round, pull through long end of A, make 6ch, skip 1ch, ss in each of next 5ch. Fasten off.

17 SCABIOUS \/

Yarn: DK wool in pale blue (A) and deep blue (B)

METHOD

Center

Using A, make a slip ring.

ROUND 1: 3ch, 15dc in ring, pull end to close ring, ss in top ch of 3ch. (16 sts)

ROUND 2: 4ch, [ss in front strand of next dc, 3ch] 15 times, ss in first ch of 4ch.

Fasten off invisibly.

Petals

ROUND 3: Working behind round 2 and into round 1: join B in top ch of 3ch, 6ch, working in back strand of each dc: [ss in next dc, 5ch] 15 times, ss in first ch of 6ch.

Fasten off invisibly.

Center

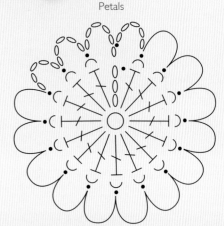

Petals

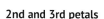

Yarn: DK wool in green (A), yellow (B), and deep pink (C)

METHOD

Center

Using A, make a slip ring.

ROUND 1: 1ch, 6sc in ring, pull end to close ring. Fasten off invisibly.

Join B in a sc of round 1.

ROUND 2: 1ch, [1sc, 3ch, 1sc] in each sc, remove hook, insert from back in first sc, catch loop and pull through. (6 picots)

ROUND 3: 1ch, [insert hook from back between 2sc of round 2, work 1sc in next sc of round 1, 1ch] 6 times, ss in 1ch. Fasten off.

First petal

Join C in a sc of round 3.

ROW 1: 1ch, 5sc in same sc as join, remove hook, insert from back in same sc of round 3, catch loop and pull through. (5 sts)

ROW 2: 1ch, 2sc in first sc, 1sc in each of next 3sc, 2sc in last sc, remove hook, insert from front in same sc of round 3, catch loop and pull through. (7 sts)

ROW 3: 1ch, 2sc in first sc, 1sc in each of next 5sc, 2sc in last sc, remove hook, insert from back in same sc of round 3, catch loop and pull through. (9 sts)

ROW 4: 1ch, 2sc in first sc, 1sc in each of next 7sc, 2sc in last sc, remove hook, insert from front in same sc of round 3, catch loop and pull through. (11 sts)

ROW 5: 1ch, 2sc in first sc, 1sc in each of next 9sc, 2sc in last sc, remove hook, insert from back in same sc of round 3, catch loop and pull through. (13 sts) Fasten off.

2nd and 3rd petals

Leaving 1ch, 1sc, 1ch of round 3 of center free between petals each time, work as first petal.

4th petal

Join C in sc between first and 2nd petals.

ROW 1: 1ch, (1sc, 3dc, 1sc) in same sc as join, remove hook, insert from back in same sc of round 3, catch loop and pull through. (5 sts)

ROW 2: 1ch, 2sc in first sc, 1dc in each of next 3dc, 2sc in last sc, insert hook from front in same sc of round 3, catch loop and pull through. (7 sts)

ROW 3: 1ch, 2sc in first sc, 1dc in each of next 5 sts, 2sc in last sc, insert hook from back in same sc of round 3, catch loop and pull through. (9 sts)

ROW 4: 1ch, 2sc in first sc, 2dc in each of next 7 sts, 2sc in last sc, insert hook from front in same sc of round 3, catch loop and pull through. (18 sts)

ROW 5: 1ch, 2sc in first sc, 1sc in each of next 16 sts, 2sc in last sc, insert hook from back in same sc of round 3, catch loop and pull through. (20 sts) Fasten off.

5th and 6th petals

Joining C between next 2 petals each time, work as 4th petal.

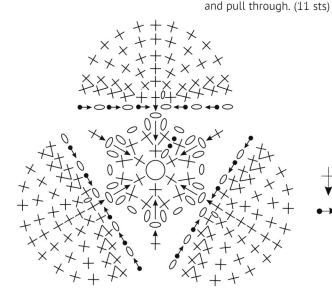

Specific symbols

1sc from back in sc of round 1.

Remove hook, insert in sc of round 3 (from back on RS rows, from front on WS rows), catch loop and pull through.

19 AURICULA \/

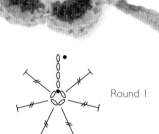

Yarn: Single strand of embroidery wool or fine wool in lime (A), cream (B), purple (C), and mauve (D)

METHOD

Flower

Using A and leaving an end of approximately 2in (5cm), make 4ch, join with ss into a ring.

ROUND 1: 4ch, 6tr in ring, ss to top ch of 4ch. (7 sts)
Fasten off invisibly.

ROUND 2: With inside of cup facing, join B in a tr, 4ch, 2tr in same tr, [1ch, 3tr in next st]

6 times, 1ch, with C ss in top ch of 4ch. (21 sts)
Continue with C.

ROUND 3: 3ch, 3dc in next tr, 1dc in next tr, [skip 1ch, 1ch, 1dc in next tr, 3dc in next tr, 1dc in next tr] 6 times, 1ch, with D ss in top ch of 3ch.
Continue with D.

ROUND 4: 1ch, 2dc in next dc, 2tr in next dc, 2dc in next dc, 1sc in next dc, 1sc around 1ch of round 3 and 1ch of round 2, [1sc in next dc, 2dc in next dc, 2tr in

next dc, 2dc in next dc, 1sc in next dc, 1sc around 1ch of round 3 and 1ch of round 2] 6 times, ss in 1ch. Fasten off invisibly.

Stem

Using A, make 15ch, skip 1ch, 1sc in each of next 14ch. Fasten off.

Finishing

Hook first A end into center of flower, knot the end close to the flower, and trim. Attach stem.

Round I

Specific symbol

+ 1sc around 1ch of round 3
↓ and 1ch of round 2.

20 CHAMOMILE \/

Yarn: Fine wool in yellow (A), green (B), and white (C)

METHOD

Center

Using A, make a slip ring.

ROUND 1: 2ch, 5sc in ring, pull end to close ring, ss in top ch of 2ch. (6 sts)

ROUND 2: 1ch, 1sc in st below, 2sc in each of next 5sc, ss in 1ch. (12 sts)

ROUND 3: 1ch, [2sc in next sc, 1sc in next sc] 5 times, 2sc in next sc, ss in 1ch. (18 sts)

ROUND 4: 1ch, [2sc in next sc, 1sc in each of next 2sc] 5 times, 2sc in next sc, 1sc in next sc, with B ss in 1ch. (24 sts)

ROUND 5: Using B, 1ch, [2sc in next sc, 1sc in each of next 3sc] 5 times, 2sc in next sc, 1sc in each of next 2sc, with C ss in 1ch. (30 sts)
Do not break off B.

ROUND 6: Using C, 3ch, [1dc in each of next 2sc, 7ch, skip 1sc] 9 times, 2dc in each of next 2sc, 3ch, ss in first ch of 3ch.
Fasten off.

ROUND 7: Using B, insert hook in st below join and make a sc over this, [3ch, folding petal forward, insert hook in empty sc of previous round, pull yarn through, then take hook over 7ch to make 1sc enclosing 7ch] 9 times, 3ch, ss in first sc. Fasten off.

Specific symbol

+ 1sc worked over ch and
↓ into sc of previous round.

Rounds 2–4

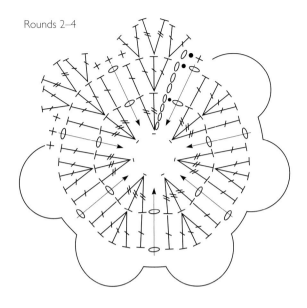

Yarn: Fine wool in mauve (A) and green (B)

METHOD

Petals

Using A, [make 9ch, skip 1ch, ss in each of next 8ch] 37 times. Fasten off. Pin out row of petals and press.

Center

With same side facing and using B, join yarn in space between first and 2nd petals, 3ch, 3dc tog in next 3 spaces, *4dc tog in next 4 spaces; repeat from * to end. Fasten off, leaving a long end.

Finishing

Coil the center so that there are 3 layers of petals. Gathering center slightly, stitch in place. Take yarn end from center and make stem: 15ch, skip 1ch, ss in each of next 14ch. Fasten off.

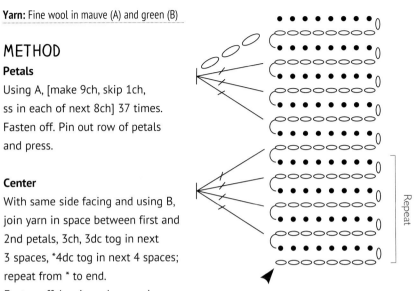

Repeat

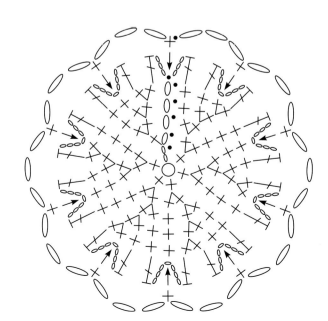

MARIGOLD \\/

Yarn: Fine cotton in orange (A) and green (B)

METHOD

Petals

Using A, make a slip ring.

ROUND 1: 2ch, 9sc in ring, pull end to close ring, ss in top ch of 2ch. (10 sts)

ROUND 2: [5ch, skip 1ch, ss in each of next 4ch, ss in front strand only of next st] 10 times. (10 petals)

ROUND 3: Bending petals forward in order to work into remaining strand of each st of round 1, ss in first st, 2ch, 1sc in each of next 9 sts, ss in top ch of 2ch. (10 sts)

ROUND 4: [5ch, skip 1ch, ss in each of next 4ch, ss in front strand only of st below, 5ch, skip 4ch, ss in each of next 4ch, ss in front strand of next st] 10 times. (20 petals)

ROUND 5: Bending petals forward in order to work into remaining strand of each st of round 3, ss in first st, then work as round 4, ending ss in first ss. (20 petals)
Fasten off.

Stem and sepals

Using B, make 11ch, skip 1ch, ss in each of next 10ch, 3ch, 7dc in remaining strand of top ch of stem, ss in top ch of 3ch, turn to work around inside of cup: [2ch, skip 1ch, ss in next ch, ss in next st] 8 times.
Fasten off invisibly.

Finishing

Using A, make a small tassel and string it with B. Thread B onto a yarn needle, take it through the center of the flower, and use it to secure the sepals and stem. Trim tassel.

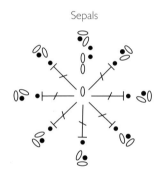

Sepals

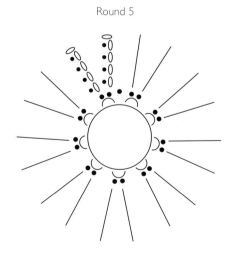

Rounds 1–2

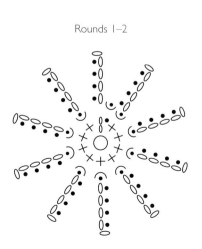

Rounds 3–4

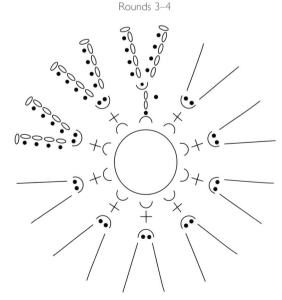

Round 5

23 TRADESCANTIA |

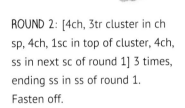

Yarn: DK wool in yellow (A) and purple (B)

METHOD

Using A, make 4ch, join with ss into a ring.

ROUND 1: 3ch, [1sc, 2ch] twice in ring, with B ss in first ch of 3ch. (3 sts and 3 ch sp)
Continue with B.

ROUND 2: [4ch, 3tr cluster in ch sp, 4ch, 1sc in top of cluster, 4ch, ss in next sc of round 1] 3 times, ending ss in ss of round 1.
Fasten off.

24 PELARGONIUM \/

Yarn: Fine cotton in pink (A) and green (B)

METHOD

Flower (make 5)

PETALS: Using A, [6ch, skip 5ch, 3dtr in next ch, 5ch, ss in first ch of 6ch] 5 times, join into a ring with ss in first ch.
Fasten off invisibly.

CENTER: RS facing and holding yarn underneath, join B by pulling a loop through the base of one petal, ss in base of each of next 4 petals, ss in join. Leaving a long end of approximately 8in (20cm), fasten off invisibly. Thread this end onto a yarn needle and take through the center to the WS. Fasten off all ends except this one.

Stem

Knot the 5 long ends close to the flowers. Starting at the knot, use one end to work 16sc over the other 4 ends. Fasten off invisibly. One at a time, thread an end onto a fine yarn needle, take it over a sc and then through the stem to the flower, work 2 or 3sc above the knot to secure the flower. Fasten off.

25 HELENIUM \/

Yarn: DK wool in orange (A), yellow (B), and lemon (C)

METHOD
Center
Using A, make a slip ring.
ROUND 1: 2ch, 7sc in ring, pull end to close ring, ss in top ch of 2ch. (8 sts)
ROUND 2: 1ch, 2sc in next sc, [1sc in next sc, 2sc in next sc] 3 times, with B ss in 1ch. (12 sts)
ROUND 3: Using B, [4ch, ss in front strand of next sc] 12 times, ending ss in ss of previous round. (12 loops) Fasten off invisibly.

ROUND 4: Join C in the back strand of first sc in round 2, [10ch, 1sc in back strand of next st] 12 times, ending ss in first ch. (12 loops) Fasten off invisibly.

Specific symbol

$+$ 1sc in back strand of sc of round 2.

26 SANTOLINA \/

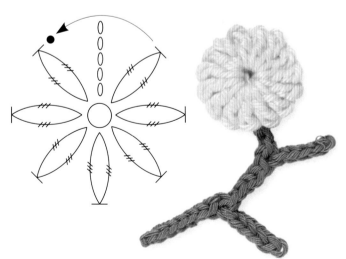

Yarn: DK cotton in yellow (A) and green (B)

METHOD
Flower
Using A, make a slip ring.
ROUND 1: 5ch, [2dtr cluster in ring] 7 times, pull end to close ring, skip 5ch and ss in top of first cluster. Fasten off, leaving an end long enough to gather top of clusters.

Stem
Using B, make 12ch, skip 1ch, ss in each of next 5ch, 10ch, skip 1ch, ss in each of next 4ch, 8ch, skip 1ch, ss in each of next 7ch, 1ch, ss in each of next 5ch, 1ch, ss in each of remaining 6ch. Fasten off invisibly.

Finishing
The long clusters will have curled to the back naturally, so use the yarn end to gather them a little more and secure them. Attach a stem.

LILY OF THE VALLEY   \/

Yarn: Fine cotton in white (A) and green (B)

METHOD

Flower (make 3)

Using A, make a slip ring.

ROUND 1: 3ch, 9dc in ring, pull end to close ring, ss in top ch of 3ch. (10 sts)

ROUND 2: 2ch, 1dc in next dc, 1ch, [2dc tog in next 2dc, 1ch] 4 times, ss in top of first dc.

ROUND 3: 4ch, ss in first ch of 4ch, [ss in 1ch of round 2, ss in top of next 2dc tog, 4ch, ss in first ch of 4ch] 4 times, ss in next ch. Fasten off invisibly.

Stem

Using B, make 31ch. Skip 1ch, ss in each of next 15ch, [3ch, skip first of 3ch, ss in each of next 2ch, on main stem ss in each of next 7ch] twice, 1sc in last ch. Fasten off invisibly.

Leaf

Worked in one round with RS facing.

Using B, make 14ch. Skip 1ch, 1sc in each of next 3ch, 1hdc in next ch, 1dc in each of next 6ch, 1hdc in next ch, 1sc in each of next 2ch, 5ch, skip 3ch, 1sc in next ch, 1ch. Working in the remaining strands of original base ch: 1sc in each of first 2ch, 1hdc in next ch, 1dc in each of next 6ch, 1hdc in next ch, 1sc in each of next 3ch. Working in both strands of each ch: 1sc in next ch, 15ch, skip 1ch, ss in each of next 14ch, 1sc in next ch. Fasten off invisibly.

Finishing

Sew a flower to the top of the stem and one to each side branch. Join stem and leaf.

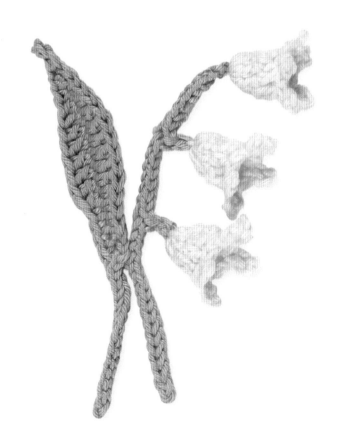

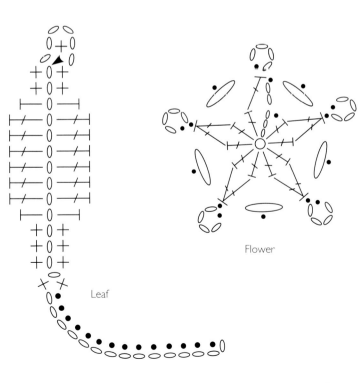

Leaf

Flower

28 PERIWINKLE \/

Yarn: Fine cotton in pale blue (A), deep blue (B), and pale green (C)

METHOD

Flower

Using A, make 4ch, join with ss into a ring.

ROUND 1: 4ch, 4tr in ring, ss in top ch of 4ch. (5 sts)

ROUND 2: 5ch, [1sc in next tr, 4ch] 4 times, ss in first ch of 5ch. (5 ch loops)
Fasten off.

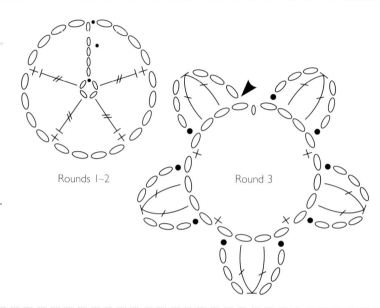

Rounds 1–2   Round 3

ROUND 3: With center of flower facing, join B in first ch loop, 3ch, 2dc cluster around ch loop, 3ch, ss in same loop, [ss, 3ch, 2dc cluster, 3ch, ss in next loop] 4 times, ss in first ch. Fasten off invisibly.

29 CORNFLOWER \|/

Yarn: DK wool in green (A), deep blue (B), and mid-blue (C)

METHOD

SPECIFIC INSTRUCTION

Loop st = insert hook in st, extend left middle finger and catch the strand behind the finger, together with the strand in front of the finger to make a loop, pull both strands through, yo and pull through 3 loops on hook.

Back

Using A and leaving a long end to form stem, make a slip ring.

ROUND 1 (RS): 1ch, 3sc in ring, pull end to close ring, ss in first sc. (3sc)*

ROUND 2: 1ch, 2sc in each sc, ss in first sc. (6sc)

ROUND 3: 1ch, 1sc in each sc, ss in first sc. Fasten off.

Center

Using B, work as back to *, noting that round 1 is now WS.

ROUND 2: 1ch, 2 loop sts in each sc, ss in 1ch. (6 loops)

JOINING ROUND: Place center on back with loops facing, using B work through 1 st from each piece each time: 2sc in each pair of sts, ss in first sc. (12 sts) Fasten off.

Florets

With center facing, join C in a sc of joining round.

ROUND 1: 1ch, 5sc in same sc as join, ss in first sc.

ROUND 2: 1ch, 1sc in each sc, ss in first sc.

ROUND 3: 1ch, (1sc, 1dc, 1sc) in each sc, ss in first sc. Fasten off invisibly.

Work 6 more florets, placing some next to each other, and spacing others 1 or 2sc apart to distribute them unevenly around the joining round.

Stem

Using C, make 11ch, skip 1ch, ss in each of next 10ch. Fasten off.

Finishing

Press petals. Thread one yarn end from the stem through the center of the flower from below. Knot it close to the flower and trim. Use 2nd end to attach stem to base of flower.

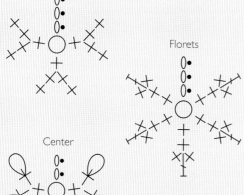

Back

Center

Florets

Specific symbol

Ⓞ Loop st

Yarn: Fine wool in yellow (A), mauve (B), and purple (C); single strand of embroidery wool in dark olive

Extras: Dark olive embroidery wool

METHOD

First petal

Using A, make 5ch, join with ss into a ring.

ROW 1: 3ch, 6dc in ring. (7 sts)
ROW 2: 5ch, 2tr tog in next 2 sts, 1dc in next st, 2tr tog in next 2 sts, 5ch, ss in top ch of 3ch.
Fasten off invisibly.

2nd and 3rd petals

*ROW 1: Join B in 5ch ring, 3ch, 4dc in ring. (5 sts)
ROW 2: 4ch, 3dc tog in next 3 sts, 4ch, ss in top ch of 3ch.
Fasten off invisibly.**
Repeat from * to ** for 3rd petal.

4th petal

Turn to WS. Join C in 5ch ring between first and 2nd petals, 4ch, ss in ring between first and 3rd petals, turn.

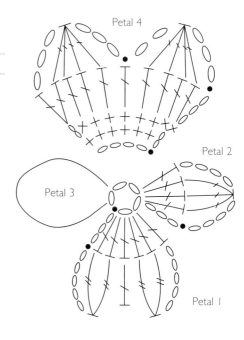

Petal 4

Petal 3

Petal 2

Petal 1

Now work behind 2nd and 3rd petals:
ROW 1: 2ch, 6sc around 4ch bar. (7 sts)
ROW 2: 2ch, 1sc in st below, 1sc in each of next 5sc, 2sc in top ch of 2ch. (9 sts)
ROW 3: 3ch, 1dc in st below, 1dc in each of next 7sc, 2dc in top ch of 2ch. (11 sts)
ROW 4: 3ch, 4dc tog in next 4dc, 3ch, ss in next dc, 2ch, 4dc tog in next 4dc, 3ch, ss in top ch of 3ch.
Fasten off invisibly.

Finishing

Press each petal. Using embroidery wool, sew straight sts along line of dc sts, 3 on first petal and 2 each on 2nd and 3rd petals.

31 ROSETTE \|/

Yarn: DK wool in yellow (A), pink (R), deep pink (C), light wine (D), and dark wine (E)

METHOD

SPECIFIC INSTRUCTION

Move loop to next ch sp = remove hook from loop, insert from back in same ch sp, catch loop and pull through, remove hook from loop, insert from front in next ch sp, catch loop and pull through.

Center

Using A, make a slip ring.
ROUND 1: 1ch, 6sc in ring, pull end to close ring, ss in 1ch.
ROUND 2: 1ch, 1sc in same sc as join, 3ch, [1sc in next sc, 3ch] 5 times, ss in 1ch.
Fasten off invisibly.

First ring of petals

Join B in a 3ch sp.
ROUND 1: *(1ch, 1sc, 3hdc, 1sc) in 3ch sp, move loop to next 3ch sp; repeat from * 5 times, omitting last pull through.
ROUND 2: 1ch, take hook behind petals, inserting it from back, make 1sc around post of first sc of round 2 of center, 3ch, [1sc around post of next sc of round 2 of center, 3ch] 5 times, ss in first sc.
Fasten off.

2nd ring of petals

Join C in a 3ch sp.
ROUND 1: *(1ch, 1sc, 1hdc, 3dc, 1hdc, 1sc) in 3ch sp, move loop to next 3ch sp; repeat from * 5 times, omitting last pull through.
ROUND 2: 1ch, take hook behind petals, inserting it from back, make 1sc around post of first sc of round 2 of first ring of petals, 4ch, [1sc around post of next sc of round 2 of first ring of petals, 4ch] 5 times, ss in first sc.
Fasten off.

3rd ring of petals

Join D in a 4ch sp.
ROUND 1: *(1ch, 1sc, 1hdc, 1dc, 3tr, 1dc, 1hdc, 1sc) in 4ch sp, move loop to next 4ch sp; repeat from * 5 times, omitting last pull through.
ROUND 2: 1ch, take hook behind petals, inserting it from back, make 1sc around post of first sc of round 2 of 2nd ring of petals, 5ch, [1sc around post of next sc of round 2 of 2nd ring of petals, 5ch] 5 times, ss in first sc.
Fasten off.

4th ring of petals

Join E in a 5ch sp.
LAST ROUND: *(1ch, 1sc, 1hdc, 1dc, 5tr, 1dc, 1hdc, 1sc) in 5ch sp, move loop to next 5ch sp; repeat from * 5 times, omitting last pull through. Fasten off.

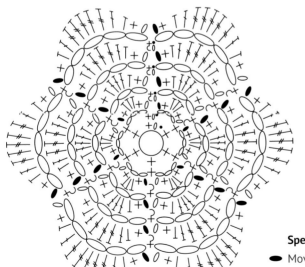

Specific symbol
● Move loop to next ch sp.

GERBERA

Yarn: DK wool in yellow (A), orange (B), and green (C)

METHOD

Center

Using A, make a slip ring.

ROUND 1: 1ch, 12sc in ring, remove hook, insert from back in first sc, catch loop and pull through, pull end to close ring.

ROUND 2: 1ch, inserting hook from back, make 1sc around post of each sc, remove hook, insert from back in first sc, catch loop and pull through.

Fasten off invisibly.

First round of petals

Join B in a sc of round 2 of center.

PETAL 1: Make 8ch loosely, working into back loop only of each ch each time, skip 1ch, ss in next ch, 1sc in each of next 2ch, 1hdc in each of next 4ch, remove hook, insert from back in same sc of round 2, catch loop and pull through.

PETALS 2-12: Remove hook, insert from front in next sc of round 2, catch loop and pull through, then work as first petal.

2nd round of petals

NEXT ROUND: Working behind first round of petals, remove hook, insert from front in strand at base of first petal, catch loop and pull through, 1ch, 1sc in same strand, [1ch, 1sc in strand between next 2 petals] 11 times, remove hook, insert in front of first sc, catch loop and pull through.

PETALS 1-12: Work 1 petal in each sc of previous round as petals of first round.

Stem

Join C in strand between petals of 2nd round.

ROUND 1: Working behind petals, 1ch, 1sc in same place as join, [1sc in 2 strands between next 2 petals] 11 times, ss in first sc. (12 sts)

ROUND 2: 1ch, 1sc in each sc, ss in first sc.

ROUND 3: 1ch, [2sc tog in next 2sc, 1sc in next sc] 4 times, ss in first st. (8 sts)

ROUND 4: 1ch, [2sc tog in next 2 sts] 4 times. (4 sts)

Work 5 rounds sc.

Fasten off.

33 GERANIUM \/

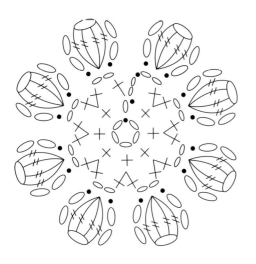

Yarn: Fine cotton in orange (A), yellow (B), and purple (C)

METHOD
Center

Using A, make 5ch, join with ss into a ring.
ROUND 1: 1ch, 7sc in ring, with B ss in 1ch.
(8 sts)
Continue with B.
ROUND 2: 2ch, 1sc in 1ch below, 2ch, [2sc in next sc, 2ch] 7 times, ss in top ch of 2ch.
Fasten off.

ROUND 3: Join C in a ch sp, 2ch, 4tr popcorn in ch sp below, 2ch, ss in same ch sp, [ss in next ch sp, (2ch, 4tr popcorn, 2ch, ss) in same ch sp] 7 times.
Fasten off invisibly.

34 ZINNIA \/

Yarn: DK wool in yellow (A) and lime (B)

METHOD
Petals

Using A, [make 7ch, skip 3ch, 5dc in next ch, skip 2ch, ss in next ch] 9 times. (9 petals)
Fasten off.
JOINING ROW: RS facing, place petals flat, straight edges uppermost, and join A with a sc in 4th ch of first petal, working behind petals, [1ch, 1sc in 4th ch of next petal] 8 times, 1ch, ss in first sc.
Fasten off.

Center

Using B, make 5ch, join with ss into ring. Working over yarn end for additional padding, 1ch, 9sc in ring, ss in 1ch. Fasten off invisibly, leaving an end to sew with.

Finishing

Weave in ends on petals. Turn center to WS and, using backstitch over edge chain, stitch to center of flower.

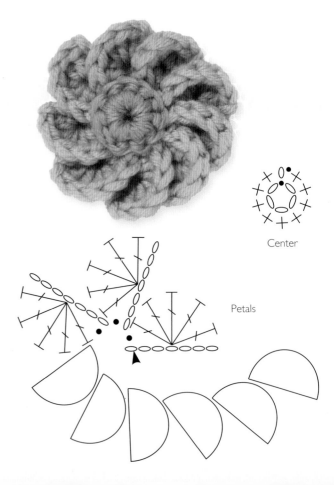

Center

Petals

Yarn: DK wool in black (A) and red (B)

METHOD

Center

Using A, make a slip ring.

ROUND 1: 3ch, [2dc tog in ring] 8 times, pull end to close ring, ss in top ch of 3ch. (9 sts)

ROUND 2: 3ch, 1dc in each of next 8 sts, with B ss in top ch of 3ch.

Continue with B.

First petal

ROW 1: 1ch, 1sc in each of next 2dc, turn. (3 sts)

ROW 2: 3ch, 1dc in sc below, 1dc in next sc, 2dc in 1ch. (5 sts)

ROW 3: 3ch, making last wrap with A 1dc in dc below, with A 1dc in each of next 2dc, making last wrap with B 1dc in next dc, with B 2dc in top ch of 3ch. (7 sts)

Continue with B.

ROW 4: 3ch, 1dc in dc below, 1dc in each of next 5dc, 2dc in top ch of 3ch. (9 sts)

ROW 5: 3ch, 2dc tog in next 2dc, 3dc tog in next 3dc, 2dc tog in next 2dc, 1dc in top ch of 3ch. (5 sts)

Fasten off invisibly.

2nd petal

RS facing, join B in next st of center and complete as rows 1–5 of first petal.

3rd petal

As 2nd petal.

Bars to hold remaining 3 petals

RS facing and working behind petals, join B in back of center sc at base of first row of 1 petal, 4ch, [1sc in back of center sc of first row of next petal, 3ch] twice, ss in first ch of 4ch.

4th petal

Around next bar work 1ch, 2sc. Complete as rows 2–5 of first petal.

5th and 6th petals

As 4th petal.

Stamens

Thread a yarn needle with A and make loops around the center, anchoring them with backstitches. Trim the loops and use the needle to fray the strands of yarn.

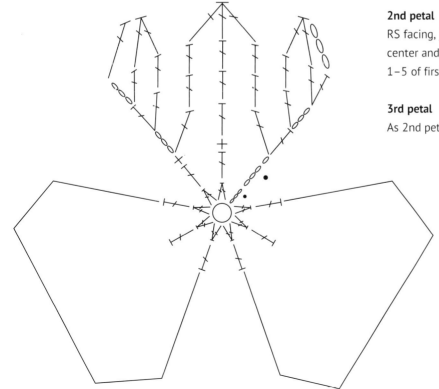

36 BACHELOR'S BUTTON \/

Yarn: Sport-weight yarn in pink

Extras: Small wooden plant stake

METHOD
SPECIFIC INSTRUCTIONS
Petal = 7ch, skip 3ch, ss in each of next 4ch.

Picot = 5ch, skip 3ch, ss in each of next 2ch.

Flower
Make a slip ring.

ROUND 1: 2ch, 7sc in ring, pull end to close ring, ss in top ch of 2ch. (8 sts)

ROUND 2: 1ch, working in back strand each time (1sc, 1 petal) in each of 7sc, ss in 1ch. (7 petals)

ROUND 3: Folding back the petals of the previous round to work in front of them and working in both strands of each st, (1sc, 1 petal, 1sc, 1 petal) in each sc of previous round, ss in first sc. (14 petals) Fasten off.

ROUND 4: Working in front strand of sts of round 1, join yarn in a sc, 1 picot in this sc, [ss in next sc, 1 picot in this sc] 6 times, ss in base of first picot.
Fasten off.

Rounds 1–3

37 SCOTTISH THISTLE \/

Yarn: Fine cotton in gray-green (A) and pale mauve (B)

METHOD
Using A, make 5ch, join with ss into a ring.

ROUND 1: 2ch, 7sc in ring, ss in top ch of 2ch. (8 sts)

ROUND 2: 1ch, [2sc in next sc, 1sc in next sc] 3 times, 2sc in next sc, ss to 1ch. (12 sts)

ROUND 3: 1ch, [2sc in next sc, 1sc in next sc] 5 times, 2sc in next sc, ss in 1ch. (18 sts)

Insert a marker and work 3 rounds of sc continuously.

ROUND 7: [2sc tog in next 2sc, 1sc in next sc] 6 times. (12 sts) Work 2 rounds straight, ending ss in next sc.

ROUND 10: *2ch, ss in first ch, ss in next st; repeat from *, ending ss in first ch.
Fasten off invisibly.

Top
Cut strands of B approximately 5in (13cm) long and enough to fill thistle head when doubled. Fold in half and tie in a tassel. Insert tassel along with a little spare yarn for padding. Secure and trim.

Stem
Using A, make 12ch, skip 1ch, ss in next 11ch, turn, 1ch, skip 1ss, ss in single strand of each remaining ss. Fasten off. Sew to base of thistle.

Round 4

Stem

Insert top of stake in the flower center.

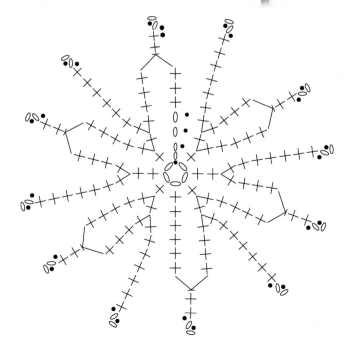

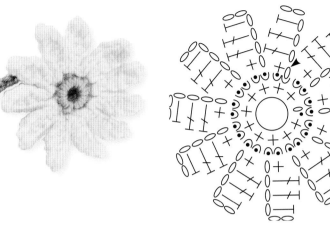

Yarn: DK yarn in yellow (A), white (B), and green (C)

METHOD

Flower

Using A, make a slip ring.

ROUND 1: 1ch, 10sc in ring, pull end to close ring, ss in 1ch. (11 sts)

Fasten off.

ROUND 2: Working in front strand only of sc, join B in a sc, *6ch, skip 2ch, 1hdc in next ch, 1dc in each of next 2ch, 1sc in next ch, ss in front strand of same sc below, ss in front strand of next sc; repeat from *, ending ss in front strand of first sc. (11 petals)

Fasten off.

Base and stem

Fasten off ends. Turn flower over and join C in back strand of a sc in ring. Working each st in back strand, 3ch, [2dc tog in next 2 sts] 5 times, ss in top ch of 3ch, 1sc in top of a dc on opposite side of group, make 24ch, skip 1ch, ss in each remaining ch. Fasten off.

DAFFODIL

Yarn: DK cotton

METHOD

Petals

RING 1: Make 12ch, join with ss into a ring. 5ch, 2dtr tog in next 2ch of ring, 2ch, skip 1ch, ss in next ch, 5ch, ss in next ch of ring, [ss in next ch, 5ch, 2dtr tog in next 2ch, 2ch, skip 1ch, ss in next ch, 5ch, ss in next ch] twice. (3 petals)

Fasten off invisibly.

RING 2: As first ring.

Trumpet

JOIN RINGS: RS uppermost, place one ring of petals on top of the other, the top petals lying at an angle to those below. Holding the yarn underneath and using a smaller size hook, insert the hook from the top in a remaining single strand of a ch in the top ring and in the remaining strand of the ch in the ring immediately below, yo, pull loop through both ch, inserting hook in center sp, catch yarn and pull it through 2 loops on hook to make a sc. Work into each pair of ch in this way until 12sc have been completed. Leave loop. Cut yarn to approximately 4½yd (4m) length and pull this through center ring in order to work into the sc just made.

ROUND 1: 1ch, 1sc in each of next 11sc, ss in 1ch.

ROUND 2: 3ch, 1dc in each of next 11sc, ss in top ch of 3ch.

ROUND 3: [2ch, skip 1ch, ss in next ch, ss in next dc] 12 times, ending ss in first ch. Fasten off invisibly.

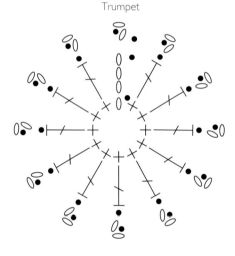

Trumpet

Petals

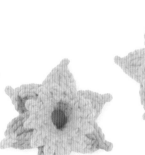

40 APPLE BLOSSOM \/

Yarn: DK wool in lime (A) and pink (B)

METHOD
Center
Using A, make a slip ring.
ROUND 1: 2ch, 9sc in ring, pull
end to close ring, using B ss in
top ch of 2ch. (10 sts)
Continue with B.

Petals
ROUND 2: 1ch, *(1tr, 2dtr, 1tr)
in next sc, ss in next sc; repeat
from * 3 times, (1tr, 2dtr, 1tr) in
next sc, ss in 1ch. (5 petals)
Fasten off invisibly.

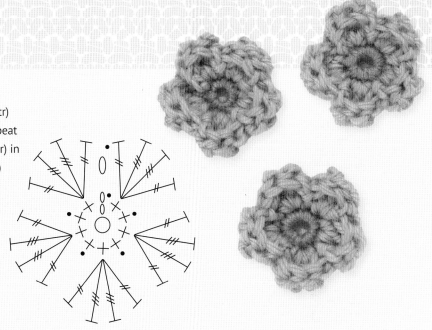

41 FORGET-ME-NOT |

Yarn: Fine wool in yellow (A), blue (B),
and green (C)

METHOD
Flower
Using A, make 4ch, join with ss
into a ring.
ROUND 1 (RS): 2ch, 9sc in ring,
with B ss in top ch of 2ch.
(10 sts)
Continue with B.
ROUND 2: 5ch, 1dtr in each of
next 9sc, ss in top ch of 5ch.
Fasten off.

Stem
Using C, make 12ch, skip 1ch, ss
in each of next 7ch; make a leaf
by working 5ch, skip 2ch, 1dc in
next ch, 1sc in next ch, ss in
next ch; ss in each of remaining
4ch of stem. Fasten off.

Finishing
Press stem and leaf only, then
attach to back of flower.

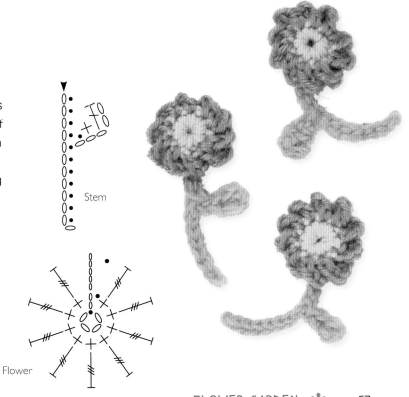

Stem

Flower

Yarn: Embroidery cotton in pale pink (A), mid-pink (B), deep pink (C), and green (D)

METHOD

Rose petals

PICOT ROW: Using A, make 5ch, skip 4ch, 1sc in next ch, [8ch, skip 4ch, 1sc in next ch] 6 times, turn. (7 picots)

ROW 1 (WS): 1ch, 7sc in first picot sp, [1ss over 3ch, 7sc in next picot] 6 times.
Fasten off.

Do not turn, join B in first ch.

ROW 2: 1ch, [1sc in each of 2sc, 2hdc in each of next 3sc, 1sc in each of next 2sc, 1ss over 3ch between picots] 5 times.
Fasten off.

Do not turn, join C in first ch.

ROW 3: 1ch, [1sc in each of 2sc, 1hdc in next hdc, 1dc in each of next 4hdc, 1hdc in next hdc, 1sc in each of next 2sc, 1ss over 3ch between picots] 3 times.
Fasten off. With smallest petals at center, roll and stitch.

Rose stem

Leaving an end approximately 4in (10cm) long, join D at base of rose. Weaving end across between each ch, make 11ch. Skip 1ch, 1sc in each of next 10ch. Fasten off.

Rose sepals

Make 5ch, wrap ch around stem and join with ss into a ring.

ROUND 1: 1ch, 9sc in 5ch sp, ss in first sc. (9 sts)

ROUND 2: 1ch, 1sc in each sc, ss in first sc.

ROUND 3: 1ch, [2sc in first sc, 1sc in each of next 2sc] 3 times, ss in first sc. (12 sts)
Fasten off, leaving an end to stitch sepals to base of rose.

Rosebud petals (make 3)

Using A, work picot row as for rose until 6 picots have been completed, turn. Work row 1, repeating instructions in brackets 5 times. Fasten off. Noting that row 1 is RS, roll and stitch to form rosebuds.

Rosebud stem

Using D, make 12ch, ss in base of first rosebud, turn and ss in each of 4ch, make 4ch, ss in base of 2nd rosebud, turn and ss in each of 4ch, make 4ch, ss in base of 3rd rosebud, turn and ss in each of 4ch and first 8ch. Fasten off.

Rosebud sepals

Holding rosebud in left hand, wrap yarn once around finger and base of rosebud to form a ring.

ROUND 1: 1ch, 6sc in ring, pull end to close ring, ss in first sc.

ROUND 2: 1ch, 2sc in each sc, ss in first sc.
Fasten off. Finish 2nd and 3rd rosebuds in same way. Stitch sepals to base of rosebuds.

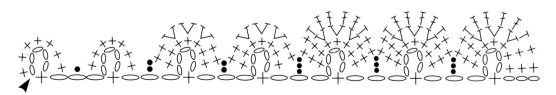

43 RUFFLED ROSE \\/

Yarn: Fine wool in pale pink (A) and deep pink (B)

METHOD

Using A, make 10ch, join with ss into a ring.

ROUND 1: 7ch, [1tr in ring, 3ch] 9 times, ss in 4th ch of 7ch. (10 ch bars)

ROUND 2: 3ch, 3dc around first 3ch bar, [4dc around next tr, 1dc in center ring, 4dc around next tr, leaving one 3ch bar free work 4dc around next 3ch bar] 4 times, 4dc around next tr, 1dc in ring, 4dc around 4ch, ss in top ch of 3ch.
Fasten off invisibly.

ROUND 3: Join B around a free 3ch bar, 7ch, [1tr around bar, 3ch] 3 times, *around next 3ch bar work [1tr, 3ch] 4 times; repeat from * 3 times, ss in 4th ch of 7ch. (20 ch bars)

ROUND 4: 3ch, 3dc around 4ch, 1dc in sp below, [4dc around next tr, leaving one 3ch bar free work 4dc around 3ch bar, 4dc around next tr, 1dc in sp below], 9 times, 4dc around next tr, 4dc around last 3ch bar, ss in top ch of 3ch.
Fasten off invisibly.
Weave in ends.

ROUND 5: This RS round will fold naturally to the back of the rose: rejoin B around a free 3ch bar, 3ch, 2tr cluster around bar, [1ch, 3tr cluster around next bar] 9 times, 1ch, ss in top ch of 3ch. (10 clusters)

ROUND 6: 3ch, [2tr cluster in next 2 sts] 10 times, ss in top ch of 3ch.
Fasten off, leaving an 8in (20cm) end. Run end through top of each cluster and draw up.

Round 1

Round 2

Round 3

Round 4

Rounds 5 and 6

Specific symbol
→ Direction of work

44 CENTIFOLIA ROSE |

Yarn: DK wool in deep pink (A) and pale pink (B)

METHOD

Large rose

Using A, make 99ch.

PETALS 1-4: Skip 3ch, 1dc in each of next 2ch, 2ch, ss in next ch, [3ch, 1dc in each of next 2ch, 2ch, ss in next ch] 3 times. Continue with B.

PETALS 5-8: [4ch, 1tr in each of next 4ch, 3ch, ss in next ch] 4 times.

PETALS 9-12: [4ch, 1tr in each of next 6ch, 3ch, ss in next ch] 4 times.

PETALS 13-16: [5ch, 1dtr in each of next 8ch, 4ch, ss in next ch] 4 times.

Fasten off.

Small rose

Using B, make 48ch.

PETALS 1-3: As petals 1-4 of large rose, but work instructions in square brackets twice.

PETALS 4-6: As petals 5-8 of large rose, but work instructions in square brackets 3 times.

PETALS 7-9: As petals 9-12 of large rose, but work instructions in square brackets 3 times.

Fasten off.

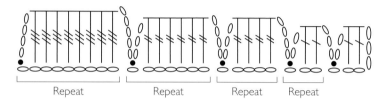

Repeat Repeat Repeat Repeat

45 IRISH ROSE \/

Yarn: Fine wool in deep pink (A), mid-pink (B), and pale pink (C)

METHOD

Using A, make a slip ring.

ROUND 1: 2ch, 7sc in ring, pull end to close ring, ss in top ch of 2ch. (8 sts)

ROUND 2: 2ch, 1sc in base of first ch, 2sc in each of next 7 sts, ss in top ch of 2ch. (16 sts)

ROUND 3: 4ch, [skip 1sc, 1sc in next sc, 3ch] 7 times, ss in first ch of 4ch. (8 ch sp)

ROUND 4: [1sc, 1hdc, 1dc, 1hdc, 1sc] in each ch sp. (8 petals)

Fasten off with A. Continue with B.

ROUND 5: Folding petals forward and working into back of petals, ss in the 2 strands that form the base of each of first 3 sts of next petal, [3ch, 1sc in base of dc at center of next petal] 7 times, 3ch, ss in 3rd of 3ss.

ROUND 6: [1sc, 1hdc, 3dc, 1hdc, 1sc] in each ch sp.

Fasten off with B. Continue with C.

ROUND 7: Folding petals forward and working into the back of petals as before, ss in base of each of next 4 sts, [5ch, 1sc in base of center dc] 7 times, 5ch, ss in 4th of 4ss.

ROUND 8: [1sc, 1hdc, 5dc, 1hdc, 1sc] in each ch sp.

Fasten off.

Specific symbols

●   Ss in the base at the back of the st below.

↓   1sc in the base at the back of the st below.

Finishing (both roses)

Press petals to shape. Starting with
the smaller petals and stitching as
you go, coil the row of petals to give
a flat base along the chain edge.

Yarn: DK wool

METHOD

Leaving a long end of yarn,
make 48ch.

ROW 1: Skip 4ch, 1tr in each of
next 43ch, 1dc in last ch. (45 sts)

ROW 2: 3ch, 3tr in each of next
43tr, 1dc in top ch of 4ch.
Fasten off, leaving a long end.

Finishing

Extend increase edge (row 2)
and press. Coil chain edge
counterclockwise, starting with
the beginning of the first row
and using the long end to stitch
as you go. When the coil is
completed, catch the yarn end of
row 2 and take it down through
the center of the rose.

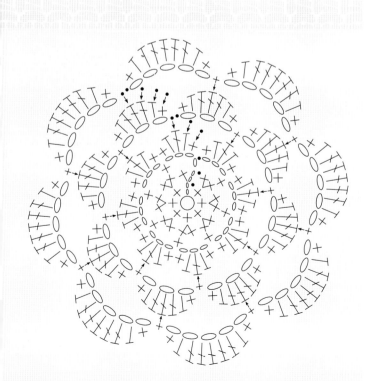

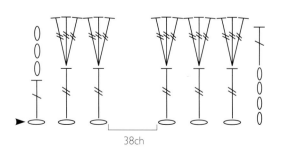

38ch

47 COMMON SUNFLOWER \||/

Yarn: Fine wool in dark olive (A) and yellow (B)

METHOD

Center

Using A, make a slip ring.

ROUND 1: 2ch, 7sc in ring, pull end to close ring, ss in top ch of 2ch. (8 sts)

ROUND 2: 3ch, *(3dc popcorn, 1ch, 1sc, 1ch) in next sc; repeat from * 6 times, 3dc popcorn in ss of previous round, 1ch, ss in 2nd ch of 3ch. (8 popcorns and 8 sts)

ROUND 3: 2ch, 2sc in ch below, [3sc in next sc] 7 times, ss in 2nd ch of 2ch. (24 sts)

ROUND 4: 3ch, [3dc popcorn in next sc, 1ch, 1sc in next sc, 1ch] 11 times, 3dc popcorn in next sc, 1ch, ss in 2nd ch of 3ch. (12 popcorns and 12 sts)

ROUND 5: 2ch, 2sc in same ch below, [3sc in next sc] 11 times, ss in 2nd ch of 2ch. (36 sts)

ROUND 6: 3ch, [3dc popcorn in next sc, 1ch, 1sc in next sc, 1ch] 17 times, 3dc popcorn in next sc,

1ch, ss in 2nd ch of 3ch. (18 popcorns and 18 sts) Fasten off.

Petals

ROUND 7: Join B in a sc, [4ch, skip 1ch, 1sc in next ch, 1hdc in next ch, 1dc in next ch, ss in next sc of round 6] 18 times. Fasten off invisibly.

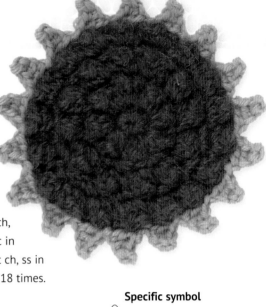

Specific symbol

〇 3dc popcorn

48 STARBURST \|/

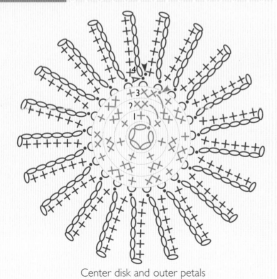

Center disk and outer petals

Yarn: Aran-weight or heavy worsted-weight wool in orange (A), fuchsia (B), and gold (C)

METHOD

Center disk

Using A, make 5ch, join with ss into a ring. Work in a spiral as follows:

ROUND 1: 7sc in ring.

ROUND 2: 2sc in each sc. (14 sts)

ROUND 3: [2sc in next sc, 1sc in next sc] 7 times. (21 sts) Fasten off with ss in next sc.

Outer petals

Join B with ss in back loop of any sc on round 3.

ROUND 4: [7ch, skip first ch, 1sc in each of next 6ch, ss in back loop of next sc on round 3] 21 times. (21 petals) Fasten off.

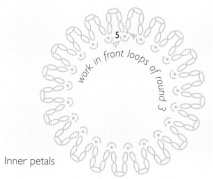

OPENWORK STAR   V

Yarn: Aran-weight or heavy worsted-weight wool in gold (A), fuchsia (B), and orange (C)

METHOD

Center disk

Using A, make 5ch, join with ss into a ring. Work in a spiral as follows:
ROUND 1: 7sc in ring.
ROUND 2: 2sc in each sc. (14 sts)
Fasten off A with ss in next sc and join B with ss in any sc on round 2.
ROUND 3: [2sc in next sc, 1sc in next sc] 7 times. (21 sts)
Fasten off B with ss in next sc and join C with ss in any sc on round 3.
ROUND 4: [2sc in next sc, 1sc in each of next 2sc] 6 times, 1sc in each of next 3sc. (27 sts)

Inner petals

Join C with ss in front loop of any sc on round 3.
ROUND 5: [5ch, ss in front loop of next sc on round 3] 21 times. (21 petals)
Fasten off.

Petals

Continue with C.
ROUND 5: [7ch, skip first ch, ss in next ch, 1sc in next ch, 1hdc in next ch, 1dc in each of next 2ch (petal made); skip last ch, skip 2sc on round 4 and attach petal with 1sc in next sc] 9 times. (9 petals)
Fasten off.

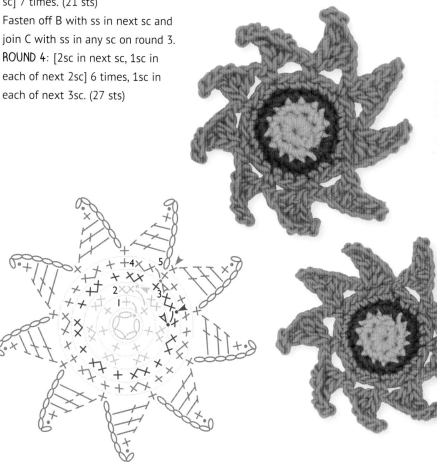

Inner petals

50 SMALL BUD |

Yarn: Worsted-weight wool in chartreuse (A) and pale gold (B)

METHOD

Center disk

Using A, make 5ch, join with ss into a ring. Work in a spiral as follows:

ROUND 1: 7sc in ring.

ROUND 2: 2sc in each sc. (14 sts)

ROUND 3: [2sc in next sc, 1sc in next sc] 7 times. (21 sts)

Fasten off with ss in next sc.

Petals

Join B with ss in any sc on round 3.

ROUND 4: [(1dc, 2tr, 1dc) in next sc, ss in each of next 2sc] 6 times, (1dc, 2tr, 1dc) in next sc, ss in next sc. (7 petals)

Fasten off with ss in next sc.

51 LARGE BUD   \|/

Yarn: Worsted-weight wool in rust (A) and chartreuse (B)

METHOD

Center disk and inner petals

Work center disk as Small Bud (above).

Join B with ss in front loop of any sc on round 3.

ROUND 4: 3ch, (1tr, 1dc) in same front loop at base of 3ch, [ss in front loop of each of next 2sc, (1dc, 1tr, 1dc) in front loop of next sc] 6 times, ss in front loop of each of next 2sc. (7 petals)

Outer petals

Work outer petals in back loops of sc on round 3 as follows:

ROUND 5: Ss in back loop of next sc (which contains an inner petal), [make 6tr bobble, working 3tr of bobble into back loops of each of next 2sc and closing bobble with 1ch, ss in back loop of next sc] 7 times. (7 petals)

Fasten off. Push a finger into each bobble from RS of work, so that fullness of bobble goes outward from center.

PURPLE PASSION \\/

Yarn: Worsted-weight wool in dusky pink (A), light pink (B), orange (C), purple (D), and green (E)

METHOD

Center disk

Using A, make 5ch, join with ss into a ring. Work in a spiral as follows:

ROUND 1: 9sc in ring.

ROUND 2: 2sc in each sc. (18 sts)

ROUND 3: [2sc in next sc, 1sc in next sc] 9 times. (27 sts)

Fasten off A with ss in next sc and join B with ss in any sc on round 3.

ROUND 4: [1sc in next sc, 4dc bobble in next sc, close bobble with 1ch, 1sc in next sc] 9 times.

Fasten off B with ss in next sc and join C with ss in sc at right of any bobble on round 4.

ROUND 5: [1sc in top of bobble, 1sc in ch closing bobble, 1sc in next sc, 5tr bobble in next sc, close bobble with 1ch] 9 times. Continue in C to work back of disk as follows:

ROUND 6: [1sc in each of next 3sc, 1sc in ch closing bobble] 9 times. (36 sts)

ROUND 7: [1sc in each of next 3sc, skip next sc] 9 times. (27 sts)

ROUND 8: 1sc in each sc.

ROUND 9: [1sc in each of next 2sc, skip next sc] 9 times. (18 sts)

ROUND 10: [1sc in next sc, skip next sc] 9 times. (9 sts) Fasten off with ss in next sc, leaving tail of yarn for sewing up.

Petals and stem

Using D, make 9 large petals (page 80). Using E, make a flower back and stem (page 80).

Finishing

Stuff center disk with scraps of yarn A (or similar color), then sew opening closed with tail of yarn. Using E (or similar color), stuff cone at top of stem and sew to back of center disk. Using D, sew base of petals evenly spaced around back of disk.

Center disk

Specific symbols

● 4dc bobble, 1ch

◯ 5tr bobble, 1ch

Yarn: Worsted-weight wool in chartreuse (A), rust (B), and pale gold (C)

METHOD

NOTE: This sunflower can be modified to have fewer petals by changing the number of stitches in round 1 of the center disk. For example, this flower begins with 9sc in round 1, then increases to 18, 27, 36, 45, 54, 63, and finally 72. If you were to begin with 6sc, the increases would be to 12, 18, 24, 30, 36, 42, and finally 48. This would make a smaller sunflower with 6 petals.

Center disk

Using A, make 7ch, join with ss into a ring.

ROUND 1: 1ch (counts as 1sc), 8sc in ring, join with ss in 1ch. (9 sts)

ROUND 2: 1ch, 1sc in st below, 2sc in each of next 8sc, join with ss in 1ch. (18 sts)

ROUND 3: 1ch, [2sc in next sc, 1sc in next sc] 8 times, 2sc in next sc, join with ss in 1ch. (27 sts)

ROUND 4: 1ch, [2sc in next sc, 1sc in each of next 2sc] 8 times, 2sc in next sc, 1sc in next sc, join with ss in 1ch. (36 sts)

ROUND 5: 1ch, [2sc in next sc, 1sc in each of next 3sc] 8 times, 2sc in next sc, 1sc in each of next 2sc, join with ss in 1ch. (45 sts)

Fasten off A and join B with ss in 1ch at beginning of round 5.

ROUND 6: 1ch, [2sc in next sc, 1sc in each of next 4sc] 8 times, 2sc in next sc, 1sc in each of next 3sc, join with ss in 1ch. (54 sts)

ROUND 7: 1ch, [2sc in next sc, 1sc in each of next 5sc] 8 times, 2sc in next sc, 1sc in each of next 4sc, join with ss in 1ch. (63 sts)

ROUND 8: 1ch, [2sc in next sc, 1sc in each of next 6sc] 8 times, 2sc in next sc, 1sc in each of next 5sc, join with ss in 1ch. (72 sts)

Fasten off.

Petals (make 9)

Join C with ss in first of any 2sc in same place on round 8 and work each petal back and forth in rows as follows:

Yarn: Worsted-weight wool in chartreuse (A), pink (B), and maroon (C)

METHOD

Center disk

Using A, make 5ch, join with ss into a ring. Work in a spiral as follows:

ROUND 1: 7sc in ring.

ROUND 2: 2sc in each sc. (14 sts)

Fasten off with ss in next sc.

Outer petals

Join B with ss in back loop of any sc on round 2.

ROUND 3: [6ch, skip first ch, 1sc in next ch, 1hdc in next ch, 1dc in next ch, 1tr in next ch, 1dtr in next ch, ss in back loop of next sc on round 2] 14 times. (14 petals)

Fasten off.

Inner petals

Join C with ss in front loop of any sc on round 2.

ROUND 4: [5ch, ss in front loop of next sc on round 2] 14 times. (14 petals)

Fasten off.

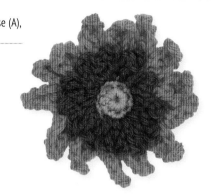

ROW 1 (RS): 1ch (counts as 1sc), 1sc in each of next 8sc, ending in first of next 2sc in same place, turn. (9 sts)

ROW 2: 1ch, skip first sc, 1sc in each of next 7sc, 1sc in 1ch, turn.

ROW 3: As row 2.

ROW 4: 1ch, skip first sc, 1sc in each remaining sc, turn leaving 1ch unworked. (8 sts)

Repeat row 4 five times. (3 sts)

ROW 10: 1ch, skip first sc, 2sc tog over (next sc and 1ch). Fasten off.

Repeat to make next petal, beginning in same sc of round 8 as final st of row 1 of petal just made. Continue all around, making 9 petals in total.

55 BICOLOR GEM \|/

Yarn: Worsted-weight wool in dark gray (A), chartreuse (B), pale gold (C), and orange (D)

METHOD

Lower center disk
Using A, make 5ch, join with ss into a ring.
Work in a spiral as follows:
ROUND 1: 7sc in ring.
ROUND 2: 2sc in each sc. (14 sts)
ROUND 3: [2sc in next sc, 1sc in next sc]
7 times. (21 sts)
Fasten off with ss in next sc.

Petals (make 7)
The petals are worked separately around center disk. They are packed tightly and will ruffle slightly when finished. Each petal is worked back and forth in rows, beginning over 3sc of round 3.
With RS facing, join B with ss in any sc on round 3.
ROW 1: 1ch, 1sc in each of next 2sc, turn. (3 sts)
ROW 2: 3ch, 1dc in sc below, 1dc in next sc, 1dc in 1ch, 3ch.
Fasten off with ss in same sc on round 3 where B was joined.
With WS facing, join C with ss in same sc on round 3 as last st of petal row 1.
ROW 3: Working around edge of inner petal, 1sc in side of row 1, 4sc up side of 3ch, 1sc in top of each of next 3dc, 4sc down side of 3ch, 1sc in side of row 1, ss in same sc on round 3 as first st of petal row 1.

ROW 4: Turn to RS, skip first ss, 1sc in each of next 4sc, 2ch, 2dc in next sc, 1tr in next sc, 1dtr in next sc, 1tr in next sc, 2dc in next sc, 2ch, 1sc in each of next 4sc.
Fasten off with ss in same sc on round 3 as last st of petal row 1.
Repeat to make next petal, beginning in next sc on round 3 of center disk. Continue all around, making 7 petals in total.

Raised center disk
Using D, make 5ch, join with ss into a ring.
Work in a spiral as follows:
ROUND 1: 7sc in ring.
ROUND 2: 2sc in each sc. (14 sts)
ROUND 3: [2sc in next sc, 1sc in next sc]
7 times. (21 sts)

ROUND 4: [1sc in next sc, skip next sc]
10 times, 1sc in last sc. (11 sts)
Break off D, leaving a long tail, and thread tail through last round. Pull to tighten and form a circle, then sew onto center of flower.

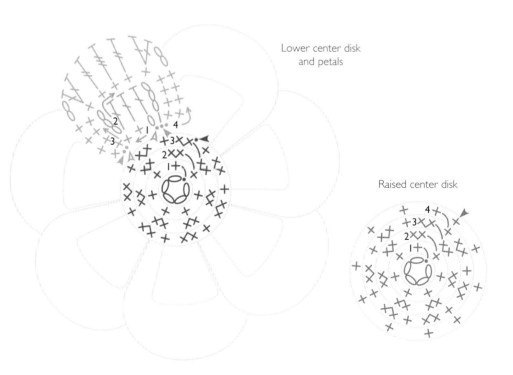

Lower center disk
and petals

Raised center disk

Yarn: Worsted-weight tweed wool in mid-brown (A) and dark brown (B); worsted-weight wool in golden yellow (C)

METHOD

Center disk

Using A, make a slip ring.

ROUND 1: 1ch (counts as 1sc), 5sc in ring, pull end to close ring, join with ss in 1ch. (6 sts)

ROUND 2: 1ch, 1sc in same place, 2sc in each of next 5sc, join with ss in 1ch. (12 sts)

ROUND 3: 1ch, [2sc in next sc, 1sc in next sc] 5 times, 2sc in next sc, join with ss in 1ch. (18 sts)

ROUND 4: 1ch, [2sc in next sc, 1sc in each of next 2sc] 5 times, 2sc in next sc, 1sc in next sc, join with ss in 1ch. (24 sts)
Fasten off A and join B with ss in 1ch at beginning of round 4.

ROUND 5: 1ch, [1sc in each of next 2sc, 5dc bobble in next sc, close bobble with 1ch, 1sc in next sc] 5 times, 1sc in each of next 2sc, 5dc bobble in next sc, close bobble with 1ch, join with ss in 1ch. (24 sts)
Fasten off B and join C with ss in 1ch at beginning of round 5.

ROUND 6: 1ch, [1sc in each of next 2sc, 2sc in ch closing bobble, 1sc in next sc] 5 times, 1sc in each of next 2sc, 2sc in ch closing bobble, join with ss in 1ch. (30 sts)
Fasten off.

Petals (make 12)

Using C and leaving tail of yarn for sewing petal to center disk, make 5ch.

ROW 1 (RS): Skip first ch, 1sc in each of next 4ch, turn.

ROW 2: 1ch (counts as 1sc), 1sc in first sc, 2sc in each of next 3sc, turn leaving 1ch unworked. (8 sts)

ROW 3: 3ch, skip first sc, 1dc in each of next 6sc, 1dc in 1ch, turn.

ROW 4: 1ch, skip first dc, 1sc in each of next 6dc, 1sc in top of 3ch, turn.

ROW 5: 1ch, skip first sc, [1sc in next sc, skip next sc] 3 times, 1sc in 1ch, turn.

ROW 6: 3ch (counts as 1dc), skip first sc, 1dc in each of next 3sc, turn leaving 1ch unworked. (4 sts)

ROW 7: 1ch (counts as 1sc), skip first dc, 1sc in next dc, skip next dc, 1sc in top of 3ch, turn. (3 sts)

ROW 8: 1ch, skip 2sc, 1sc in 1ch.
Fasten off.

Finishing

Using tails of yarn, sew straight edge of 6 petals evenly spaced around edge of center disk, aligning center of each petal to a bobble. Sew base of remaining 6 petals around disk, positioning them behind the spaces between the first 6 petals.

Specific symbol
◯ 5dc bobble, 1ch

Center disk

Petal

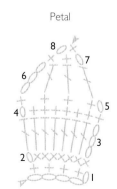

Yarn: Worsted-weight wool in golden yellow (A), rust (B), chartreuse (C), and orange (D)

METHOD

Center disk

Using A, make 5ch, join with ss into a ring.

Work in a spiral as follows:

ROUND 1: 8sc in ring.

ROUND 2: 2sc in each sc. (16 sts)

ROUND 3: [2sc in next sc, 1sc in next sc] 8 times. (24 sts)

ROUND 4: [2sc in next sc, 1sc in each of next 2sc] 7 times, 2sc in each of next 2sc, 1sc in next sc. (33 sts)

Fasten off with ss in next sc.

Specific symbol

◯ 5dc bobble, 1ch

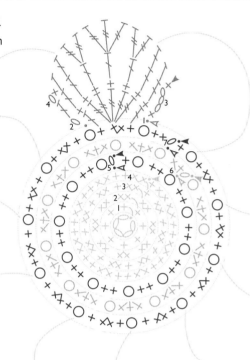

Bobble border

Join B with ss in any sc on round 4.

ROUND 5: 1ch (counts as 1sc), [5dc bobble in next sc, close bobble with 1ch, 1sc in each of next 2sc] 10 times, 5dc bobble in next sc, close bobble with 1ch, 1sc in next sc, join with ss in 1ch.

Fasten off B and join C with ss in ch closing any bobble on round 5.

ROUND 6: 1ch (counts as 1sc), 2sc in same place, [skip next sc, 5dc bobble in next sc, close bobble with 1ch, 3sc in ch closing next bobble] 10 times, skip next sc, 5dc bobble in next sc, close bobble with 1ch, join with ss in 1ch.

Fasten off C and rejoin B with ss in ch closing any bobble on round 6.

ROUND 7: 1ch (counts as 1sc), 1sc in same place, [1sc in next sc, 5dc bobble in next sc, close bobble with 1ch, 1sc in next sc, 2sc in ch closing next bobble] 10 times, 1sc in next sc, 5dc bobble in next sc, close bobble with 1ch, 1sc in next sc, join with ss in 1ch.
Fasten off.

Petals (make 11)

Join D with ss in ch closing any bobble on round 7 and work each petal back and forth in rows.

ROW 1 (RS): 1dc in next sc, skip next sc, 5tr in next sc, 1dc in next sc, ss in ch closing next bobble, turn.

ROW 2: 1ch (counts as 1sc), skip first ss, 1sc in each of next 8 sts, turn. (9 sts)

ROW 3: 3ch, skip first sc, 1dc in each of next 7sc, 1dc in 1ch, turn.

ROW 4: 1ch, 1sc in first dc, 1hdc in next dc, 1dc in next dc, 2tr in next dc, 3tr in next dc, 2tr in next dc, 1dc in next dc, 1hdc in next dc, 1sc in 3rd of 3ch.
Fasten off.

Repeat to make next petal, beginning in ch closing same bobble as last st of row 1 of petal just made. Continue all around, making 11 petals in total.

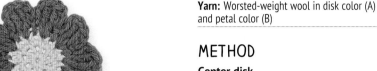

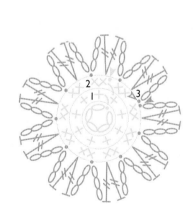

Felted variation with French knot embroidery.

Yarn: Worsted-weight wool in disk color (A) and petal color (B)

METHOD

Center disk

Using A, make 5ch, join with ss into a ring. Work in a spiral as follows:
ROUND 1: 9sc in ring.
ROUND 2: 2sc in each sc. (18 sts)
Fasten off with ss in next sc.

Petals

Join B with ss in any sc on round 2.
ROUND 3: [3ch, 2tr in next sc, 3ch, ss in next sc] 9 times. (9 petals)
Fasten off.

59 SUNBRIGHT |

Yarn: Aran-weight or heavy worsted-weight wool in fuchsia (A) and orange (B)

METHOD

Center disk

Using A, make 5ch, join with ss into a ring. Work in a spiral as follows:

ROUND 1: 7sc in ring.

ROUND 2: 2sc in each sc. (14 sts)

ROUND 3: [2sc in next sc, 1sc in next sc] 7 times. (21 sts) Fasten off with ss in next sc.

Petals

Join B with ss in any sc on round 3.

ROUND 4: [7ch, ss in next sc] 21 times. (21 petals) Fasten off.

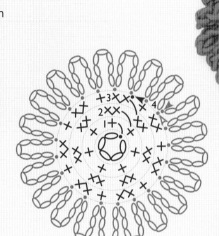

60 SUNBURST |

Yarn: Aran-weight or heavy worsted-weight wool in fuchsia (A) and gold (B)

METHOD

Center disk

Using A, make 5ch, join with ss into a ring. Work in a spiral as follows.

ROUND 1: 7sc in ring.

ROUND 2: 2sc in each sc. (14 sts)

ROUND 3: [2sc in next sc, 1sc in next sc] 7 times. (21 sts) Fasten off with ss in next sc.

Petals

Join B with ss in any sc on round 3.

ROUND 4: [7ch, skip first ch, 1sc in each of next 6ch, ss in next sc] 21 times. (21 petals) Fasten off.

61 RASPBERRY RUFFLE \/

Yarn: DK or light worsted-weight wool/cotton in brown (A), pink (B), and green (C)

METHOD

Center disk

Using A, make 5ch, join with ss into a ring. Work in a spiral as follows:

ROUND 1: 6sc in ring.

ROUND 2: 2sc in each sc. (12 sts)

ROUND 3: [2sc in next sc, 1sc in next sc] 6 times. (18 sts)

ROUND 4: [2sc in next sc, 1sc in each of next 2sc] 6 times. (24 sts)

ROUND 5: [2sc in next sc, 1sc in each of next 3sc] 6 times. (30 sts)
Fasten off with ss in next sc.

Petals

Join B with ss in any sc on round 5.

ROUND 6: [6ch, ss in 2nd ch from hook, 1sc in next ch, 1hdc in next ch, 2dc in each of next 2ch (petal made); skip next sc on round 5 and attach petal with 1sc in next sc] 15 times. (15 petals)
Fasten off.

If you leave the flower unblocked, the petals will curl around the center disk and form a double ruffle.

Ruffle border

Join C with ss in any empty sc on round 5 and work in front of petals as follows:

ROUND 7: [3ch, ss in 2nd ch from hook, 1sc in next ch (ruffle made), ss in next empty sc on round 5] 15 times. (15 ruffles)
Fasten off.

For a flower in full bloom, block the sunflower with the petals pinned out.

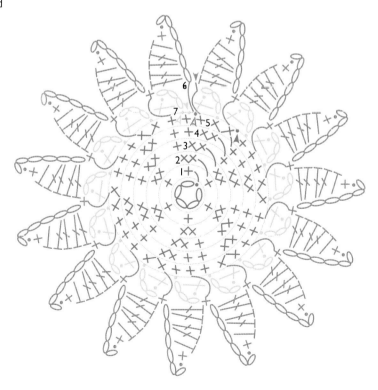

Yarn: Worsted-weight tweed wool in chartreuse (A) (optional), brown (B), green (C), and orange or pale yellow (D)

METHOD

Center disk and stem

Using A for two-color center or B for single-color center, make 4ch, join with ss into a ring.

Work in a spiral as follows:

ROUND 1: 5sc in ring.

ROUND 2: 2sc in each sc. (10 sts)

ROUND 3: [2sc in next sc, 1sc in next sc] 5 times. (15 sts)

ROUND 4: [2sc in next sc, 1sc in each of next 2sc] 5 times. (20 sts)

ROUND 5: [2sc in next sc, 1sc in each of next 3sc] 5 times. (25 sts)

ROUND 6: [2sc in next sc, 1sc in each of next 4sc] 5 times. (30 sts)

If working two-color center, fasten off A and join B in same place.

ROUND 7: [2sc in next sc, 1sc in each of next 5sc] 5 times. (35 sts)

ROUND 8: [2sc in next sc, 1sc in each of next 6sc] 5 times. (40 sts)

ROUNDS 9-10: 1sc in each sc.

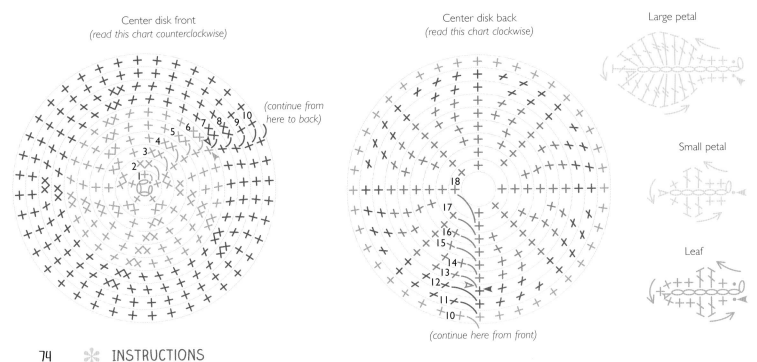

Center disk front
(read this chart counterclockwise)

(continue from here to back)

Center disk back
(read this chart clockwise)

(continue here from front)

Large petal

Small petal

Leaf

ROUND 11: [Skip next sc, 1sc in each of next 4sc] 8 times. (32 sts).

ROUND 12: [Skip next sc, 1sc in each of next 3sc] 8 times. (24 sts).

Fasten off B and join C in same place.

ROUNDS 13-14: 1sc in each sc.

ROUND 15: [Skip next sc, 1sc in each of next 2sc] 8 times. (16 sts)

ROUND 16: 1sc in each sc.

ROUND 17: [Skip next sc, 1sc in next sc] 8 times. (8 sts)

Stuff center disk with scraps of yarn in matching color.

ROUND 18: [Skip next sc, 1sc in each of next 3sc] twice. (6 sts)

Continue by working 1sc in each sc, forming a spiral tube on these 6 sts to length of stem required, then fasten off with ss in next sc.

Large petals (make 11)

Using D, make 10ch.

ROW 1: Skip first ch, ss in next ch, 1sc in each of next 3ch, 1dc in next ch, 2dc in next ch, 2tr in next ch, 1dc in next ch, 5dc in last ch (base of petal). Continuing along other side of chain, 1dc in next ch, 2tr in next ch, 2dc in next ch, 1dc in next ch, 1sc in each of next 3ch.

Fasten off with ss at top of petal.

Small petals (make 11)

Using D, make 6ch.

ROW 1: Skip first ch, 1sc in each of next 2ch, 1dc in each of next 2ch, 2sc in last ch (base of petal). Continuing along other side of chain, 1dc in each of next 2ch, 1sc in each of next 2ch.

Fasten off with ss at top of petal.

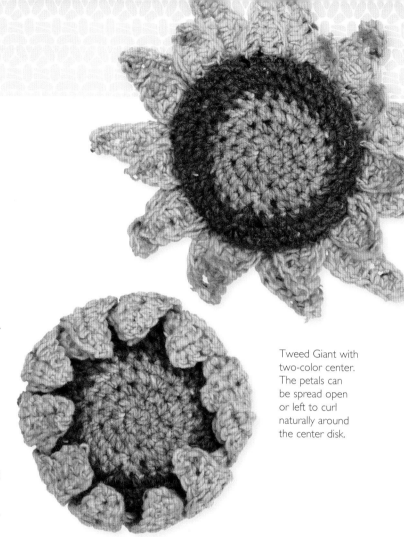

Tweed Giant with two-color center. The petals can be spread open or left to curl naturally around the center disk.

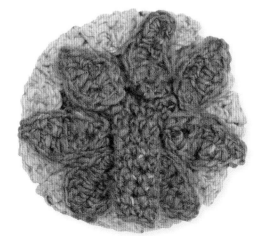

Leaves (make 7)

Using C, make 7ch.

ROW 1: Skip first ch, ss in next ch, 1sc in next ch, 1dc in each of next 2ch, 1sc in next ch, 5sc in last ch (base of leaf). Continuing along other side of chain, 1sc in next ch, 1dc in each of next 2ch, 1sc in next ch.

Fasten off with ss at top of leaf.

Finishing

Using D, sew base of small petals evenly spaced around back of center disk. Sew base of large petals around disk, positioning them behind the spaces between the small petals. Using C, sew base of leaves around top of stem.

Yarn: Worsted-weight cotton in dark brown (A); fringed yarn in copper (B); worsted-weight wool in maroon (C)

METHOD

Center disk

Using A, make 5ch, join with ss into a ring. Work in a spiral as follows:

ROUND 1: 9sc in ring.

ROUND 2: 2sc in each sc. (18 sts)

ROUND 3: [2sc in next sc, 1sc in next sc] 9 times. (27 sts)

ROUND 4: [2sc in next sc, 1sc in each of next 2sc] 9 times. (36 sts)

ROUND 5: [2sc in next sc, 1sc in each of next 3sc] 9 times. (45 sts)

Fasten off A and join B in same place.

ROUND 6: [2sc in next sc, 1sc in each of next 4sc] 9 times. (54 sts)

ROUND 7: [2sc in next sc, 1sc in each of next 5sc] 9 times. (63 sts)

Fasten off B and rejoin A in same place to work back of disk.

ROUND 8: [1sc in each of next 6sc, skip next sc] 9 times. (54 sts)

ROUND 9: [1sc in each of next 5sc, skip next sc] 9 times. (45 sts)

ROUND 10: [1sc in each of next 4sc, skip next sc] 9 times. (36 sts)

ROUND 11: [1sc in each of next 3sc, skip next sc] 9 times. (27 sts)

ROUND 12: [1sc in each of next 2sc, skip next sc] 9 times. (18 sts)

ROUND 13: [1sc in next sc, skip next sc] 9 times. (9 sts)

Fasten off with ss in next sc, leaving tail of yarn for sewing up.

Petals (make 16)

Using C, make 8ch.

ROW 1: Skip first ch, ss in next ch, 1sc in each of next 3ch, 1hdc in each of next 2ch, 3sc in last chain (base of petal). Continuing along other side of chain, 1hdc in each of next 2ch, 1sc in each of next 3ch.

Fasten off with ss at top of petal.

Finishing

Stuff center disk with scraps of yarn A (or similar color), then sew opening closed with tail of yarn. Using C, sew base of petals evenly spaced around back of disk.

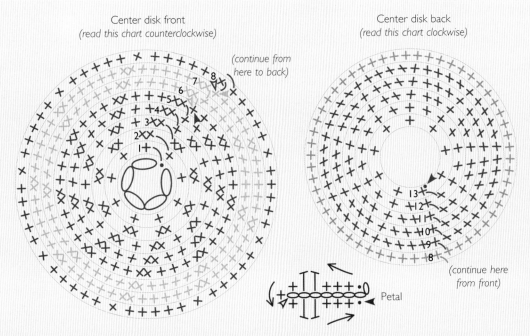

Center disk front
(read this chart counterclockwise)

(continue from here to back)

Center disk back
(read this chart clockwise)

(continue here from front)

Petal

Yarn: Worsted-weight wool in brown (A), red (B), pale gold (C), and chartreuse (D)

METHOD

Center disk

Using A, make 5ch and join with ss to form a ring. Work in a spiral as follows:

ROUND 1: 7sc in ring.

ROUND 2: 2sc in each sc. (14 sts)

ROUND 3: [2sc in next sc, 1sc in next sc] 7 times. (21 sts)

Fasten off A with ss in next sc and join B with ss in any sc on round 3.

ROUND 4: [1sc in next sc, 5dc bobble in next sc, close bobble with 1ch, 1sc in next sc] 7 times.

ROUND 5: 1sc in each sc and 1sc in each ch closing bobble. (21 sts)

ROUND 6: 1sc in each sc.

ROUND 7: [1sc in each of next 2sc, skip next sc] 7 times. (14 sts)

ROUND 8: 1sc in each sc.

ROUND 9: [1sc in next sc, skip next sc] 7 times. (7 sts)

Fasten off with ss in next sc, leaving tail of yarn for sewing up.

Petals, stem, and leaves

Using C, make 14 small petals (page 80).
Using D, make a flower back and stem (page 80) and 3 small leaves (page 82).

Finishing

Stuff center disk with scraps of yarn A (or similar color), then sew opening closed with tail of yarn. Using D (or similar color), stuff cone at top of stem and sew to back of center disk. Using C, sew base of 7 petals evenly spaced around back of disk. Sew base of remaining 7 petals around disk, positioning them behind the spaces between the first 7 petals. Using D, sew base of leaves around top of stem.

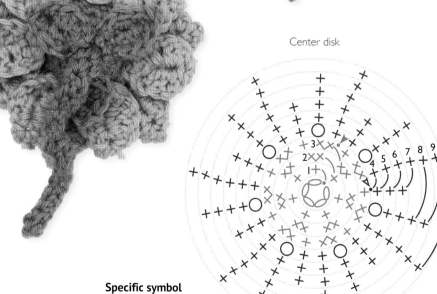

Center disk

Specific symbol

◯ 5dc bobble, 1ch

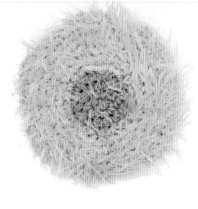

Yarn: DK or light worsted-weight cotton in green (A) and yellow (C); fringed yarn in yellow (B)

METHOD

Using A, make 5ch, join with ss into a ring. Work in a spiral as follows:

ROUND 1: 6sc in ring.

ROUND 2: 2sc in each sc. (12 sts)

ROUND 3: [2sc in next sc, 1sc in next sc] 6 times. (18 sts) Fasten off A and join B in same place.

ROUND 4: [2sc in next sc, 1sc in each of next 2sc] 6 times. (24 sts)

ROUND 5: [2sc in next sc, 1sc in each of next 3sc] 6 times. (30 sts)

ROUND 6: [2sc in next sc, 1sc in each of next 4sc] 6 times. (36 sts)

ROUND 7: [2sc in next sc, 1sc in each of next 5sc] 6 times. (42 sts)

ROUND 8: [2sc in next sc, 1sc in each of next 6sc] 6 times. (48 sts)

ROUND 9: [2sc in next sc, 1sc in each of next 7sc] 6 times. (54 sts)

ROUND 10: [2sc in next sc, 1sc in each of next 8sc] 6 times. (60 sts)

ROUND 11: [2sc in next sc, 1sc in each of next 9sc] 6 times. (66 sts)

ROUND 12: [2sc in next sc, 1sc in each of next 10sc] 6 times. (72 sts)

Fasten off B and join C in same place to work back of flower.

ROUND 13: [1sc in each of next 11sc, skip next sc] 6 times. (66 sts)

ROUND 14: [1sc in each of next 10sc, skip next sc] 6 times. (60 sts)

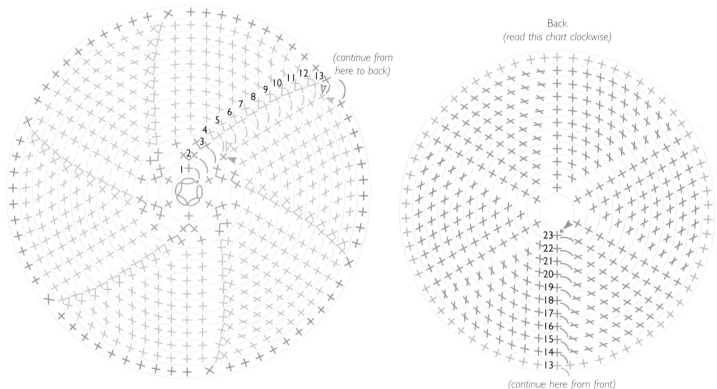

Front
(read this chart counterclockwise)

(continue from here to back)

Back
(read this chart clockwise)

(continue here from front)

ROUND 15: [1sc in each of next 9sc, skip next sc] 6 times. (54 sts)

ROUND 16: [1sc in each of next 8sc, skip next sc] 6 times. (48 sts)

ROUND 17: [1sc in each of next 7sc, skip next sc] 6 times. (42 sts)

ROUND 18: [1sc in each of next 6sc, skip next sc] 6 times. (36 sts)

ROUND 19: [1sc in each of next 5sc, skip next sc] 6 times. (30 sts)

ROUND 20: [1sc in each of next 4sc, skip next sc] 6 times. (24 sts)

ROUND 21: [1sc in each of next 3sc, skip next sc] 6 times. (18 sts)

ROUND 22: [1sc in each of next 2sc, skip next sc] 6 times. (12 sts)

ROUND 23: [1sc in next sc, skip next sc] 6 times. (6 sts) Fasten off with ss in next sc, leaving tail of yarn for sewing up.

Finishing

Stuff sunflower with scraps of yarn B (or similar color), then sew opening closed with tail of yarn.

Yarn: Worsted-weight wool in disk color (A) and petal color (C); fringed yarn in toning color (B) (optional)

METHOD
SPECIAL INSTRUCTION

3ch picot = 3ch, ss in 3rd ch from hook.

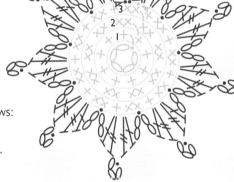

Center disk

Using A, make 5ch, join with ss into a ring. Work in a spiral as follows:

ROUND 1: 9sc in ring.

ROUND 2: 2sc in each sc. (18 sts)

Continue using A or change to B for next round.

ROUND 3: [2sc in next sc, 1sc in next sc] 9 times. (27 sts) Fasten off with ss in next sc.

Petals

Join C with ss in any sc on round 3.

ROUND 4: [2ch, (1dc, 1tr) in next sc, 3ch picot, (1tr, 1dc) in next sc, 2ch, ss in next sc] 9 times. (9 petals) Fasten off.

FLOWER BACK AND STEM \/

Yarn: Worsted-weight wool

METHOD

Cone

Make 5ch, join with ss into a ring. Work in a spiral as follows:

ROUND 1: 6sc in ring.

ROUND 2: 2sc in each sc. (12 sts)

ROUND 3: 1sc in each sc.

ROUND 4: [2sc in next sc, 1sc in next sc] 6 times. (18 sts)

ROUND 5: 1sc in each sc.

You can continue in this way, working an increase round followed by a plain round of sc, to fit the back of a larger flower. Fasten off with ss in next sc, leaving tail of yarn for sewing to flower.

Stem

Make 15ch.

ROW 1: Skip first ch (counts as 1sc), 1sc in each ch to end, turn. (15 sts)

ROW 2: 1ch, skip first sc, 1sc in each of next 13sc, 1sc in 1ch, turn.

ROW 3: As row 2.

Fasten off, leaving tail of yarn for sewing seam along length of stem.

For a longer or shorter stem, begin with as many ch as required.

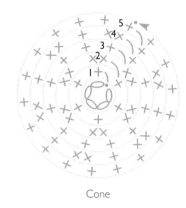

Cone

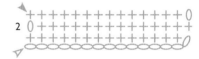

Stem

SUNFLOWER PETALS |

Yarn: Worsted-weight wool

METHOD

Small

Make 6ch.

ROW 1: Skip first ch, ss in next ch, 1sc in next ch, 2dc in next ch, 1sc in next ch, 2sc in last ch (base of petal). Continuing along other side of chain, 1sc in next ch, 2dc in next ch, 1sc in next ch.

Fasten off with ss at top of petal.

Large

Make 9ch.

ROW 1: Skip first ch, ss in next ch, 1sc in next ch, 1hdc in next ch, 1dc in next ch, 2dc in next ch, 1tr in next ch, (1tr, 1dc) in next ch, 5dc in last ch (base of petal). Continuing along other side of chain, (1dc, 1tr) in next ch, 1tr in next ch, 2dc in next ch, 1dc in next ch, 1hdc in next ch, 1sc in next ch.

Fasten off with ss at top of petal.

Square-ended

Make 10ch.

ROW 1: Skip first 3ch, 1dc in each of next 4ch, 1hdc in next ch, 1sc in next ch, ss in last ch, 2ch (top of petal). Continuing along other side of chain, ss in next ch, 1sc in next ch, 1hdc in next ch, 1dc in each of next 4ch, 1dc in base of skipped 3ch at beg of row.

Fasten off.

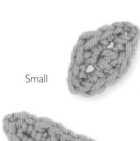

Small

Large

Square-ended

Finishing

Fold stem in half lengthwise and sew long edges together. Sew top of stem to back of cone. Stuff cone with scraps of yarn in matching color and sew to back of flower.

Yarn: Worsted-weight wool in rust (A) and amber (B)

METHOD
Center disk
Using A, make 5ch, join with ss into a ring.
Work in a spiral as follows:

ROUND 1: 7sc in ring.

ROUND 2: 2sc in each sc. (14 sts)

ROUND 3: [2sc in next sc, 1sc in next sc] 7 times. (21 sts)

ROUND 4: [2sc in next sc, 1sc in each of next 2sc] 7 times. (28 sts)

ROUND 5: [2sc in next sc, 1sc in each of next 3sc] 7 times. (35 sts)

ROUND 6: 1sc in each sc.

ROUND 7: [2sc tog in next 2sc, 1sc in each of next 3sc] 7 times. (28 sts)

ROUND 8: [2sc tog in next 2 sts, 1sc in each of next 2sc] 7 times. (21 sts)

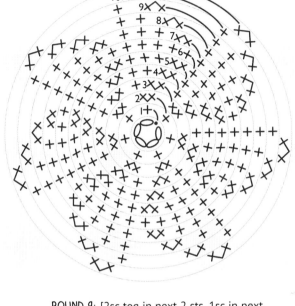

Center disk

ROUND 9: [2sc tog in next 2 sts, 1sc in next sc] 7 times. (14 sts)

ROUND 10: [2sc tog in next 2 sts] 7 times. (7 sts)

Fasten off with ss in next st, leaving tail of yarn for sewing up.

Petals (make 7)
Using B, make 7 square-ended petals (page 80).

Finishing
Stuff center disk with scraps of yarn A (or similar color), then sew opening closed with tail of yarn, and at the same time stitch center front and back of disk together to pull center of sunflower in a little to shape it. Using B, sew straight edge of petals evenly spaced around back of disk.

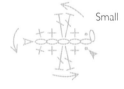

Small

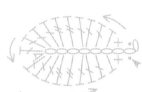

Large

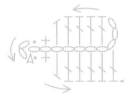

Square-ended

Small

Medium

Large

Extra large

Yarn: Worsted-weight wool

METHOD

Small
Make 6ch.

ROW 1: Skip first ch, ss in next ch, 1sc in next ch, 2dc in next ch, 1sc in next ch, 2sc in last ch (base of leaf). Continuing along other side of chain, 1sc in next ch, 2dc in next ch, 1sc in next ch.

Fasten off with ss at top of leaf.

Medium
Make 8ch.

ROW 1: Skip first ch, ss in next ch, 1sc in each of next 2ch, (1hdc, 1dc) in next ch, 2dc in next ch, 2tr in next ch, 5dc in last ch (base of leaf). Continuing along other side of chain, 2tr in next ch, 2dc in next ch, (1dc, 1hdc) in next ch, 1sc in each of next 2ch.

Fasten off with ss at top of leaf.

Large
Make 9ch.

ROW 1: Skip first ch, ss in next ch, 1sc in each of next 2ch, 1hdc in next ch, 2dc in next ch, (1dc, 1tr) in next ch, 2tr in next ch, 7dc in last ch (base of leaf). Continuing along other side of chain, 2tr in next ch, (1tr, 1dc) in next ch, 2dc in next ch, 1hdc in next ch, 1sc in each of next 2ch, ss in next ch.

Fasten off or add picot edge as follows:

ROW 2: 2ch, [1sc in each of next 3 sts, 2ch, 1sc in 2nd ch from hook] 8 times, 1sc in each of next 3 sts.

Fasten off with ss at top of leaf.

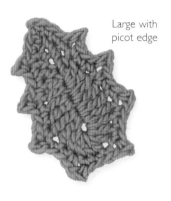

Large with picot edge

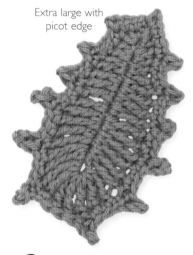

Extra large with picot edge

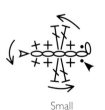

Small

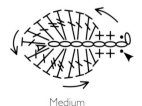

Medium

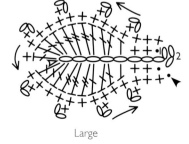

Large

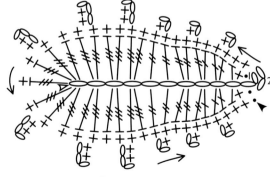

Extra large

71 TULIP TREE LEAF

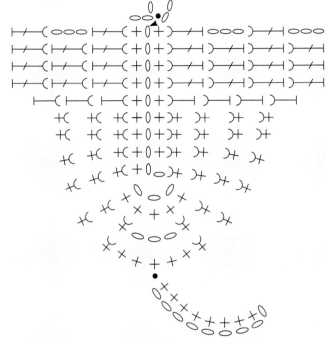

Extra large

Make 12ch.

ROW 1: Skip first ch, ss in next ch, (1sc, 1hdc) in next ch, 2dc in next ch, (1dc, 1tr) in next ch, 2tr in next ch, 1tr in each of next 2ch, 2dtr in each of next 3ch, 7dtr in last ch (base of leaf). Continuing along other side of chain, 2dtr in each of next 3ch, 1tr in each of next 2ch, 2tr in next ch, (1tr, 1dc) in next ch, 2dc in next ch, (1hdc, 1sc) in next ch, ss in next ch.

Fasten off or add picot edge as follows:

ROW 2: 2ch, skip first ss, [1sc in each of next 3 sts, 2ch, 1sc in 2nd ch from hook] 3 times, [1sc in each of next 3 sts, 3ch, skip first ch from hook, 1sc in each of next 2ch] 6 times, [1sc in each of next 3 sts, 2ch, 1sc in 2nd ch from hook] 3 times, 1sc in each of next 3 sts.

Fasten off with ss at top of leaf.

Yarn: DK wool

METHOD

Make 10ch.

ROW 1: Skip 2ch, 1sc in each of next 8ch, 5ch, ss in first of 5ch, 2ch, working in remaining strand of base ch: 1sc in each of next 8ch, 1sc in top ch of 2ch, 3ch; working in back loop only from now on: 1sc in 1ch, 1sc in each of next 3sc, 1hdc in next sc, 1dc in each of next 4sc, turn.

ROW 2: 3ch, 1dc in each of next 3dc, 1hdc in hdc, 1sc in each of next 4sc, 5sc in 3ch sp, 1sc in each of next 4sc, 1hdc in next sc, 1dc in each of next 4 sts, turn.

ROW 3: 3ch, 1dc in each of next 3dc, 1hdc in hdc, 1sc in each of next 6sc, 3ch, skip 1sc, 1sc in each of next 6sc, 1hdc in hdc, 1dc in each of next 4 sts, turn.

ROW 4: 3ch, 1dc in each of next 3dc, 1hdc in hdc, 1sc in each of next 6sc, 5sc in ch sp, 1sc in each of next 6sc, 1hdc in hdc, 1dc in each of next 4 sts.

Fasten off invisibly.

Stem

Turn leaf to WS, join yarn in back of center sc of base, 9ch, skip 1ch, 1sc in each of next 8ch, ss in base of leaf.

Fasten off.

72 IRISH LEAF \/

Yarn: DK wool

METHOD

Leaf

Make 12ch.

ROW 1 (WS): Skip 1ch, 1sc in each of next 10ch, 5sc in next ch, without turning over and working in the remaining strand of base ch: 1sc in each of next 10ch, 3ch, working under both loops of each st: 1sc in each of next 9sc, turn.

ROW 2: 1ch, working in back loop only: 1sc in each of next 8sc, [1sc in back loop of next ch, 1ch] twice, 1sc in next ch, 1sc in each of next 9sc, turn.

ROW 3: 1ch, skip 1sc, working under both loops: 1sc in each of next 9sc, [1ch, 1sc in next st] 4 times, 1sc in each of next 6sc, turn.

ROW 4: 1ch, skip 1sc, working in back loop only: 1sc in each of next 20 sts, turn.

ROW 5: 1ch, skip 1sc, working in both loops: 1sc in each of next 9 sts.

Stem

7ch, skip 1ch, ss in each of next 6ch, ss in last sc of row 5. Fasten off invisibly.

See also chart opposite

73 IVY LEAF \/

Yarn: Fine wool in dark green (A) and pale green (B)

METHOD

Stem

Using A, make 12ch, skip 2ch, 1sc in next ch, ss in each of next 9ch. Do not fasten off.

Leaf

ROW 1 (RS): [5ch, skip 4ch, 1sc in next ch] 3 times, ss in remaining strand of top ch of stem, turn. (3 ch loops)

ROW 2: In first loop: (2sc, 1ch, 1dc, 1ch, 2sc); in 2nd loop: (1sc, 1dc, 1ch, [1tr, 1ch] twice, 1dc, 1sc); in 3rd loop: (2sc, 1ch, 1dc, 1ch, 2sc), turn. Fasten off.

ROW 3: Join B in last sc of row 2; first lobe: 1ch, 2sc in next sc, 2sc in 1ch, 1ch, 1dc in dc, 1ch, 2sc in 1ch, 2sc in next sc, ss in next sc; 2nd lobe: 1sc in sc, (1sc, 1dc) in dc, 2dc in 1ch, 1ch, (2tr, 1ch, 1dtr) in tr, skip 1ch, 2dc in next tr, 1dc in 1ch, (1dc, 1sc) in next dc, ss in 1sc; 3rd lobe: 1sc in sc, 2sc in next sc, 2sc in 1ch, 1ch, 1dc in dc, 1ch, 2sc in 1ch, 2sc in sc, 1sc in next sc. Fasten off invisibly.

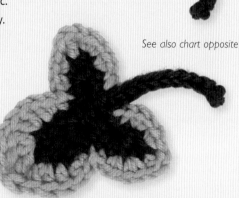

See also chart opposite

FERN LEAF \\/

Yarn: DK cotton

METHOD

LEAF 1: Make 12ch, *skip 1ch, 1sc in next ch, 1hdc in next ch, 1dc in next ch, 1tr in next ch, 1dc in next ch, 1hdc in next ch, 1sc in next ch.**

LEAF 2: Make 12ch, *skip 1ch, 1sc in next ch, 1hdc in next ch, 1dc in next ch, 1tr in each of next 2ch, 1dc in next ch, 1hdc in next ch, 1sc in next ch.**

LEAF 3: As leaf 2.

LEAF 4: Make 11ch, then work as leaf 1 from * to **.

LEAF 5: Make 8ch, then work as leaf 1 from * to **.

LEAF 6: As leaf 5.

STEM: Ss in each of next 3ch.

LEAF 7: Make 9ch, then work as leaf 2 from * to **.

STEM: Ss in each of next 3ch.

LEAF 8: As leaf 7.

STEM: Ss in each of next 3ch.

LEAF 9: As leaf 5.

STEM: Ss in each of next 4 ch.
Fasten off invisibly.

See also chart below

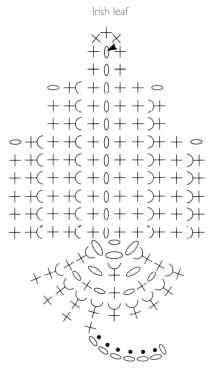

Irish leaf

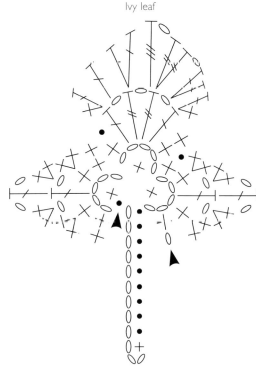

Ivy leaf

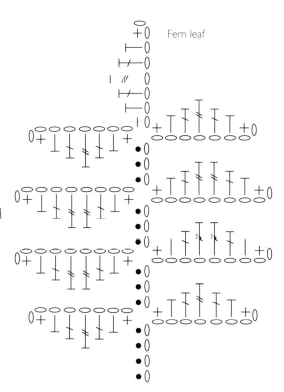

Fern leaf

Yarn: DK wool

METHOD

Leaf

Make 11ch.

ROW 1: Skip 1ch, 1sc in each of next 4ch, 1hdc in next ch, 1dc in each of next 5ch. (11 sts)

From now on, work in the back loop of each st:

ROW 2: 3ch, 1dc in each of next 4dc, 1hdc in hdc, 1sc in each of next 4sc, 1sc in 1ch.

ROW 3: 1ch, 1sc in each of next 4sc, 1hdc in hdc, 1dc in each of next 4dc, 1dc in top ch of 3ch.

ROW 4: As row 2.

ROW 5: 1ch, 1sc in each of next 4sc, 1hdc in hdc, 1dc in each of next 3dc, turn.

ROW 6: 4ch, skip 3ch, 1dc in next ch, 1dc in each of next 3dc, 1hdc in hdc, 1sc in each of next 4sc, 1sc in 1ch.

ROW 7: As row 3.

ROW 8: As row 2.

ROW 9: As row 3.

Fasten off invisibly.

Base

Turn to RS. Working under 2 strands, join yarn in 1ch at beginning of first row, 2ch, 4dc cluster in 1ch of rows 3, 5, 7, and 9. Do not fasten off.

Stem

Make 10ch, skip 1ch, 1sc in each of next 9ch. Fasten off.

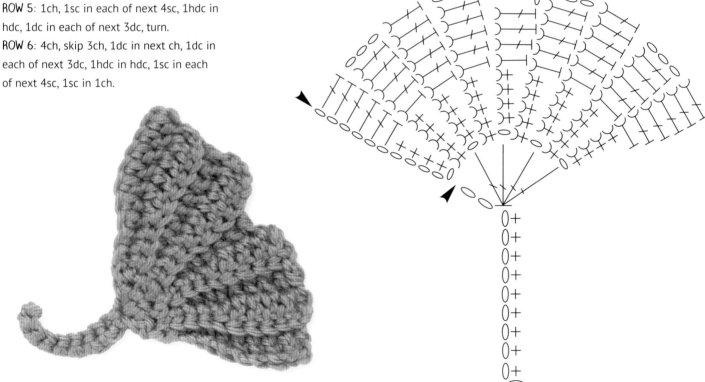

76 PLAIN CLOVER LEAF

Yarn: Fine wool

METHOD

First lobe

Make 5ch. RS facing, skip 2ch, 1sc in next ch, 1dc in next ch, 10tr in last ch; working in remaining strand of each ch: 1dc in next ch, 1sc in next ch, ss in next ch. Fasten off.

2nd and 3rd lobes

Make 2 more lobes the same as first lobe but without fastening off the last one.

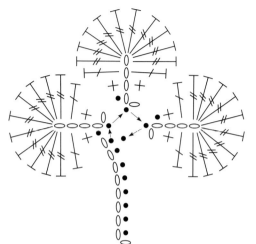

Stem

Using attached yarn and with RS facing, make 9ch, skip 1ch, ss in each of next 8ch, ss in first st of attached lobe, ss in first st of 2nd lobe, ss in first st of first lobe, ss in 8th ss of stem. Fasten off invisibly.

77 VARIEGATED CLOVER LEAF

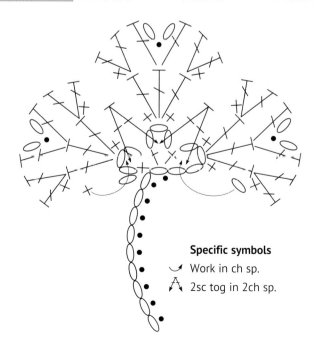

Specific symbols

⌣ Work in ch sp.

⋀ 2sc tog in 2ch sp.

Yarn: DK yarn in pale green (A) and dark green (B)

METHOD

ROUND 1: Using A, make 15ch, skip 4ch, 1sc in next ch, [3ch, 1sc in same ch as before] twice, turn.

ROUND 2 (RS): 1ch, (3dc, 1sc) in first ch sp, (1sc, 3dc, 1sc) in each of next 2 ch sp, ss in same ch as 3sc of round 1, ss in each of 10ch of stem. Fasten off. Do not turn.

ROUND 3: Using B, join yarn in center of first ch sp, 1ch, *(1sc, 2dc) in first dc, (1dc, 1ch, ss, 1ch, 1dc) in 2nd dc, (2dc, 1sc) in 3rd dc, skip 1sc, insert hook in ch sp below, yo, pull loop through, insert hook in next ch sp, yo, pull loop through, yo, pull yarn through all 3 loops on hook; repeat from * once, (1sc, 2dc) in next dc, (1dc, 1ch, ss, 1ch, 1dc) in next dc, (2dc, 1sc) in last dc, 1sc in 3rd ch sp. Fasten off.

78 SPRING OAK LEAF \/

Yarn: DK wool in olive (A) and lime (B)

Using A, make 23ch.

ROW 1 (RS): Skip 2ch, (1dc, 3tr, 1dc, 1sc) in next ch, skip 1ch, (1sc, 1dc) in next ch, 3tr in next ch, (1dc, 1sc) in next ch, skip 1ch, (1dc, 1tr) in next ch, 3dtr in next ch, (1tr, 1dc) in next ch, skip 1ch, (1sc, 3dc, 1sc) in next ch, ss in each of next 8ch, 1sc in each of last 2ch. Fasten off.

ROW 2 (RS): Rejoin A in single strand of ch that forms base of last group, 2ch, (3dc, 1sc) in same ch, skip 1ch, (1dc, 1tr) in next ch, 3dtr in next ch, (1tr, 1dc) in next ch, skip 1ch, (1sc, 1dc) in next ch, 3tr in next ch, (1dc, 1sc) in next ch, skip 1ch and base of first group, ss in next ch. Fasten off.

ROW 3 (RS): Join B in first ch of row 2, 1ch, 2sc in each of 3dc, ss in each of 1sc and 1dc, 1sc in tr, 2sc in each of 3dtr, 1sc in tr, ss in each of 1dc and 1sc, 1sc in dc, 2sc in each of 3tr, 1sc in dc, ss in sc, skip ss, ss in 23rd ch, 2sc in dc, 2sc in each of 3tr, 2sc in dc, ss in each of next 2sc, 1sc in dc, 2sc in each of 3tr, 1sc in dc, ss in each of 1sc and 1dc, 1sc in tr, 2sc in each of 3dtr, 1sc in tr, ss in each of 1dc and 1sc, 2sc in each of 3dc, ss in sc. Fasten off.

See also chart opposite

79 AUTUMN OAK LEAF \/

Yarn: DK wool in rust (A) and olive (B)

METHOD

ROW 1 (RS): Using A, make 10ch, skip 1ch, ss in each of next 9ch; 7ch, skip 3ch, 1dc in each of next 2ch, 1sc in each of next 2ch; 9ch, skip 3ch, 1dc in each of next 2ch, 1sc in next ch; 8ch, skip 3ch, 1dc in next ch, 1sc in next ch; 6ch, skip 3ch, 1dc in next ch; 1sc in each of next 2ch; 5ch, skip 3ch, 1dc in next ch, 1sc in next ch; 1sc in each of 3ch stem; 6ch, skip 3ch, 1dc in each of next 2ch, 1sc in next ch, 1sc in each of 3ch stem; 7ch, skip 3ch, 1dc in each of next 2ch, 1sc in each of next 2ch, ss in top ch of stem. Fasten off.

ROW 2 (RS): Working in single remaining strand of ch at base of sts from now on: join B in first ch of first 7ch, 1ch, 1sc in each of next 3 sts; working into 2 strands of 3 free ch and tops of sts from now on: 1sc in first ch, 2sc in 2nd ch, 1sc in 3rd ch, 1sc in each of next 3 sts; 1sc in center ch of stem, 1sc in each of next 3 sts, (1sc, 2sc, 1sc) in 3ch, 1sc in each of next 3 sts, 1sc in center ch of stem, 1sc in each of next 2 sts, (1sc, 2sc, 1sc) in 3ch, 1sc in next st, skip 1ch of stem, 1sc in each of next 2ch, (1sc, 2sc, 1sc) in 3ch, 1sc in each of next 5 sts, (1sc, 2sc, 1sc) in 3ch, 1sc in each of the next 2 sts, skip 1sc, 1sc in next sc, skip next sc, 1sc in each of next 3 sts, (1sc, 2sc, 1sc) in 3ch, 1sc in each of next 3 sts, skip 1sc, 1sc in next sc, skip next sc, 1sc in each of next 4 sts, (1sc, 2sc, 1sc) in 3ch, 1sc in each of next 3 sts, ss in next st.

Fasten off invisibly.

See also chart opposite

Yarn: DK wool in dark olive (A) and
light olive (B)

METHOD

Acorn

Using A, make 5ch, join with ss
into a ring.

ROUND 1 (RS): 1ch, 7sc in ring,
ss in 1ch. (8 sts)

ROUND 2: 1ch, [2sc in next sc,
1sc in next sc] 3 times, 2sc in
next sc, ss in 1ch. (12 sts)

ROUND 3: 1ch, 1sc in each sc, ss
in 1ch. Fasten off invisibly. Allow
the cup shape to curl so that the
WS of the sts is facing.

ROUND 4: Now working in
the opposite direction to the
previous round, inserting the
hook in the back loop of each st:

join B, 4ch, 3dtr tog in next
3 sts, [4dtr tog in next 4 sts]
twice, ss in top ch of 4ch.
Fasten off.
Gather the top, stuffing the
acorn with yarn B.

Stem

Using A, make 11ch, skip 1ch, ss
in each of next 10ch. Fasten off
invisibly. Attach to base of acorn.

Autumn oak leaf

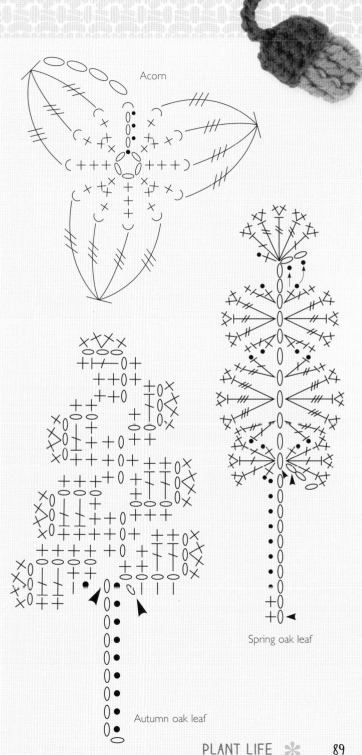

Acorn

Spring oak leaf

Autumn oak leaf

81 NETTLE LEAF |

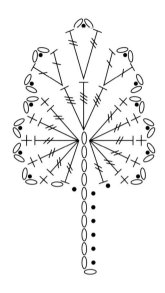

Yarn: DK cotton

METHOD
SPECIFIC INSTRUCTION
2ch picot = 2ch, skip 1ch, ss in next ch.

Make 11ch.
ROW 1: Skip 1ch, ss in each of next 6ch, skip 3ch, (6tr, 3dtr, 6tr) in next ch, ss in same ch as last ss of stem, turn.

ROW 2: 1ch, skip 1tr, (1sc, 2ch picot) in each of next 5tr, (1dc, 2ch picot, 1dc) in first dtr, (1tr, 2ch picot, 1tr) in next dtr, (1dc, 2ch picot, 1dc) in next dtr, (2ch picot, 1sc) in each of next 5tr, ss in last tr. Fasten off.

82 MISTLETOE |

Yarn: DK wool in green (A) and white (B)

METHOD
Leaves
Using A, *make 14ch, skip 5ch, 1dtr in each of next 2ch, 1tr in each of next 2ch, 1dc in each of next 2ch, 1hdc in next ch, 1sc in each of next 2ch; repeat from * once, ss in remaining strand of first ch. Do not fasten off.

Stem
Make 9ch, skip 1ch, ss in each of next 8ch. Fasten off invisibly.

Berry (make 2)
Using B, make 2ch, skip 1ch, (1dc, 1sc) in next ch. Fasten off invisibly.

Finishing
Press leaves. Tie both yarn ends of each berry, then sew onto leaves.

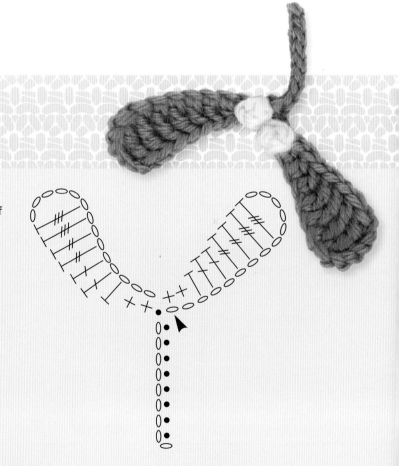

Yarn: DK wool in dark green (A); fine wool in red (B)

METHOD

Leaf and stem

ROUND 1: Using A, make 12ch, skip 1ch, *1sc in next ch, 1hdc in next ch, 1dc in next ch, 2dc in next ch, 2tr in next ch, 1tr in next ch, 2tr in next ch, 2dc in next ch, 1dc in next ch, 1hdc in next ch, 1sc in next ch,** 4ch, skip 1ch, ss in next ch, 1sc in next ch, 1ch; working in remaining strand of 11 original base ch, repeat from * to **.

STEM: 9ch, skip 1ch, ss in each of next 7ch, 1ch.

Prickled edge

FIRST EDGE: Continue along sts of round 1: ***1sc in sc, 1sc in hdc, 3ch, skip 1ch, ss in next ch, 1sc in next ch, 1sc in each of next 3 sts, [4ch, skip 1ch, ss in next ch, 1sc in next ch, 1hdc in next ch, skip next st, 1sc in each of next 3 sts] twice, 3ch, skip 1ch, ss in next ch, 1sc in next ch, 1sc in hdc, ss in sc.**** Fasten off invisibly.

2ND EDGE: Turn to WS to work along remaining straight edge of round 1: join A in 1ch above stem, then work from *** to ****. Do not fasten off. Pin out and press points, then fold leaf along center and on WS, using a smaller size hook and A, work 1sc in each bar of original base ch. Fasten off.

Berry (make 3)

Using B, make 4ch, skip 3ch, 4tr cluster in first ch, 2ch, from back ss in first ch. Fasten off. Use one yarn end to pad the berry and the other to attach it to the leaf.

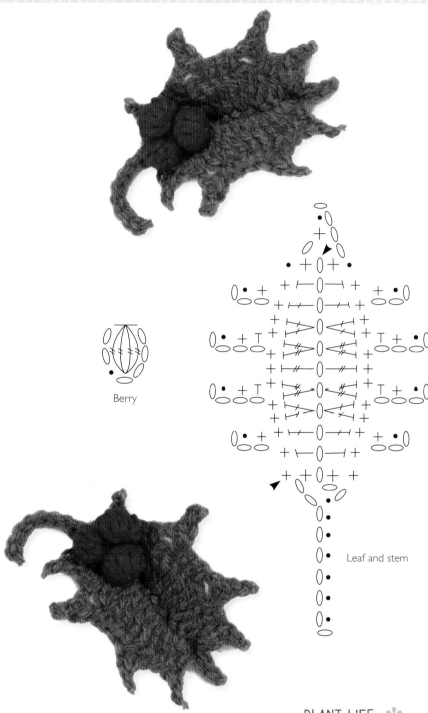

Berry

Leaf and stem

STRAWBERRY LEAF \/

Yarn: DK yarn

METHOD

Leaf (make 3)

Make 8ch.

ROUND 1: Skip 1ch, 1sc in next ch, 1hdc in next ch, 1dc in next ch, 2tr in next ch, 1dc in next ch, 1hdc in next ch, 1sc in last ch, 2ch, working into remaining strands of ch: 1sc in next ch, 1hdc in next ch, 1dc in next ch, 2tr in next ch, 1dc in next ch, 1hdc in next ch, 1sc in last ch, join with ss in first sc.

ROUND 2: 1ch, 1sc in each sc, hdc, and dc of previous round, 2sc in each tr and 2ch sp, ending 1sc in ss at end of round 1, join with ss in first sc. (23 sc)

ROUND 3: 1ch, *1sc in next sc, 2ch, skip 1ch, ss in next ch; repeat from * to end, join with ss in first sc. Fasten off.

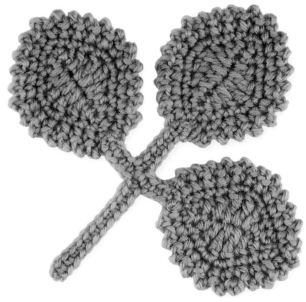

Branched stalk

Make 18ch. Working in back strand of each ch, skip 1ch, 1sc in each of next 4ch, 7ch, skip 1ch, 1sc in each of next 6ch, 5ch, skip 1ch, 1sc in each of next 4ch, 1sc in each of next 13ch. Fasten off.

Finishing

Stitch one leaf onto each branch of the stalk, overlapping the base of the leaf with about 1⁄16in (2mm) of stalk.

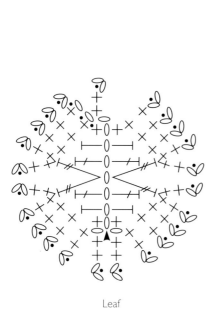

Leaf

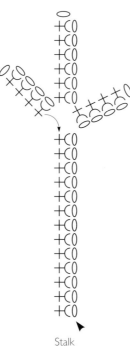

Stalk

Yarn: DK cotton in red (A) and green (B)

Extras: Yellow glass beads; embroidery thread to match A; batting

METHOD

NOTE: The strawberry is worked in continuous rounds without joining. Use a marker to count rounds.

Strawberry

Using A, make 2ch.

ROUND 1: Skip 1ch, 6sc in next ch.

ROUND 2: [1sc in next sc, 2sc in next sc] 3 times. (9 sts)

ROUND 3: [1sc in each of next 2sc, 2sc in next sc] 3 times. (12 sts)

ROUND 4: 1sc in each sc.

ROUND 5: [1sc in each of next 3sc, 2sc in next sc] 3 times. (15 sts)

ROUND 6: [1sc in each of next 4sc, 2sc in next sc] 3 times. (18 sts)

ROUND 7: 1sc in each sc.

ROUND 8: [1sc in each of next 5sc, 2sc in next sc] 3 times. (21 sts)

ROUND 9: [1sc in each of next 6sc, 2sc in next sc] 3 times. (24 sts)

ROUND 10: 1sc in each sc.

ROUND 11: [2sc tog] to end of round. (12 sts)

At this point stitch beads onto the RS of the strawberry using 2 strands of embroidery thread and positioning the beads randomly across the surface. Fasten off securely. Stuff the strawberry firmly and continue.

ROUND 12: [2sc tog] to end. (6 sts)

Fasten off. Stitch from side to side of the strawberry to close the opening, tightening each stitch before making the next one.

Calyx

Using B, make 8ch.

ROW 1: Skip 1ch, 1sc in each ch to end. (7 sc)

ROW 2: 1ch, *1sc in next sc, 5ch, skip 1ch, 1sc in each of next 4ch, ss into sc at base of ch; repeat from * to end. Fasten off.

With RS to inside, roll calyx and secure with a couple of stitches, then stitch to top of strawberry.

Strawberry

Yarn: Fine wool in pale green (A) and purple (B)

METHOD

NOTE: Work all tr around posts by inserting hook from back.

Using A, make a slip ring.
ROUND 1: 3ch, 11dc in ring, pull end to close ring, ss in top ch of 3ch. (12 sts)
ROUND 2: 3ch, [2dc in each of next 2dc, 1dc in next dc] 3 times, 2dc in each of next 2dc, ss in top ch of 3ch. (20 sts)
ROUND 3: 3ch, [1tr around post of next dc, 2dc in next dc] 9 times, 1tr around post of next dc, 1dc in ss at base of 3ch, with B ss in top ch of 3ch. (30 sts)
Continue with B.
ROUND 4: 3ch, [1tr around post of next st, 1dc in each of next 2dc] 9 times, 1tr around post of next st, 1dc in next dc, ss to top ch of 3ch.

ROUND 5: 3ch, 1tr around post of next st, [2dc tog in next 2dc, 1tr around post of next st] 9 times, 1dc in next dc, ss in top ch of 3ch. (21 sts)
ROUND 6: 3ch, [1tr around post of next st, 1dc in next dc] 10 times, ss in top ch of 3ch.
ROUND 7: 3ch, [(1tr around post, 1dc) tog in next 2 sts] 10 times, ss in top ch of 3ch. (11 sts)

Use coiled yarn B as filler and push it into the fig with the end of a pencil.
ROUND 8: 3ch, [(1tr around post of (1tr, 1dc) tog] 10 times, ss in top ch of 3ch.
ROUND 9: 3ch, [1tr around post of next st] 10 times, ss in top ch of 3ch.
Fasten off, leaving an end to gather the stitches underneath ribs of last few rows to form the stalk.

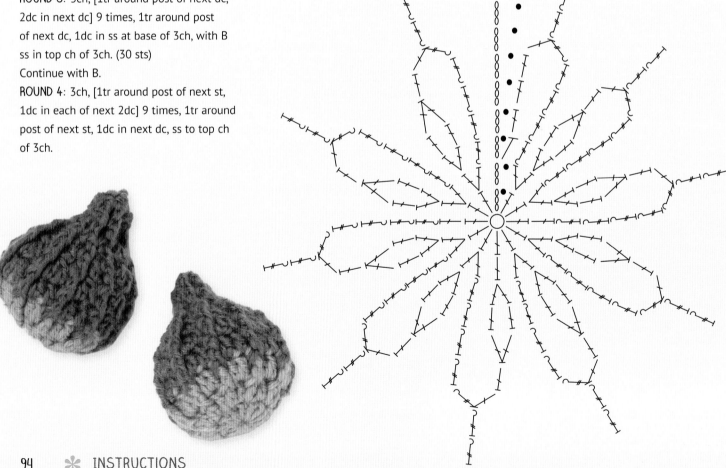

FIG LEAF \|/

Yarn: DK wool

METHOD

Stem

Make 14ch, skip 2ch, 1sc in each of next 2ch, ss in each of next 10ch. Do not fasten off.

Leaf—round 1

LOBE 1 (RS): 11ch, *skip 3ch, 1dc in each of next 3ch, 1hdc in next ch, 1sc in next ch, 1hdc in next ch, 1dc in next ch, 1tr in next ch.**

LOBE 2: 12ch, ***skip 3ch, 1tr in each of next 3ch, 1dc in next ch, 1hdc in next ch, 1sc in next ch, 1hdc in next ch, 1dc in next ch, 1tr in next ch.****

LOBE 3: 14ch, skip 3ch, 1tr in each of next 5ch, 1dc in each of next 4ch, 1hdc in next ch, 1sc in next ch, [3sc in post of next tr] twice, ss in top ch of post, turn. Now continue round 1 in opposite direction:

LOBE 4 (WS): 11ch, work as lobe 1 from * to **, ss in first of 3sc in post of tr of lobe 1.

LOBE 5: 12ch, work as lobe 2 from *** to ****, ss in first of 3sc in post of tr of lobe 2. Fasten off. From now on work in single remaining strand of ch where necessary, otherwise under 2 strands of each st, including ch.

Leaf—round 2

LOBE 1 (RS): Rejoin yarn in 2nd ch of lobe 1, 1ch, 1sc in next ch, 1hdc in next ch, 1dc in next ch, 1tr in each of next 2ch, 2tr in each of next 5 sts, 1dc in next dc, 1hdc in next dc, 1sc in hdc, ss in each of next 3 sts, skip tr.

LOBE 2: Ss in each of next 3ch, 1sc in next ch, 1hdc in next ch, 1dc in next ch, 1tr in each of next 2ch, 2tr in each of next 5 sts, 1tr in next tr, 1dc in next tr, 1hdc in dc, 1sc in hdc, [2sc tog in next 2 sts] twice.

LOBE 3: 2sc tog in next 2ch, 1sc in next ch, 1hdc in next ch, 1dc in each of next 3ch, 1tr in each of next 3ch, 2tr in each of next 5 sts, 1tr in each of next 3 sts, 1dc in each of next 3 sts, 1hdc in next dc, 1sc in next dc, 2sc tog in next 2 sts.

LOBE 5: [2sc tog in next 2 sts] twice, 1sc in hdc, 1hdc in dc, 1dc in tr, 1tr in next tr, 2tr in each of next 5 sts, 1tr in each of next 2ch, 1dc in next ch, 1hdc in next ch, 1sc in next ch, ss in each of next 3ch.

LOBE 4: Skip tr, ss in each of next 3 sts, 1sc in hdc, 1hdc in dc, 1dc in next dc, 2dc in each of next 5 sts, 1dc in each of next 3ch, 1hdc in next ch, 1sc in next ch, ss in next ch.

Fasten off invisibly.

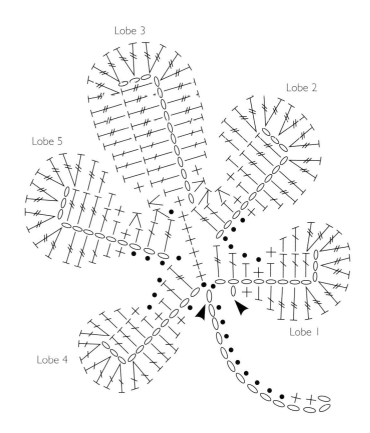

Lobe 3

Lobe 2

Lobe 5

Lobe 1

Lobe 4

LIME AND LEAF \/

Yarn: DK yarn in lime green (A), dark green (B), and brown (C)

Extras: Batting

METHOD

NOTE: The lime is worked in continuous rounds without joining. Use a marker to count rounds.

Lime

Using A, make 2ch.

ROUND 1 (RS): Skip 1ch, 6sc in next ch. (6 sts)

ROUND 2: 2sc in each sc. (12 sts)

ROUND 3: As round 2. (24 sts)

ROUNDS 4-5: 1sc in each st.

ROUND 6: [1sc in next st, 2sc in next st] 12 times. (36 sts)

ROUNDS 7-16: 1sc in each st.

ROUND 17: [1sc in next st, 2sc tog in next 2 sts] 12 times. (24 sts)

ROUNDS 18-19: 1sc in each st.

Stuff the lime very firmly and then continue.

ROUND 20: [2sc tog] to end. (12 sts)

ROUND 21: As round 20. (6 sts)

ROUND 22: 1sc in each st. Fasten off.

Leaf (make 2)

Using B, make 21ch.

ROUND 1 (RS): Skip 1ch, working in single strand of each ch, ss in each of next 2ch, 1sc in each of next 2ch, 1hdc in each of next 2ch, 1dc in each of next 8ch, 1hdc in each of next 2ch, 1sc in each of next 2ch, ss in each of last 2ch. (20 sts, excluding 1ch)

Working in single strand along opposite side of ch, 1ch, ss in each of next 2ch, 1sc in each of next 2ch, 1hdc in each of next 2ch, 1dc in each of next 8ch, 1hdc in each of next 2ch, 1sc in each of next 2ch, ss in each of last 2ch, join with ss in 1ch. (20 sts, excluding 1ch)

ROUND 2: *Ss in each of first 2 sts, 1sc in each of next 2 sts, 1hdc in each of next 12 sts, 1sc in each of next 2 sts, ss in each of next 2 sts; repeat from * along opposite side of leaf, join with ss in first ss. Fasten off.

Branching stem

Using C, make 23ch. Skip 1ch, 1sc in each of next 7ch, 12ch, skip 1ch, 1sc each of next 8ch, 9ch, skip 1ch, 1sc in each of next 8ch, 1sc in each of next 18ch. Fasten off.

Finishing

Stitch the lime onto the first branch worked, overlapping the stem end by about ⅜in (1cm). Stitch a leaf onto each of the remaining 2 branches.

89 GRAPES \//

Yarn: DK wool in shades of purple (A) and olive (B)

METHOD

Grape (make 19)

Using A, make 5ch. Skip 4ch, 6tr cluster in next ch. Pull yarn tight so that stitches curve with smooth side (RS) to the outside. Make 4ch, from the back ss in ch at base of cluster. Fasten off.

Stem

Using B, make 18ch. Skip 1ch, 1sc in each of next 6ch, 5ch, skip 1ch, 1sc in each of next 4ch, 1sc in each of remaining 11ch. Fasten off invisibly.

Finishing

Sew grapes in a formation of 1, 2, 3, 4, 5, 4 as shown in diagram, varying direction of sts. Attach the shortest branch of the stem behind the bunch.

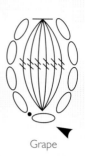

Grape

Finishing formation

90 EAR OF WHEAT \//

Yarn: Natural raffia

Extras: Fine wire (optional)

METHOD

Make 29ch, skip 3ch, 2dc in next ch, *remove hook leaving loop, insert hook in top ch of 3ch and then in loop, yo, pull yarn through both loops on hook, yo, pull yarn tightly through remaining loop. Cut yarn, leaving an end of approximately 2in (5cm).** Skip 1ch, join yarn in next of 29ch (base ch), 3ch, 2dc in base ch, repeat from * to **. Rejoin yarn in remaining strand of same base ch, 3ch, 2dc in same ch, repeat from * to **. Skipping 1ch between each pair of clusters, make 4 more pairs in this way.

Specific symbol

 3ch, 2dc in ch below, then work as * to **.

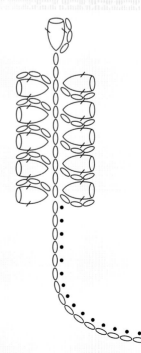

Finishing

Take a length of fine raffia and ss in each of remaining base ch. Take the first end of each group through the st at the top. Trim and fray the ends. Catch together the groups and wire the stem if necessary.

Yarn: DK yarn in white (A), apple green (B), and dark green (C); sport-weight yarn in brown (D)

Hooks: 2 hooks, one a size smaller than the other

Extras: Heavy non-woven interfacing; embroidery thread to match B; batting

METHOD

Front

Using larger hook and A, make 8ch.

ROUND 1: Skip 1ch, working in a single strand of each ch, 1sc in next ch, 1hdc in next ch, 1dc in next ch, 2tr in next ch, 1dc in next ch, 1hdc in next ch, 1sc and 1ss in last ch. Working in single strands along opposite side, 1sc in first ch, 1hdc in next ch, 1dc in next ch, 2tr in next ch, 1dc in next ch, 1hdc in next ch, 1sc in last ch, ss in first sc. (17 sts)

ROUND 2: 1ch, 1sc in st below, 1sc in each st of previous round, working 2sc in each tr and 2sc in ss at center, ss in first sc. (22 sts)

ROUND 3: 1ch, 1sc in st below, 1dc in next st, 3tr in next st, 2tr in next st, 3tr in next st, 1dc in next st, 2hdc in each of next 3 sts, 1hdc in next st, (1sc, 1ss) in next st, (1ss, 1sc) in next st, 1hdc in next st, 2hdc in each of next 3 sts, 1dc in next st, 3tr in next st, 2tr in next st, 3tr in next st, 1dc in next st, 1sc in next st, ss in first sc. (40 sts)

ROUND 4: (1sc, 1hdc) in next st, 2dc in next st, 3dc in each of next 2 sts, 2dc in each of next 3 sts, 1hdc in each of next 3 sts, 1sc in each of next 8 sts, ss in each of next 2 sts, 1sc in each of next 8 sts, 1hdc in each of next 3 sts, 2dc in each of next 3 sts, 3dc in each of next 2 sts, 2dc in next st, (1hdc, 1sc) in next st, ss in last st, ss in ss at end of last row. Fasten off.

ROUND 5: Join B in any sc along side edge of piece, 1ch, 1sc in same st, 1sc in each st of previous round, working (skip 1 st, ss in each of next 2 sts, skip next st) in 4 sts at center of top of apple and (ss in next st, skip 1 st, ss in next st) at center of base of apple, join with ss in first sc. Fasten off.

Back

Using larger hook and B, join yarn at top, make 3ch.

ROW 1 (RS): Skip 1ch, 2sc in each of next 2ch. (4sc)

ROW 2: 1ch, 2sc in first sc, 1sc in each of next 2sc, 2sc in next sc. (6sc)

ROW 3: 1ch, 2sc in each of first 2sc, 1sc in each of next 2sc, 2sc in each of next 2sc. (10sc)

ROW 4: 1ch, 2sc in each of first 2sc, 1sc in each of next 6sc, 2sc in each of next 2sc. (14sc)

ROW 5: 1ch, 1sc in each sc.

ROW 6: 1ch, 2sc in first sc, 1sc in each of next 12sc, 2sc in next sc. (16sc)

ROW 7: As row 5.

ROW 8: 1ch, 1sc in each of first 3sc, 2sc in next sc, 1sc in each of next 3sc, 2sc in each of next 2sc, 1sc in each of next 3sc, 2sc in next sc, 1sc in each of next 3sc. (20sc)

ROW 9: 1ch, 1sc in each of first 4sc, 2sc in next sc, 1sc into each of next 4sc, 2sc in each of next 2sc, 1sc in each of next 4sc, 2sc in next sc, 1sc in each of next 4sc. (24sc)

ROWS 10-15: As row 5.

ROW 16: 1ch, 1sc in first sc, 2sc tog, 1sc in each sc to last 3 sts, 2sc tog, 1sc in next sc. (22 sts)

ROW 17: As row 16. (20 sts)

ROW 18: 1ch, 1sc in each of first 3sc, 2sc tog, 1sc in each of next 3sc, [2sc tog] twice, 1sc in each of next 3sc, 2sc tog, 1sc in each of next 3sc. (16 sts)

ROW 19: As row 16. (14 sts)

ROW 20: As row 5.

ROWS 21-24: As row 16. (6 sts)

ROW 25: 1ch, 1sc in first sc, [2sc tog] twice, 1sc in next sc. (4 sts)

Fasten off.

Stalk

Using larger hook and C, make 9ch. Skip 1ch, 1sc in each of next 4ch, ss in each of next 4ch. Fasten off.

Pips (make 2)

Using smaller hook and D, make 2ch. Skip 1ch, 3dc tog in next ch. Fasten off. Tighten each yarn end to form a tiny bobble.

Finishing

Press front to shape. Place front WS down on interfacing and baste to secure. Using 4 strands of embroidery thread, backstitch around the front, following the base of stitches worked in B. Work a row of backstitches down the center, then work the same stitch in an oval shape between the stitches of rounds 2 and 3. Carefully trim away the interfacing close to the edge. Using yarn ends, sew pips in place either side of the central stitched line, then sew the base of the stalk to the top of the front. Beginning at the top near the stalk, WS together, overcast front to back, aligning edges and taking each stitch through edge of back and behind outer round of sc on front. Leave a small opening on the 2nd side, insert batting, then continue stitching up to the top.

Yarn: DK yarn in dark olive (A) and light gray-green (B)

METHOD

NOTE: Either side of olive piece can be used as RS.

Olive (make 4)

Using A, make 6ch.

ROW 1: Skip 1ch, 1sc in next ch, 1hdc in each of next 3ch, 1sc in next ch.

ROW 2: 1ch, 1sc in first sc, 1hdc in each of next 3hdc, 1sc in next sc.

Repeat row 2 five times.

Fasten off.

Fold olive into tube. Join seam, stitch across end, and turn to RS. Stuff olive firmly with the same yarn, then close the top, using the yarn end to make 3ch for stalk.

Leaf (make 6)

Using B, make 17ch. Skip 1ch, working in single strand along edge of ch, ss in each of next 2ch, 1sc in each of next 2ch, 1hdc in each of next 2ch, 1dc in each of next 4ch, 1hdc in each of next 2ch, 1sc in each of next 2ch, ss in each of last 2ch. (16 sts)

1ch, working in single edge strand again, ss in each of next 2ch, 1sc in each of next 2ch, 1hdc in each of next 2ch, 1dc in each of next 4ch, 1hdc in each of next 2ch, 1sc in each of next 2ch, ss in each of last 2ch, join with ss in first ss. (16 sts) Fasten off.

Branching stem

Using B, make 15ch. Skip 1ch, working in back strand of each ch, ss in each of next 5ch, 9ch, skip 1ch, ss in each of next 5ch, 9ch, skip 1ch, ss in each of next 5ch, 6ch, skip 1ch, ss in each of next 5ch, ss in each of next 3ch, 6ch, skip 1ch, ss in each of next 5ch, ss in each of next 3ch, 6ch, skip 1ch, ss in each of next 5ch, ss in next 9ch. Fasten off.

Finishing

Stitch a leaf onto each branch of the stem. Stitch the olives randomly onto the stems.

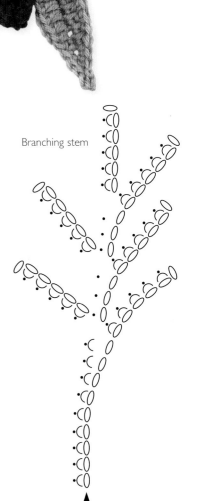

Branching stem

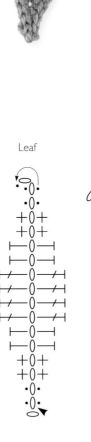

Leaf

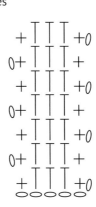

Olive

WAXCAP V

Yarn: DK yarn in yellow ocher (A) and white (B)

METHOD

Cap

Using A, make a slip ring.

ROUND 1 (RS): 1ch, 5sc in ring, pull end to close ring, ss in 1ch. (6 sts)

ROUND 2: 3ch, 1dc in each of 5sc, ss in top ch of 3ch.

ROUND 3: 3ch, 2dc in next dc, [1dc in next dc, 2dc in next dc] twice, ss in top ch of 3ch. (9 sts)

ROUND 4: 3ch, 1dc in st below, 2dc in each of next 8dc, ss in top ch of 3ch. (18 sts)

ROUND 5: 1ch, *(1dc, 1tr) in next dc, (1tr, 1dc) in next dc, 1sc in next dc, 1dc in each of next 2dc, 1sc in next sc; repeat from *, ending 1dc in each of next 2dc, ss in 1ch.

Fasten off.

Stalk

Using B, make 4ch, join with ss into a ring.

ROUND 1: 3ch, enclosing yarn end work 5dc in ring, ss in top ch of 3ch. (6 sts)

ROUND 2: 3ch, 1dc in each of 5dc, ss in top ch of 3ch.

Repeat round 2 once, making ss with A. Continue with A.

Repeat round 2 six times, making last ss with B. Continue with B.

ROUND 10: 3ch, 2dc in st below, 3dc in each of next 5dc, ss in top ch of 3ch. (18 sts)

Fasten off.

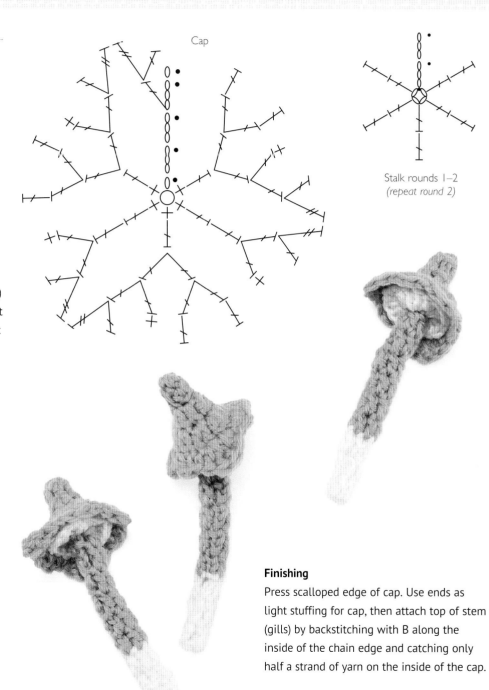

Cap

Stalk rounds 1–2
(repeat round 2)

Finishing

Press scalloped edge of cap. Use ends as light stuffing for cap, then attach top of stem (gills) by backstitching with B along the inside of the chain edge and catching only half a strand of yarn on the inside of the cap.

Yarn: Single strands of tapestry yarn in beige (A) and yellow ocher or orange (B)

Extras: Batting

METHOD

NOTE: If you wish to avoid a ss join between rounds, work continuously, substituting 1sc for 1ch at the beginning and omitting the ss at the end of each round. Use a marker to count rounds.

Large mushroom stalk

Using A, make a slip ring.

ROUND 1: 1ch, 7sc in ring, pull end to close ring, ss in 1ch. (8 sts)

ROUND 2: 1ch, 2sc in next sc, [1sc in next sc, 2sc in next sc] 3 times, ss in 1ch. (12 sts)

ROUND 3: 1ch, 2sc in next sc, [1sc in next sc, 2sc in next sc] 5 times, ss in 1ch. (18 sts)*

ROUND 4: 1ch, 2sc in next sc, [1sc in next sc, 2sc in next sc] 8 times, ss in 1ch. (27 sts)

ROUND 5: 1ch, 1sc in next sc, 2sc in next sc, [1sc in each of next 2sc, 2sc in next sc] 8 times, ss in 1ch. (36 sts)

ROUNDS 6-8: 1ch, 1sc in each sc, ss in 1ch.

ROUND 9: 1ch, 1sc in each of next 3sc, 2sc tog in next 2sc, [1sc in each of next 4sc, 2sc tog in next 2sc] 5 times. (30 sts)

ROUNDS 10-11: As round 6.

ROUND 12: 1ch, 1sc in each of next 2sc, 2sc tog in next 2sc, [1sc in each of next 3sc, 2sc tog in next 2sc] 5 times, ss in 1ch. (24 sts)

ROUNDS 13-14: As round 6.

ROUND 15: 1ch, 1sc in next sc, 2sc tog in next 2sc, [1sc in each of next 2sc, 2sc tog in next 2sc] 5 times, ss in 1ch. (18 sts)

ROUNDS 16-19: As round 6.

ROUND 20: 3ch, 1dc in st below, [2dc in next sc] 17 times, ss in top ch of 3ch. (36 sts) Fasten off.

Large mushroom cap

Using B, make a slip ring.

ROUND: 1ch, 5sc in ring, pull end to close ring, ss in 1ch. (6 sts)

ROUND 2: 1ch, 1sc in st below, 2sc in each of next 5sc, ss in 1ch. (12 sts)

ROUND 3: 1ch, 2sc in next sc, [1sc in next sc, 2sc in next sc] 5 times, ss in 1ch. (18 sts)

ROUND 4: 1ch, 1sc in next sc, 2sc in next sc, [1sc in each of next 2sc, 2sc in next sc] 5 times, ss in 1ch. (24 sts)

ROUND 5: 1ch, 1sc in each of next 2sc, 2sc in next sc, [1sc in each of next 3sc, 2sc in next sc] 5 times, ss in 1ch. (30 sts)

ROUND 6: 1ch, 1sc in each of next 3sc, 2sc in next sc, [1sc in each of next 4sc, 2sc in next sc] 5 times, ss in 1ch. (36 sts)**

ROUND 7: 1ch, 1sc in each sc, ss in 1ch.

ROUND 8: 1ch, 1sc in each of next 4sc, 2sc in next sc, [1sc in each of next 5sc, 2sc in next sc] 5 times, ss in 1ch. (42 sts)

ROUNDS 9-11: As round 7.

Turn to work last round on WS.

ROUND 12: 1ch, 1sc in each of next 4sc, 2sc tog in next 2sc, [1sc in each of next 6sc, 2sc tog in next 2sc] 5 times, ss in 1ch. (36 sts)

Fasten off.

Small mushroom stalk

Work as large mushroom stalk to *.

ROUNDS 4-5: 1ch, 1sc in each sc, ss in 1ch.

ROUND 6: 1ch, 1sc in each of next 3sc, 2sc tog in next 2sc, [1sc in each of next 4sc, 2sc tog in next 2sc] twice, ss in 1ch. (15 sts)

ROUND 7: As round 4.

ROUND 8: 1ch, 1sc in each of next 2sc, 2sc tog in next 2sc, [1sc in each of next 3sc, 2sc tog in next 2sc] twice, ss in 1ch. (12 sts)

ROUNDS 9-11: As round 4.

ROUND 12: 3ch, 1dc in st below, [2dc in next sc] 11 times, ss in top ch of 3ch. (24 sts) Fasten off.

Small mushroom cap

Work as large mushroom cap to **.

ROUNDS 7-8: 1ch, 1sc in each sc, ss in 1ch.

Turn to work last round on WS.

ROUND 9: 1ch, 2sc tog in next 2sc, [1sc in next sc, 2sc tog in next 2sc] 11 times, ss in 1ch. (24 sts) Fasten off.

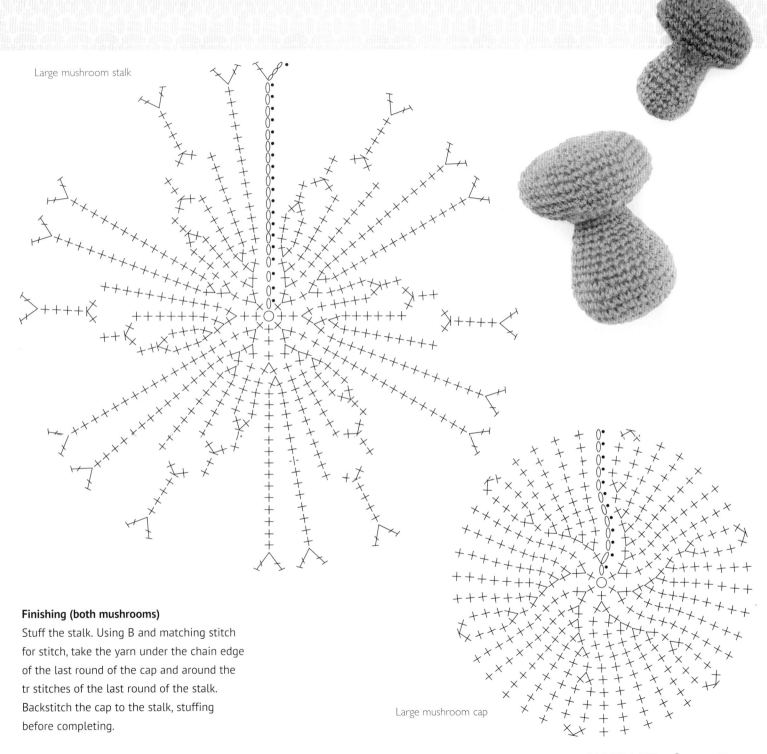

Large mushroom stalk

Large mushroom cap

Finishing (both mushrooms)

Stuff the stalk. Using B and matching stitch
for stitch, take the yarn under the chain edge
of the last round of the cap and around the
tr stitches of the last round of the stalk.
Backstitch the cap to the stalk, stuffing
before completing.

95 RADISHES \/

Yarn: Stranded embroidery wool or fine wool in white (A), pale pink (B), deep pink (C), and 2 shades of green (D)

Extras: Batting

METHOD

Radish

Using A and leaving an end of approximately 2in (5cm), make 6ch, skip 3ch, ss in next ch.

ROUND 1: 2ch, 5sc in ring, ss in top ch of 2ch. (6 sts)

ROUND 2: 2ch, 1sc in st below, 2sc in each sc, with B ss in top ch of 2ch. (12 sts)

Continue with B.

ROUND 3: 1sc in each st.

ROUND 4: [2sc in next sc, 1sc in next sc] 6 times. (18 sts)

Change to C.

ROUNDS 5-8: 1sc in each sc.

ROUND 9: [2sc tog in next 2sc] 9 times. (9 sts)

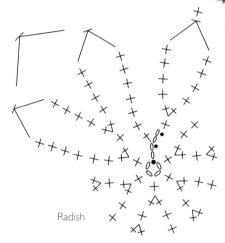

Leaf

Radish

96 CHILI \/

Yarn: Sport-weight yarn in red (A) and green (B)

METHOD

Using A, make a slip ring.

ROUND 1: 3ch, 3dc in ring, pull end to close ring, ss in top ch of 3ch. (4 sts)

ROUND 2: 3ch, 2dc in next dc, 1dc in next dc, 2dc in next dc, ss in top ch of 3ch. (6 sts)

ROUND 3: 3ch, 2dc in next dc, [1dc in next dc, 2dc in next dc] twice, ss in top ch of 3ch. (9 sts)

ROUND 4: 3ch, 1dc in next dc, 2dc in next dc, [1dc in each of next 2 dc, 2dc in next dc] twice, ss in top of 3ch. (12 sts)

ROUNDS 5-8: 3ch, 1dc in each of next 11dc, ss in top ch of 3ch.

ROUND 9: 1ch, 2sc tog in next 2dc, [1sc in next dc, 2sc tog in next 2dc] 3 times, with B ss in 1ch. (8 sts)

Continue with B.

ROUND 10: 1ch, ss in each of next 7 sts, ss in 1ch.

Without breaking off yarn, insert spare yarn A as stuffing.

PEAPOD

Hook first end to RS, then insert batting into cavity.
ROUND 10: 1sc in next st, [2sc tog in next 2 sts] 4 times. (5 sts)
Fasten off.

Leaf (make 3 for each radish)

Using D, make 9ch, skip 1ch, 1sc in each of next 8ch, 1ch, working in remaining strand of ch, 1sc in each of next 6ch, turn, 1ch, 1sc in each of next 5sc, 3sc in 1ch sp, 1sc in each of next 6sc. Fasten off. Attach leaf to radish.

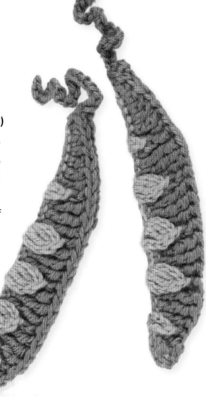

ROUND 11: 1ch, working in back loop of each st, 2sc tog in next 2 sts, 1sc in next st, [2sc tog in next 2 sts] twice, ss in 1ch. (5 sts)
Do not break off yarn.

Stem

9ch, skip 2ch, 1sc in next ch, ss in each of next 6ch. Fasten off and use end to secure base of stem.

Yarn: DK wool in mid-green (A); fine wool in pale green (B)

METHOD

Pod front

*Using A, make 28ch.
ROW 1 (RS): Skip 1ch, 1sc in next ch, 1hdc in next ch, 1dc in next ch, 1tr in next ch, 1dtr in each of next 15ch, 1tr in each of next 2ch, 1dc in each of next 2ch, 1hdc in each of next 2ch, 1sc in next ch, ss in next ch.**
Make 20ch. Fasten off invisibly.
ROW 2: Turn work to WS and using a smaller size hook, join B in 1ch at base of pod. Working in the remaining strand of original base ch, ss in each of next 4ch.
PEA 1: 2ch, turn to RS, inserting hook from right to left ss in top wrap of tr, 2ch, turn to WS and ss in same base ch as before, ss in each of next 4 base ch.
PEA 2: [3ch, 2tr cluster in same base ch, turn to RS, ss in top wrap of dtr above, 3ch, turn to WS and ss in first of 3ch, then ss in same base ch as before, ss in each of next 4 base ch] 3 times, make last pea as first, ss in each of next 6 base ch.
Fasten off invisibly.

Pod back

Work as pod front from * to **.
Fasten off invisibly.

Finishing

Place back underneath front, edges matching, insert a stiff paper cutout if needed, and backstitch together underneath the ch edge on RS. Curl stem by twisting it around a pencil.

Specific symbol

Ss in top wrap of st indicated.

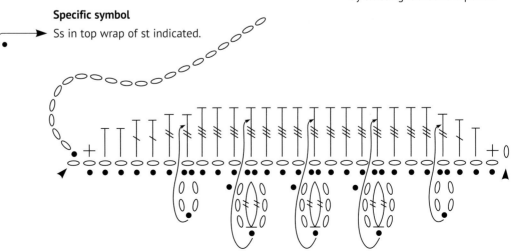

Yarn: DK yarn in soft yellow (A), bright green (B), and mid-green (C); tapestry wool in pale yellow

Extras: Batting

METHOD

Corn

Using A, make 22ch.

SET-UP ROW (RS): Skip 1ch, 1sc in each of 21ch. (21sc)

ROW 1: 1ch, 1sc in first st, [3dc bobble in next st, 1sc in next st] 10 times.

ROW 2: 1ch, 1sc in each st and top of each bobble.

Repeat rows 1–2 eight times.

ROWS 19, 21 & 23: 1ch, 1sc in first st, [2dc bobble in next st, 1sc in next st] 10 times.

ROWS 20 & 22: As row 2.

ROW 24: Ss in first 2sc, 1ch, 1sc in st below, 1sc in each st and top of each bobble, omitting last st. (19sc)

ROW 25: 1ch, 1sc in first st, [2dc bobble in next st, 1sc in next st] to end.

Repeat rows 24–25 three times. (13sc)

ROW 32: 1ch, skip first st, [2sc tog] to end. (6 sts)

Fasten off.

WS facing, fold corn in half lengthwise. Stitch across top and down seam.

Turn corn to RS and stuff firmly.

Stalk

Join B to base of corn at seam, 1ch, work 21sc evenly around base, join with ss in first sc.

ROUNDS 2–3: 1ch, 1sc in each dc, ss in first sc.

ROUND 4: 3ch, 2dc tog, [3dc tog] to end of round, join with ss in top ch of 3ch. Gather edge of last round tightly to close gap at center.

Leaves (make 1B and 2C)

Make 10ch.

ROW 1: Skip 1ch, working into strand that lies behind each ch, work 1sc in each of 9ch. (9sc)

ROW 2: 1ch, 1sc in each sc.

ROW 3 (RS): 3ch (counts as 1dc), 1dc in st below, [1dc in next st, 2dc in next st] 4 times. (14dc)

ROW 4: 1ch, 1sc in each dc. (14sc)

ROW 5: 3ch, skip 1sc, 1dc in each sc.

ROW 6: 1ch, 1sc in each dc.

Repeat rows 5–6 ten times.

ROW 27: 3ch, 2dc tog, 1dc in each sc to last 3 sts, 2dc tog, 1dc in last st.

ROW 28: 1ch, 1sc in each dc.

Repeat rows 27–28 three times. (6 sts)

ROW 35: 3ch, [2dc tog] twice, 1dc in last sc. (4 sts)

ROW 36: 1ch, [2sc tog] twice.

Fasten off.

Silk

Cut fourteen 8in (20cm) lengths of tapestry wool. Thread each length in a yarn needle and insert randomly around top of corn, aligning ends and securing in place with an overhand knot. When all the lengths have been attached, trim to required length and fray out the ends of each.

Finishing

Center B leaf over seam on corn, aligning straight end of leaf with base of stalk and placing WS of leaf to RS of corn. Leaving chain edge at base of leaf free, stitch in place through base of each sc on row 1. Repeat with other 2 leaves, overlapping first leaf by about ⅝in (1.5cm). Arrange leaves, pin in place, then secure leaf edges at back of corn with rows of stitches worked in matching yarn, making sure the stitches go through both leaf and corn.

99 BELL PEPPER

Yarn: DK yarn in red (A) and green (B)
Extras: Batting

METHOD

Segment (make 3)
Using A, make 26ch.
ROW 1 (RS): Skip 1ch, 1sc in each of next 25ch. (25 sts)
ROW 2: 1ch, ss in first sc, 1sc in each of next 4sc, 1hdc in each of next 4sc, 1dc in each of next 13sc, 1hdc in next sc, 1sc in next sc, ss in last sc.
ROW 3: 1ch, ss in ss, 1sc in next sc, 1hdc in next hdc, 1dc in each of next 13dc, 1hdc in each of next 4hdc, 1sc in each of next 4sc, ss in ss.
ROW 4: 1ch, 1sc in each st. (25sc)
ROW 5: 1ch, ss in first sc, 1sc in next sc, 1hdc in next sc, 1dc in each of next 13sc, 1hdc in each of next 4sc, 1sc in each of next 4sc, ss in next sc.
ROW 6: 1ch, ss in ss, 1sc in each of next 4sc, 1hdc in each of next 4hdc, 1dc in each of next 13dc, 1hdc in next hdc, 1sc in next sc, ss in ss.

ROW 7: As row 4.
ROWS 8-12: As rows 2-6.
ROW 13: 1ch, 1sc in each st. (25sc)
Fasten off.

Finishing

RS together, pin long edges of segments to make a tube. Backstitch them, taking stitches through both loops of adjoining stitches. Aligning seams, fold each narrow end of segments and overcast edges together. Turn to RS and stuff.

Stalk

With RS facing, join B to edge of opening at top of bell pepper, 1ch, making first sc in same st as 1ch, work 4sc in each segment and 2sc tog over sts at either side of seams, then ss in first sc. (15sc)
ROUNDS 1-2: 1ch, 1sc in each sc, ss in first sc.
ROUND 3: 1ch, 1sc, [2sc tog] 7 times, ss in 1sc. (8dc)
Omitting 1ch, work in continuous rounds of sc without joining until narrow part of stalk measures ¾in (2cm). Break off yarn and stitch across top of stalk to close.

Yarn: DK yarn in pale green (A), mid-green (B), and light brown (C)

Extras: Batting

METHOD

NOTE: Do not break off yarn at each color change, but carry yarn not in use up side of work. Change color by working final yarn over of last st of row in new color before turning to work next row.

Body

Using A, make 25ch.

SET-UP ROW (RS): Skip 1ch, 1sc in each of next 4ch, 1hdc in each of next 2ch, 1dc in each of next 12ch, 1hdc in each of next 2ch, 1sc in each of next 4ch.

ROW 1: Using A, 1ch, 1sc in each of next 4sc, 1hdc in each of next 2hdc, 1dc in each of next 12dc, 1hdc in each of next 2hdc, 1sc in each of next 4sc. Change to B.

ROW 2: Using B, 1ch, 1sc in each of next 4sc, 1hdc in each of next 2hdc, 1dc in each of next 12dc, 1hdc in each of next 2hdc, 1sc in each of next 4sc.

ROW 3: Using B, 1ch, 1sc in each st of previous row. (24sc)

ROW 4: Using A, 1ch, 1sc in each of next 4sc, 1hdc in each of next 2sc, 1dc in each of next 12sc, 1hdc in each of next 2sc, 1sc in each of next 4sc.

Repeat rows 1–4 eight times, then rows 1–3 once again.

WS facing, fold body to form a tube, aligning edge of last row with starting chain. Ss through both layers. Fasten off. With A, work running stitches around the end of the tube where you changed yarns, draw up the stitches to close the tube, and fasten off securely. Turn body to RS. Stuff squash body fairly firmly so that it will stand upright on the gathered base.

Stalk

With RS facing and using A, work sc around top of squash, starting at seam and working 1sc in top of each stripe, join with ss in first sc. (20sc)

ROUND 1: 1ch, 1sc in each sc, ss in first sc. Repeat round 1 once.

Change to C and repeat round 1 twice.

NEXT ROUND: 1ch, [2sc tog] to end of round, join with ss in first 2sc tog. Adding more stuffing as required, work sc continuously (do not join rounds). When stalk measures ⅝in (1.5cm), work a round of 2sc tog. Fasten off yarn, leaving top of stalk open.

101 YELLOW SQUASH V/

Yarn: DK yarn in soft yellow (A) and light brown (B)
Extras: Batting

METHOD
NOTE: On body, stitches are worked through both loops, single back loops, or single front loops on different rows.

Body
Using A, make 25ch.
SET-UP ROW (RS): Skip 1ch, 1sc in each of next 5ch, 1hdc in next ch, 1dc in each of next 12ch, 1hdc in next ch, 1sc in each of next 5ch. (24 sts, excluding 1ch)
ROW 1: 1ch, working into back loops only of previous row, 1sc in each of next 5sc, 1hdc in hdc, 1dc in each of next 12dc, 1hdc in hdc, 1sc in each of next 5 sts.
ROW 2: 1ch, working into both loops of previous row, 1sc in each of next 5sc, 1hdc in hdc, 1dc in each of next 12dc, 1hdc in hdc, 1sc in each of next 5 sts.
ROW 3: 1ch, working into front loops only of previous row, 1sc in each of next 5sc, 1hdc in hdc, 1dc in each of next 12dc, 1hdc in hdc, 1sc in each of next 5sc.
ROW 4: As row 2.
Repeat rows 1–4 eight times, then rows 1–3 once again.
WS facing, fold body to form a tube, aligning edge of last row with starting chain. Ss through both layers and turn tube to RS.

Stalk
With RS facing, join B to one end of tube, 1ch, work round of sc (1sc for every 2 row-ends), join with ss in first sc. (20sc)
NEXT ROUND: 1ch, 1sc in each sc, ss in first sc.
NEXT ROUND: 1ch, [2sc tog] to end, ss in first 2sc tog. (10 sts)
Begin working sc continuously (do not join rounds). When stalk measures ⅝in (1.5cm), work a round of 2sc tog, fasten off, then stitch across top of stalk to close.
Cut ten 10in (25cm) lengths of A. Secure one end of each length on WS of squash below stalk where grooves form between rows 1 and 4 (note that first groove is formed between row 1 and set-up row). Bring each length through to RS, work row of running stitches along groove, pull yarn end gently to tighten up running stitches and accentuate groove, then finish off each end securely. Stuff squash body lightly, forming it first into a doughnut shape, then stuffing center of doughnut.

Base
Using B, make 4ch, join with ss into a ring.
ROUND 1: 1ch, 10sc in ring, ss in first sc.
ROUND 2: 1ch, [1sc in next sc, 2sc in next sc] to end, ss in first sc. (15sc)
ROUND 3: 1ch, [1sc in each of next 2sc, 2sc in next sc] to end, ss in first sc. (20sc)
Continue with A.
ROUND 4: 3ch, 1dc in st below, 2dc in each sc, ss in top ch of 3ch. (40 sts)
ROUND 5: 1ch, 1sc in each dc, ss in first sc. Fasten off.
Lay base over gap at bottom of squash. Leaving front loop of each sc free, sew in place.

102 BEETLE |

Yarn: Metallic yarn (used double)

Extras: 2 beads; sewing thread in darker color

METHOD

Body

Using yarn double, make 9ch, skip 2ch, 3sc in next ch, 2dc tog in next 2ch, 2tr tog in next 2ch, 2dc tog in next 2ch, 2ch, ss in last ch worked into, 2ch, working in remaining strands of original ch, 2dc tog in next 2ch, 2tr tog in next 2ch, 2dc tog in next 2ch, ss in top ch of 9ch. Fasten off.

Underside

Using yarn double, make a slip ring. 3ch, 7dc in ring, pull end to close ring, ss in top ch of 3ch. Fasten off.

Finishing

With concave side to the inside, stitch the underside to the body, filling with a little spare yarn if necessary. Using sewing thread double, backstitch along the center back line of chain and around the cluster forming the head. Sew on beads for eyes.

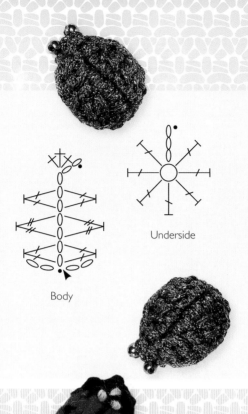

Underside

Body

103 SLEEPING LADYBUG |

Yarn: Sport-weight yarn in black (A), red (B), and white (C)

METHOD

Body

Using A, make 3ch.

ROW 1: Skip 2ch, (2dc, 1sc) in next ch, making last wrap of sc with B. (4 sts) Continue with B.

ROW 2: 2ch, (1dc, 1tr) in first dc, (1tr, 1dc) in next dc, 1sc in top ch of 3ch. (6 sts)

ROW 3: 3ch, 1dc in dc, [2tr in tr] twice, 1dc in dc, 1sc in top ch of 2ch. (8 sts) Fasten off.

Underside

Using A, make 2ch.

ROW 1: Skip 1ch, 2sc in next ch. (3 sts)

ROW 2: 2ch, 1sc in st below, 1sc in next sc, 2sc in top ch of 2ch. (5 sts)

ROW 3: 2ch, 1sc in each of next 3sc, 1sc in top ch of 2ch.

ROW 4: 2ch, skip 1sc, 1sc in next sc, skip 1sc, 1sc in top ch of 2ch. (3 sts)

ROW 5: 2ch, skip 1sc, 1sc in top ch of 2ch. (2 sts) Fasten off.

Finishing

Using split yarn, stitch 3 spots on either side of body with B. Use C to embroider 3 spots on head. RS facing and using A for head, B for body, use running stitch to join body and underside, stuffing with ends and spare yarn B before closing.

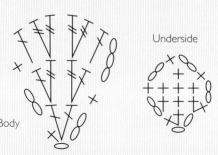

Body

Underside

Yarn: Worsted-weight wool in black (A), red (B), and white (C)

Extras: 3 bobby pins; round-nose pliers; glue suitable for use with metal

METHOD

Body (make 2 pieces)

Using A, make 13ch.

ROW 1: Skip first ch, 1sc in each ch to end, turn. (12sc)

ROW 2: 1ch, 1sc in each sc to end, turn.

ROW 3: 1ch, 1sc in first sc, 1hdc in each of next 2sc, 2dc in next sc, 1dc in next sc, 2tr in next sc, 1tr in each of next 3sc, 1dc in next sc, 1hdc in each of next 2sc, 1sc in 1ch. Continue along other side of foundation chain to make other side of body as follows:

ROW 4: (1sc, 1ch, 1sc) in first ch made, 1sc in of each of next 11ch, turn.

ROW 5: 1ch, 1sc in first sc, 1hdc in each of next 2sc, 2dc in next sc, 1dc in next sc, 2tr in next sc, 1tr in each of next 3sc, 1dc in next sc, 1hdc in each of next 2sc. Fasten off with ss in next ch.

Wings (make 2)

Using B, make 8ch.

ROW 1: Skip first ch, 1sc in each of next 7sc.

ROW 2: 1ch, 1 sc in each sc to end, turn. (7sc)

ROW 3: 3ch, 1tr in first sc, 2tr in next sc, 1dc in next sc, 2dc in next sc, 1hdc in each of next 2sc, 1sc in last sc, 1sc in first ch made. Fasten off.

Finishing

Using A, sew body pieces together, stuffing with scraps of yarn as you do so. Allow about one quarter of body length for head area. Sew wings to top of body behind head, attaching them only along the shorter straight edge and letting them flap open at center back. Using double strand of A, work several French knots on each wing. Using double strand of C, work a French knot at center top of each wing and work several straight stitches to form a large spot at each side of head. Using single strand of C, work two French knots for eyes. Using single strand of A, stitch a small spot in middle of each eye. Use pliers to bend bobby pins into the shape of three pairs of legs. Thread legs through body. To steady them, apply a small amount of glue to the points that join the crochet piece.

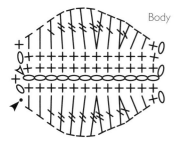
Body

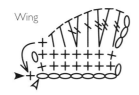
Wing

Yarn: Sport-weight cotton (A) and metallic yarn (B)

Extras: 2 beads

METHOD

Body

Using A, make 12ch. Skip 4ch, 4tr in next ch, remove hook leaving loop, insert hook in top ch of 4ch and then in loop, yo, pull yarn through (popcorn made), 4ch, skip 2ch, 2dc cluster in next ch, 3ch, ss in first of 4ch, 4ch, ss in same ch as base of popcorn, ss in each of remaining 7ch, 1ch, working in single remaining strand each time, ss in each of 7ch. Fasten off.

Upper wings (make 2)

Using B, make 11ch. Skip 2ch, 1sc in each of next 4ch, 1hdc in next ch, 1dc in each of next 3ch, 9dc in next ch; working in remaining strand of each ch and enclosing yarn end, 1dc in each of next 3ch, 1hdc in next ch, 1sc in each of next 2ch, ss in each of next 2ch. Fasten off.

Right lower wing

Using B, make 12ch. Skip 2ch, 1sc in each of next 2ch, 1hdc in next ch, 1dc in next ch, (1dc, 1tr) in next ch, 1dtr in each of next 2ch, 1tr in next ch, 1dc in next ch, 1hdc in next ch. Fasten off.

Left lower wing

Using B, make 12ch. Skip 2ch, 1dc in next ch, 1tr in next ch, 1dtr in each of next 2ch, (1tr, 1dc) in next ch, 1dc in next ch, 1hdc in next ch, 1sc in each of next 3ch. Fasten off.

Finishing

Carefully fasten off ends of right lower wing, running them back along the set-up chain. Pair upper wings and join. Do the same with lower wings, noting that the foundation chain runs along the top edge of the lower wings. Position them underneath the body and stitch. Join upper and lower wings with a single invisible stitch halfway along. Sew on beads for eyes.

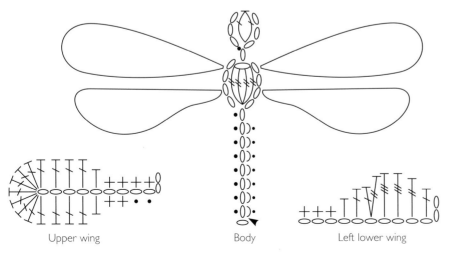

Upper wing   Body   Left lower wing   Right lower wing

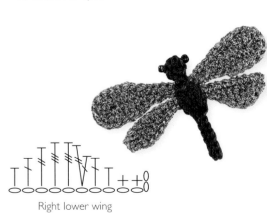

106 BUMBLEBEE \/

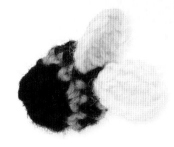

Yarn: DK wool in black (A), yellow (B), and white (C)

METHOD

Body

Using A, make a slip ring.

ROUND 1: 3ch, 7dc in ring, pull end to close ring, with B ss in top ch of 3ch. (8 sts)

Continue with B.

ROUND 2: 2ch, [2sc in next dc, 1sc in next dc] 3 times, 2sc in next dc, with A ss in top ch of 2ch. (12 sts)

Continue with A.

ROUND 3: 2ch, 1sc in each of next 11sc, with B ss in top ch of 2ch.

Continue with B.

ROUND 4: As round 3, working ss with A.

Continue with A.

ROUND 5: 1ch, [2tr tog in next 2sc, 1sc in next sc] 3 times, 2tr tog in next 2sc, ss to 1ch. (8 sts)

Fasten off invisibly.

Wings

Using C, [make 6ch, skip 5ch, 2dtr cluster in next ch, 5ch, ss in same ch as cluster] twice. Fasten off invisibly.

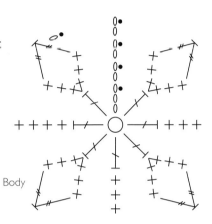

Body

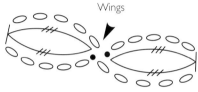

Wings

Finishing

Use yarn to fill body. With color joins underneath, flatten the body a little and with A join the two sides of the opening for the head. Attach wings with A.

---

107 FURRY CATERPILLAR |

Yarn: Fine mohair

Extras: 2 sequins; sewing thread; 16 faceted beads; 14 round beads

METHOD

Make a slip ring.

ROUND 1: 3ch, 5dc in ring, pull end to close ring, ss in top ch of 3ch. (6 sts)

ROUND 2: 3ch, working in back loop of st each time, 2dc in next dc, [1dc in next dc, 2dc in next dc] twice, ss in top ch of 3ch. (9 sts)

ROUND 3: 3ch, working in back loop of st each time, 1dc in each of 8dc, ss in top ch of 3ch. Repeat round 3 five times, then fill with spare yarn.

ROUND 9: 3ch, working in back loop of st each time, [2dc tog in next 2dc] 4 times. Insert some more filling, then ss in top ch of 3ch. Fasten off.

Finishing

Close last end and sew on sequins for eyes. For legs, sew pairs of faceted beads either side of ch joins of rounds, using top strand of dc as markers for spacing. With mohair, overcast these strands and gather slightly to form the segments of the body. Stitch loops along the back, anchoring each loop with a backstitch. Sew round beads along each side, 1 bead to each segment.

Yarn: Sport-weight space-dyed wool in beige and browns (A); fingering-weight wool in brown (B)

Hooks: 2 hooks, one a size smaller than the other

Extras: Batting; fine wire; 2 small black beads

METHOD

Shell first side

Using larger hook and A, make 5ch, join with ss into a ring.

ROUND 1 (RS): 1ch, (4sc, 2hdc, 5dc) in ring. *Now work in continuous rounds without joining. Working in back loop of each st, 3dc in each of next 7 sts, 2tr in each of next 7 sts, (1tr, 1dtr) tog in next 2 sts. Fasten off.

Shell 2nd side

As first side, but working all sts from * in the front loop of each st and noting that the back of the work will be the RS.

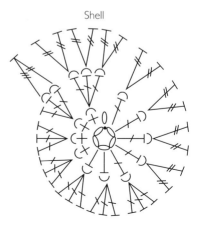

Shell

Body

Using smaller hook and B, make a slip ring.

ROUND 1 (WS): 2ch, 5sc in ring, pull end to close ring, ss in top ch of 2ch. (6 sts)

Marking the beginning of each round, work in continuous rounds of sc without joining, working in the back loop of each st.

Work 3 rounds straight.

ROUND 5: [1sc in each of next 2 sts, 2sc in next st] twice. (8 sts)

ROUND 6: [1sc in next st, 2sc in next st] 4 times. (12 sts)

ROUND 7: [1sc in next st] 12 times.

Specific symbol

 Work into back loop of st on first side of shell, but work into front loop of st on 2nd side.

ROUND 8: [1sc in each of next 2 sts, 2sc in next st] 4 times. (16 sts)

Turn work inside out (RS is now outside) and continue working with WS facing, working into back loop of each st.

ROUND 9: [1sc in next st, 2sc in next st] 8 times. (24 sts)

ROUND 10: [1sc in next st] 24 times.

ROUND 11: [1sc in each of next 3 sts, 2sc in next st] 6 times. (30 sts)

Work 6 rounds straight.

Fill the body with batting and continue to fill as you crochet.

DECREASE ROUND: [1sc in next st, 2sc tog in next 2 sts] 10 times. (20 sts)

Work 4 rounds straight.

Horns

Make first horn by making 10ch, skip 2ch, ss in each of next 8ch. Continue round by working 1sc in each of next 3sc, make a second horn to match the first, then complete the round. Making sure horns protrude on RS, work 1 round, then a part round, ending at underside. Shaping the body carefully to keep underside flat, finish stuffing, then take yarn end through top of last round of sts and draw up.

Finishing

Leaving outer strand of each st free and starting at final st of each piece, join top seam of shell for 15 sts, catch it down on either side of the body, and lightly stuff with spare yarn. Insert fine wire into the horns and sew a bead on the end of each horn.

Yarn: DK wool

Extras: Pipe cleaners; nail varnish or glue

METHOD

Head

Make 4ch, skip 3ch, 4dc in next ch, remove hook leaving loop, insert hook in top ch of 4ch and then in loop, yo, pull yarn through firmly. Fasten off and weave in end inside cavity.

Body

Make 5ch, skip 4ch, 7tr in next ch, turn, ss in top ch of 5ch. Fasten off, leaving an extra long end. Fill cavity with spare yarn, then use long end to gather top of sts.

Finishing

Join head to body. Cut the pipe cleaners into four 2⅜in (6cm) lengths. Bind each length with yarn: starting near one end, bind to that end and then work back over this to secure the yarn end; bind to the opposite end and then thread yarn onto a yarn needle and take it back under the last wraps firmly. Trim ends of yarn and ends of pipe cleaner. Secure ends with nail varnish or glue. Form a shallow X with 2 pipe cleaners, secure it, then stitch underneath the body of the spider. Bend the remaining 2 pipe cleaners into U shapes and stitch these, one above and one below the X.

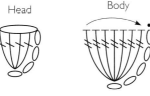

Head   Body

Legs

Yarn: Worsted-weight wool in black (A), orange (B), white (C), and gold (D)

Extras: 2 black beads; black sewing thread; fabric glue (optional)

METHOD

Body

Using A, make 2ch.

ROW 1 (RS): Skip first ch, 2sc in next ch, turn.

ROW 2: 1ch, 1sc in first sc, 1sc in next sc, 2sc in 1ch, turn.

ROW 3: 1ch, skip first sc, 1sc in each of next 3sc, 1sc in 1ch, turn.

ROW 4: 3ch, skip first sc, 1dc in each of next 3sc, 1dc in 1ch, turn.

ROW 5: 3ch, 1dc in first dc, 2dc in each of next 2dc, 1dc in next dc, 1dc in top ch of 3ch, turn.

ROW 6: 1ch, skip first dc, 1sc in next dc, 2sc in next dc, 1sc in each of next 2dc, 2sc in next dc, 1sc in next dc, 1sc in top ch of 3ch, turn.

ROW 7: 1ch, skip first sc, 1sc in each of next 8 sc, 1sc in 1ch, turn.

Repeat row 7 three times.

ROW 11: 1ch, skip first sc, [1sc in next sc, skip next sc] 4 times, 1sc in 1ch, turn.

ROW 12: 1ch, skip first sc, [1sc in next sc, skip next sc] twice, 1sc in 1ch.

Fasten off with 1sc in 1ch at beginning of row 12.

Wings

Using B, make 5ch, join with ss into a ring.

ROUND 1: 3ch (counts as 1dc; place marker on this st), 13dc in ring. (14dc)

UPPER RIGHT WING: Turn and work in rows as follows:

ROW 1 (WS): 2ch, 1dc in dc at base of ch, 1dc in each of next 2dc, turn. (4 sts)

ROW 2: 2ch, 1dc in first dc, 1dc in each of next 2dc, 2dc in top ch of 2ch, turn. (6 sts)

ROW 3: 2ch, skip first dc, 1dc in each of next 4dc, 1dc in top ch of 2ch, turn. (6 sts)

ROW 4: 1ch, 1sc in first dc, 1hdc in next dc, 1dc in each of next 2dc, 2tr in next dc, 1tr in top ch of 2ch. (7 sts)

Fasten off.

UPPER LEFT WING: With RS facing, rejoin B with ss in top of 3rd dc of round 1. Turn and work in rows as follows:

ROW 1 (WS): 2ch, 1dc in dc at base of ch, 1dc in next dc, 1dc in top ch of 3ch, turn. (4 sts)

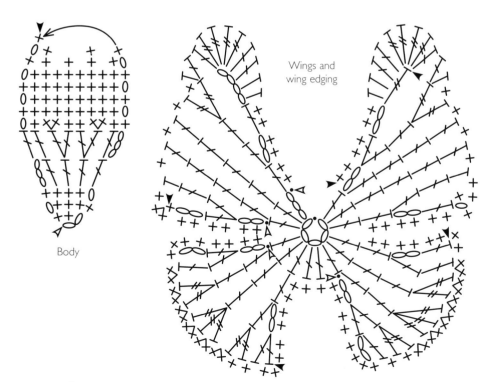

Body

Wings and wing edging

ROWS 2-3: As for upper right wing.

ROW 4: 4ch (counts as 1tr), skip first dc, 2tr in next dc, 1dc in each of next 2dc, 1hdc in next dc, 1sc in top ch of 2ch. (7 sts) Fasten off.

LOWER LEFT WING: With RS facing, rejoin B with ss in top of next (4th) dc of round 1. Do not turn. Work in rows as follows:

ROW 1 (RS): 2ch, 1dc in dc at base of ch, 1dc in each of next 2dc, turn. (4 sts)

ROW 2: 2ch, 1dc in first dc, 1dc in each of next 2dc, 2dc in top ch of 2ch, turn. (6 sts)

ROW 3: 2ch, skip first dc, 1dc in next dc, 2tr in next dc, 3tr in next dc, 2tr in next dc, 2dc in top ch of 2ch. (11 sts) Fasten off.

LOWER RIGHT WING: With RS facing, skip next 2dc of round 1 and rejoin B with ss in top of 9th dc of round 1. Do not turn. Work in rows as follows:

ROWS 1-2: As for lower left wing.

ROW 3: 2ch, 1dc in first dc, 2tr in next dc, 3tr in next dc, 2tr in next dc, 1dc in next dc, 1dc in top ch of 2ch. (11 sts) Fasten off.

Wing edging

With RS facing, join A with ss in top ch of 3ch at beginning of round 1 (marked stitch).

UPPER LEFT WING: Work edging around upper left wing as follows: 2sc in side of each of next 3 rows, (2hdc, 2dc) in side of 4ch, (4tr, 1dc) in top ch of 4ch at top corner, (1dc, 1hdc) in next tr, [1sc in space before next st] 5 times, 2sc in last sc, 2sc in side of each of next 3 rows.

LOWER LEFT WING: Continue around lower left wing: 2sc in side of each of first 2 rows, 4sc around 2ch at beginning of row 3, skip next dc, [2sc in space before next st] 6 times, [1sc in space before next st] twice, 4sc around last dc of row 3, 2sc in side of each of next 2 rows, 1sc in each of 2 skipped dc of round 1.

LOWER RIGHT WING: Continue around lower right wing: 2sc in side of each of next 2 rows, 4sc around 2ch at beginning of row 3, skip next dc, [1sc in space before next st] twice, [2sc in space before next st] 6 times, 4sc around last dc of row 3, 2sc in side of each of next 2 rows.

UPPER RIGHT WING: Continue around upper right wing: 2sc in side of each of next 3 rows, 1sc in each of ch and sc at corner, [1sc in space before next st] 5 times, (1hdc, 1dc) in next tr, (1dc, 4tr) in last tr at corner, (2dc, 2hdc) in side of same tr, 2sc in side of next 3 rows. Fasten off.

Finishing

Using A, fold body in half lengthwise and sew seam, stuffing body lightly with scraps of yarn as you do so. Sew body onto wings, centered over the round of dc. Join upper and lower wings for a short distance at each side of body. Using sewing thread, sew a bead at each side of head for eyes. Using single strand of A, add antennae at top of head, above the eyes. Trim antennae to about 1½in (4cm) and stiffen with fabric glue if desired. Using double strand of C, work running stitch around outer edge of each wing. Using double strand of D, work four random stitches at top of upper wings, just inside the white stitching. Using single strand of A, work long random stitches to simulate veins in butterfly wings.

111 GOLDEN HAIRSTREAK \\/

Yarn: Sport-weight Shetland-type yarn in ochre (A) and olive (B)

METHOD

Upper left wing
Using A, make 7ch. Skip 2ch, 1sc in next ch, 1hdc in next ch, 1dc in next ch, 1tr in next ch, 2tr in next ch, 4ch, ss in each remaining strand of the 5ch at the base of the sts.

Lower left wing
*5ch, skip 4ch, 3dtr in next ch, 4ch, ss in same ch as 3dtr. Fasten off. **

Upper right wing
Using A, make 8ch. Skip 3ch, 2tr in next ch, 1tr in next ch, 1dc in next ch, 1hdc in next ch, 1sc in next ch, 2ch, ss in each remaining strand of the 5ch at the base of the sts. Fasten off.

Lower right wing
RS facing, rejoin yarn in the ss under the 1sc. Work as lower left wing from * to **.

Body
Using B, make 5ch, skip 2ch, 2dc tog in next ch. Fasten off.

Finishing
Join wings and catch together 2 sts of upper and lower wings

See also chart opposite

invisibly on WS. Press to shape. Turn body over and stitch in place. Using B, make 2 antennae.

112 ORANGE TIP \\\/

Yarn: DK wool in white (A), pale orange (B), and black (C)

METHOD

NOTE: The butterfly is worked in rows, but these are all RS rows.

Both pairs of wings
Using A, make 15ch.
ROW 1 (RS): Skip 5ch, 3dtr in next ch, 1ch, 1dc in next ch, 2ch, 2dtr in next ch, 1tr in next ch, 3ch, ss in next ch, 3ch, 1tr in next ch, 2dtr in next ch, 1 ch, 1dc in next ch, 2ch, 3dtr in next

ch, 5ch, ss in next ch. Fasten off.
ROW 2 (RS): Using B, join yarn in 2nd ch of 2nd wing, 1ch, (1sc, 1dc) in next st, (1dc, 1ch, 1tr, 1dc) in next st, (1dc, 1sc) in next st, 1ch, ss in top ch of 3ch. Fasten off invisibly.
ROW 3 (RS): Using B, join yarn in 3rd ch of 3rd wing, 1ch, (1sc, 1dc) in next st, (1dc, 1tr, 1ch, 1dc) in next st, (1dc, 1sc) in next st, 1ch, ss in 1ch. Fasten off invisibly.

ROW 4 (RS): Using C, join yarn in 2nd dc of 2nd wing tip, 1ch, (1sc, 1ch, 1sc) in tr, 1ch, ss in dc. Fasten off invisibly.
ROW 5 (RS): Using C, join yarn in 2nd dc of 3rd wing tip, 1ch, (1sc, 1ch, 1sc) in tr, 1ch, ss in next dc. Fasten off invisibly.

Body
With C, make 6ch, skip 1ch, 2sc in next ch. Fasten off invisibly.

Finishing
Gathering up slightly, join wings in center. Sew body in place, leaving 2 ends of C for antennae; split the yarn and cut away excess strands. With C, embroider a spot on each upper wing.

See also chart opposite

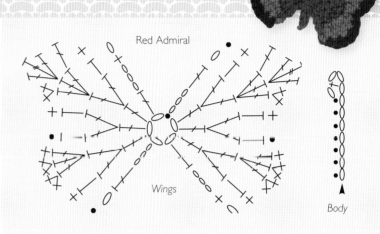

Yarn: DK wool in khaki (A), orange (B), and black (C)

METHOD

First pair of wings

Using A, make 5ch, join with ss into a ring.

ROW 1 (WS): 3ch, 4dc in ring. (5 sts)

ROW 2: 3ch, 2dc in each of next 3dc, 1dc in top ch of 3ch working last wrap with B. (8 sts)

ROW 3: Using B, 1ch, 1hdc in next dc, 3dc in next dc, 1hdc in each of next 2dc, 3dc in next dc, 1hdc in next dc, 1sc in top ch of 3ch working last wrap with C. (12 sts)

ROW 4: Using C, 1ch, 1sc in hdc, 2sc in each of next 2dc, 1sc in next dc, ss under 3 strands of next hdc, 1sc in next hdc, 2sc in next dc, (1dc, 1tr, 1dc) in next dc, 1dc in next dc, 1sc in hdc, ss in 1ch. Fasten off invisibly.

2nd pair of wings

With WS facing, join A in 5ch ring and work rows 1–3 as first pair of wings.

ROW 4: 1ch, 1sc in hdc, 1dc in next dc, (1dc, 1tr, 1dc) in next dc, 2sc in next dc, 1sc in next hdc, ss under 3 strands of next hdc, 1sc in next dc, 2sc in each of next 2dc, 1sc in hdc, ss in 1ch. Fasten off invisibly.

Body

Using A, make 10ch, skip 2ch, 1sc in next ch, 1ch, ss in each of remaining 7ch. Fasten off.

Finishing

Join wings in center and stitch body over join.

Red Admiral

Wings

Body

Golden Hairstreak

Wings

Body

Orange Tip

Wings

Body

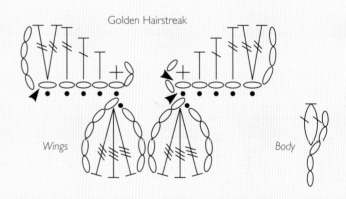

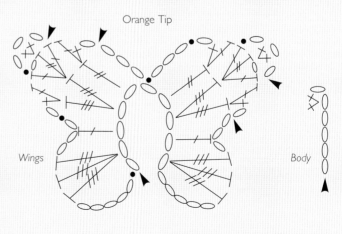

LARGE WHITE \\//

Yarn: Sport-weight yarn in pale gray (A), white (B), and charcoal gray (C)

METHOD

Upper right wing

Using A, make 6ch, join with ss into a ring.

ROW 1: 3ch, 4dc in ring, making last wrap of 4th dc with B, turn. (5 sts)

Continue with B.

ROW 2: 3ch, 2dc in next st, turn and continue on these 3 sts.

ROW 3: 3ch, 1dc in st below, 1FPtr in next st, 2dc in top ch of 3ch. (5 sts)

ROW 4: 3ch, 1dc in st below, 1dc in next st, 1BPtr in next st, 1dc in next st, 2dc in top ch of 3ch. (7 sts)

ROW 5: 3ch, 1FPtr in next st, [1dc in next st, 1FPtr in next st] twice, (1dc, 1sc) in top ch of 3ch. (8 sts)

ROW 6: 1ch, 1sc in next st, [1BPtr in next st, 1dc in next st] twice, 1BPtr in next st, 1sc in top ch of 3ch.
Fasten off.

Lower right wing

WS facing, join B in 3rd st of row 1.

ROW 2: 3ch, 2dc in next st, 2dc in top ch of 3ch. (5 sts)

ROW 3: 3ch, 1dc in st below, 1FPtr in next st, 1dc in next st, 1FPtr in next st, 2dc in top ch of 3ch. (7 sts)

ROW 4: 3ch, 1dc in st below, 1dc in next st, [1BPtr in next st, 1dc in next st] twice, 2dc in top ch of 3ch. (9 sts)

ROW 5: 2ch, 1FPtr in next st, [1dc in next st, 1FPtr in next st] 3 times, 1sc in top ch of 3ch.

ROW 6: Ss in each of next 2 sts, 1sc in each of next 3 sts, ss in each of next 2 sts. Fasten off.

NEXT ROW: RS facing, rejoin A in ring, 3ch, 4dc in ring, making last wrap of 4th dc with B. (5 sts)

Turn and continue with B.

Lower left wing

ROW 2: 3ch, 1dc in st below, 2dc in next st, 1dc in next st, turn and continue on these 5 sts.

ROW 3: 3ch, 1dc in st below, 1FPtr in next st, 1dc in next st, 1FPtr in next st, 2dc in top ch of 3ch. (7 sts)

ROW 4: 3ch, 1dc in st below, 1dc in next st, [1BPtr in next st, 1dc in next st] twice, 2dc in top ch of 3ch. (9 sts)

ROW 5: 2ch, 1FPtr in next st, [1dc in next st, 1FPtr in next st] 3 times, 1sc in top ch of 3ch.

ROW 6: Ss in each of next 2 sts, 1sc in each of next 3 sts, ss in each of next 2 sts. Fasten off.

Upper left wing

WS facing, join B in remaining dc of row 1.

ROW 2: 3ch, 1dc in st below, 1dc in top ch of 3ch. (3 sts)

ROW 3: 3ch, 1dc in st below, 1FPtr in next st, 2dc in top ch of 3ch. (5 sts)

ROW 4: 3ch, 1dc in st below, 1dc in next st, 1BPtr in next st, 1dc in next st, 2dc in top ch of 3ch. (7 sts)

ROW 5: 2ch, 1dc in st below, 1FPtr in next st, [1dc in next st, 1FPtr in next st] twice, 1dc in top ch of 3ch. (8 sts)

ROW 6: 2ch, 1BPtr in next st, [1dc in next dc, 1BPtr in next st] twice, 1sc in next st, ss in top ch of 2ch. Fasten off.

Wing tips

UPPER RIGHT: RS facing and using C, join yarn in last tr of row 6, 1ch, 1sc in each of next 4 sts, 2dc in next st, 1tr in 1ch. Fasten off.

UPPER LEFT: RS facing and using C, join yarn in ss of row 6, 4ch, 2dc in next st, 1sc in each of next 4 sts, ss in next st. Fasten off.

Body

Using C, make 7ch, skip 1ch, ss in each of next 6ch, 3ch, 2dc in last of 7ch, remove hook leaving loop, insert hook in top ch of 3ch and then in loop, yo, pull yarn through both loops on hook. Fasten off.

Finishing

Using C, embroider 2 spots on each upper wing. Sew on body and, using C, make 2 antennae. Join each upper and lower wing with a single invisible stitch.

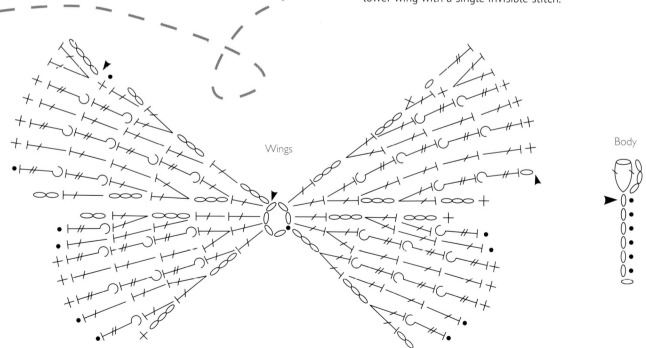

Wings

Body

CAMBERWELL BEAUTY \\//

Yarn: DK yarn in dark brown (A), pale yellow (B), and pale blue (C)

METHOD

Using A, make 5ch, join with ss into a ring.
SET-UP ROW (RS): 3ch, 16dc in ring. (17 sts)

Right upper wing

ROW 1: 2ch, 1dc in st below, 1dc in each of next 2 sts, 2dc in next st, turn.
Continue on these 6 sts.
ROW 2: 2ch, 1sc in st below, 1sc in each of next 2 sts, 1dc in next st, (1tr, 1dtr) in next st, 1dtr in top ch of 2ch of previous row. (8 sts)
ROW 3: 3ch, 1dc in st below, 1dc in each of next 2 sts, 1sc in each of next 4 sts, 1sc in top ch of 2ch making last wrap with B. (9 sts)
ROW 4: Using B, 2ch, 1sc in st below, 1dc in each of next 4 sts, 2dc in next st, 4ch, skip 3ch, ss in next ch, 2dc in next st, 1dc in next st, 1dc in top ch of 3ch. (12 sts)
Fasten off.

Left upper wing

WS facing, rejoin A in 4th st of set-up row.
ROW 1: 2ch, 1dc in st below, 1dc in each of next 2 sts, 2dc in top ch of 3ch. (6 sts)
ROW 2: 5ch, (1dtr, 1tr) in next st, 1dc in next st, 1sc in each of next 2 sts, 2sc in top ch of 2ch. (8 sts)
ROW 3: 2ch, 1sc in each of next 4 sts, 1dc in each of next 2 sts, 2dc in top ch of 5ch making last wrap with B. (9 sts)
ROW 4: Using B, 3ch, 1dc in next st, 2dc in next st, 4ch, skip 3ch, ss in next ch, 2dc in next st, 1dc in each of next 4 sts, 2sc in top ch of 2ch. (12 sts)
Fasten off.

Right lower wing

WS facing, rejoin A in set-up row in st next to right upper wing.
ROW 1: 3ch, 1dc in st below, 1dc in each of next 2 sts, 2dc in next st. (6 sts)
ROW 2: 3ch, 1dc in st below, 1dc in next st, 1tr in each of next 2 sts, 1dc in next st, (1dc, 1sc) in top ch of 3ch. (8 sts)
ROW 3: 2ch, 1sc in each of next 6 sts, 2sc in top ch of 3ch making last wrap with B. (9 sts)

ROW 4: Using B, 1ch, 1sc in each of next 2 sts, 2dc in next st, 4ch, skip 3ch, ss in next ch, 2dc in next st, 1dc in each of next 2sts, 1sc in next st, ss in top ch of 2ch. (11 sts)
Fasten off.

Left lower wing

WS facing, skip st beside right lower wing and rejoin A in next st.
ROW 1: 3ch, 1dc in st below, 1dc in each of next 2 sts, 2dc in next st. (6 sts)
ROW 2: 2ch, 1dc in st below, 1dc in next st, 1tr in each of next 2 sts, 1dc in next st, 2dc in top ch of 3ch. (8 sts)

ROW 3: 2ch, 1sc in st below, 1sc in each of next 6 sts, 1sc in top ch of 2ch making last wrap with B. (9 sts)
ROW 4: Using B, 1ch, 1sc in next st, 1dc in each of next 2 sts, 2dc in next st, 4ch, skip 3ch, ss in next ch, 2dc in next st, 1sc in each of next 2 sts, ss in top ch of 2ch. (11 sts)
Fasten off.

Body

Using A, make 6ch, skip 2ch, 1sc in each of 4ch, make 4ch, skip 4ch, 4tr in last sc. Leaving the loop, remove hook and insert it first in top ch of 4ch and then in loop, yo, pull yarn through, 3ch, skip 2ch, 1sc in next ch.
Fasten off.

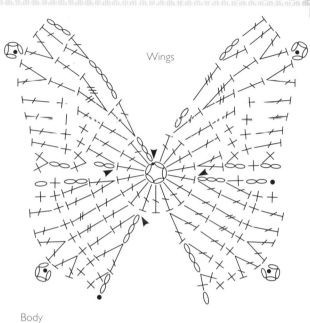

Wings

Yarn: DK yarn in yellow (A), olive green (B), and orange (C)

METHOD

Wings (RS)

Using A, make 13ch, skip 5ch, 2dtr in next ch, 5ch, 1sc in 7th of 13ch, 4ch, (1dtr, 1ttr) in 8th of 13ch, 3ch, ss in top of ttr, 6ch, ss in 9th of 13ch, 9ch, skip 2ch, ss in next ch, (1ttr, 1dtr) in 10th of 13ch, 4ch, 1sc in 11th of 13ch, 5ch, 2dtr in 12th of 13ch, 5ch, ss in 13th ch. Fasten off.

Body (WS)

Using B, make 7ch, skip 1ch, 1sc in next ch, ss in each of next 4ch. Fasten off.

Finishing

Gather center, close it, and join wings. Press. Stitch body in place. Using C, embroider a spot on each wing. Using B, make antennae.

Body

Finishing

Stretching widthwise, press to shape. Using C, stitch spots on alternate sts of row 3 of each wing. Attach body and, using A, make antennae. Stitch ends of antennae with C.

Wings

Body

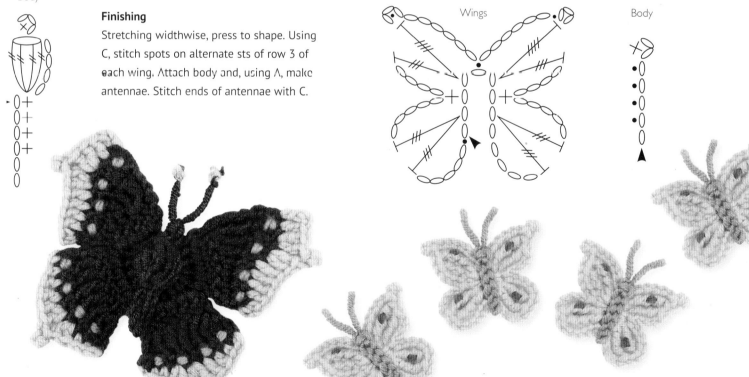

Yarn: Sport-weight cotton in yellow (A) and brown (B)

Hooks: 2 hooks, one a size smaller than the other

METHOD

Right wings

Using larger hook and A, make 9ch, join with ss into a ring.

ROW 1 (RS): 3ch, 7dc in ring, turn. (8 sts)

ROW 2: 3ch, 1dc in each of next 2 sts, 2dc in each of next 3 sts, 1dc in next st, 1dc in top ch of 3ch. (11 sts)

ROW 3: 3ch, 1dc in each of next 3 sts, 2tr in next st, 1dc in each of next 2 sts, 2ch, ss in next st, 2ch, 2dc in next st, 2tr in next st, 1tr in top ch of 3ch. (15 sts)

ROW 4: 3ch, 1dc in next st, 2tr in next st, 1dc in next st, 1sc in next st, ss in top ch of 2ch. (6 sts)

Fasten off.

ROW 5: Join B in same ch as ss, 3ch, 1dc in each of next 2 sts, 2dc in next st, 1tr in next st, 2tr tog in next st and top ch of 3ch.

Fasten off.

NEXT ROW: RS facing, join B in first dc of row 3, 1ch, 1sc in each of next 2 sts, 2sc in each of next 3 sts, 1sc in next st, ss in top ch of 2ch.

Left wings

RS facing, join A in ring.

ROW 1: 3ch, 7dc in ring, turn. (8 sts)

ROW 2: 3ch, 1dc in next st, 2dc in each of next 3 sts, 1dc in each of next 2 sts, 1dc in top ch of 3ch. (11 sts)

ROW 3: 4ch, 2tr in next st, 2dc in next st, 2ch, ss in next st, 2ch, 1dc in each of next 2 sts, 2tr in next st, 1dc in each of next 3 sts, 1dc in top ch of 3ch.

Fasten off.

ROW 4: WS facing, rejoin A in top ch of 2ch of upper wing, 1ch, 1sc in first st, 1dc in next st, 2tr in next st, 1dc in next st, 1dc in top ch of 4ch making last wrap with B.

ROW 5: Using B, 3ch, 1tr in each of next 2 sts, 2dc in next st, 1dc in each of next 2 sts, 2ch, ss in 1ch.

Fasten off.

NEXT ROW: RS facing, join B in top ch of 2ch of lower wing, 1ch, 1sc in next st, 2sc in each of next 3 sts, 1sc in each of next 3 sts, ss in last st.

Fasten off.

Edging

Using smaller hook and B, working into one strand of A only, ss along edges of upper and lower wings.

Body

Using larger hook and B, make 5ch, skip 1ch, ss in each of next 4ch, make 4ch, 3tr cluster in top ch of 5ch, 3ch, skip 2ch, 1sc in next ch. Fasten off.

Finishing

Close center and press to shape. Attach body and, using B, make antennae. Using B, embroider a spot on each upper wing.

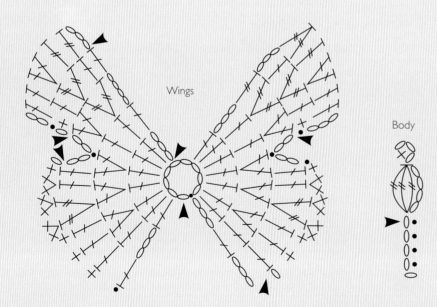

Wings

Body

STRAW NEST \/

Yarn: Natural raffia

METHOD

NOTE: When joining strands it is not necessary to knot them; just leave the ends at the back of the work – this will be the outside. The inside of the nest will be facing you as you work each round.

Make 4ch, join with ss into a ring.
ROUND 1: 1ch, 7sc in ring, ss in 1ch. (8 sts)
ROUND 2: 1ch, [2sc in next st, 1sc in next st] 3 times, 2sc in next st, ss in 1ch. (12 sts)
ROUND 3: 1ch, 1sc in next st, [2sc in next st, 1sc in each of next 2 sts] 3 times, 2sc in next st, ss in 1ch. (16 sts)
ROUND 4: 1ch, [2sc in next sc, 1sc in next st] 7 times, 2sc in next st, ss in 1ch. (24 sts)
ROUND 5: 1ch, 1sc in each of next 2 sts, [2sc in next st, 1sc in each of next 3 sts] 5 times, 2sc in next st, ss in 1ch. (30 sts)
ROUND 6: 1ch, 1sc in each of next 3 sts, [2sc in next st, 1sc in each of next 4 sts] 5 times, 2sc in next st, ss in 1ch. (36 sts)
ROUND 7: 1ch, 1sc in each st, ss in 1ch.

ROUNDS 8-12: As round 7.
In next round before joining new strands, fasten off previous strand with ss.
ROUND 13: 1ch, make loop: yarn over middle finger of left hand to make a loop, insert hook in back strand of next st, drop yarn, catch loop and pull it through st and loop on hook as for ss, release loop, pick up yarn, 1sc in back strand of next st; complete round, working random loops and sc, ss in 1ch, turn.
ROUND 14: Work sc, inserting hook in remaining strand of each sc of round 12 (not loop round).
Fasten off. Tug base of each loop to tighten. Cut loops, then trim and fray ends.

The chart shows rounds 1–7. Rounds 8–12 are as round 7. See instructions for rounds 13–14.

119 FEATHERED NEST |

Yarn: DK yarn in light gray

Hooks: 2 hooks, one a size smaller than the other

Extras: Feathers; glue (optional)

METHOD

NOTE: The inside of the nest will be facing you as you work each round.

Using larger hook, make 5ch, join with ss into a ring.
ROUND 1: 3ch, 15dc in ring, ss in top ch of 3ch. (16 sts)

ROUND 2: 3ch, 2dc in next st, [1dc in next st, 2dc in next st] 7 times, ss in top ch of 3ch. (24 sts)

ROUND 3: 3ch, 1dc in each of next 2 sts, 2dc in next st, [1dc in each of next 3 sts, 2dc in next st] 5 times, ss in top ch of 3ch. (30 sts)

ROUND 4: 3ch, 1dc in each of next 29 sts, ss in top ch of 3ch.

ROUND 5: Using smaller hook, make 1ch, 1sc in each of next 29 sts, ss in 1ch. Fasten off.

120 PIGEON FEATHER |

Yarn: DK yarn in white (A), gray (B), and charcoal (C)

METHOD

ROW 1: Using A and leaving an extra long end, make 7ch, skip 3ch, 2dc in next ch. (3 sts)

ROWS 2 & 4: 1ch, [1sc in next st] to end.

ROW 3: 4ch, 3tr in next st, 1tr in 1ch. (5 sts)

ROW 5: 5ch, 1dtr in next st, 3dtr in next st, 1dtr in next st, 1dtr in 1ch. (7 sts)

ROW 6: 1ch, 1dc in each st, making last wrap of last dc with B.

ROW 7: Using B, 5ch, 1dtr in each of next 2 sts, 3dtr in next st, 1dtr in each of next 3 sts. (9 sts)

ROW 8: 1ch, 1sc in each st, making last wrap of last sc with C.

ROW 9: Using C, 1ch, 1dc in next st, 1tr in each of next 2 sts, 3dtr in next st, 1tr in each of next 2 sts, 1dc in next st, 1sc in 1ch. Fasten off.

Finishing
Weave in long end behind first 3ch, then use it to make a few loops, anchored with a backstitch between each. Trim and fray the ends.

Finishing

Insert feathers in last round, gluing them in place if necessary.

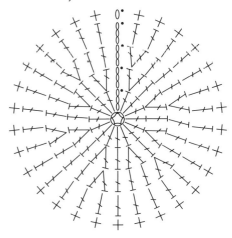

Yarn: Sport-weight yarn (preferably wool for elasticity)

Extras: Egg mold, 13cm (5in) circumference

METHOD

Make a slip ring.

ROUND 1 (RS): 2ch, 7sc in ring, pull end to close ring, ss in top ch of 2ch. (8 sts)

ROUND 2: 3ch, 1tr in ch below, 2dc in each of next 7 sts, ss in top ch of 3ch. (16 sts)

ROUND 3: 3ch, 2dc in next st, [1dc in next st, 2dc in next st] 7 times, ss in top ch of 3ch. (24 sts)

ROUND 4: 3ch, 1dc in each of next 23 sts, ss in top ch of 3ch.

ROUNDS 5-7: As round 4.

ROUND 8: 3ch, 2dc tog in next 2 sts, [1dc in next st, 2dc tog in next 2 sts] 7 times, ss in top ch of 3ch. (16 sts) Pull up inside end and fasten off. Insert mold, rounded end downward.

ROUND 9: 3ch, 1dc in next st, 2dc tog in next 2 sts, [1dc in each of next 2 sts, 2dc tog in next 2 sts] 3 times, ss in top ch of 3ch. (12 sts)

ROUND 10: 3ch, 2dc tog in next 2 sts, [1dc in next st, 2dc tog in next 2 sts] 3 times, ss in top ch of 3ch. (8 sts)

Fasten off, leaving a long end. Use this end to gather sts of last round by taking yarn under one strand of each st each time.

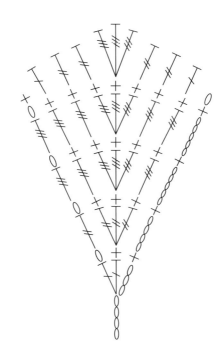

Yarn: Sport-weight yarn

Extras: Batting (optional); 2 faceted sequins; small quantity of flat sequins

METHOD

Body

Make a slip ring.

ROUND 1: 1ch, 7sc in ring, pull end to close ring, ss in 1ch. (8 sts)

ROUND 2: 1ch, 1sc in each st, ss in 1ch.

ROUND 3: 3ch, 1dc in st below, 1dc in next st, 2dc in next st, 1dc in next st, 3dc in next st, 1dc in next st, 2dc in next st, 1dc in next st, 1dc in ss of round below, ss in top ch of 3ch. (14 sts)

ROUND 4: 3ch, 1dc in st below, 1dc in each of next 6 sts, 3dc in next st, 1dc in each of next 6 sts, 1dc in ss of round below, ss in top ch of 3ch. (18 sts)

ROUND 5: 3ch, 1dc in st below, 1dc in each of next 8 sts, 3dc in next st, 1dc in each of next 8 sts, 1dc in ss of round below, ss in top ch of 3ch. (22 sts)

ROUNDS 6-7: 3ch, 1dc in each of next 21 sts, ss in top ch of 3ch.

ROUND 8: 3ch, 2dc tog over next 2 sts, 1dc in each of next 17 sts, 2dc tog over next 2 sts, ss in top ch of 3ch. (20 sts)

ROUND 9: 3ch, 2dc tog over next 2 sts, 1dc in each of next 15 sts, 2dc tog over next 2 sts, ss in top ch of 3ch. (18 sts)

ROUND 10: 3ch, [2dc tog over next 2 sts] twice, 1dc in each of next 9 sts, [2dc tog over next 2 sts] twice, ss in top ch of 3ch. (14 sts)

ROUND 11: 3ch, [2dc tog over next 2 sts] twice, 1dc in each of next 5 sts, [2dc tog over next 2 sts] twice, ss in top ch of 3ch. (10 sts)

Fasten off.

Dorsal fin

Turn fish so that mouth is to the right. Join yarn around post of center st of 3-st increase of round 5.

ROW 1: 1ch, 1sc around this st, 2sc around each center st of rounds 6, 7, 8, and 9, 1sc around center st of round 10. (11 sts)

ROW 2: 2ch, 1dc in each of next 2 sts, 1ch, 1sc in each of next 2 sts, 1ch, 1dc in next st, 2tr in next st, 1tr in each of next 2 sts, 2tr tog over next st and 1ch.

Fasten off.

Smaller pair of underside fins

Turn fish so that mouth is to the left.

FIRST FIN: Join yarn in st beside 3ch at start of round 5, 4ch, 2tr in st below. Fasten off.

2ND FIN: Turn fish over and join yarn in corresponding st beside 3ch of round 4, 4ch, 2tr in st below. Fasten off.

Larger pair of underside fins

In round 8, position as smaller pair of fins but work: 5ch, 2dtr in st below. Fasten off.

Ventral fin

ROW 1: With mouth to the left, join yarn in first ch of 3ch at beginning of round 10: (1ch, 1sc) in this group of 3ch, 2sc in next group. (4 sts)

ROW 2: Skip 1sc, 1sc in next st, 1dc in next st, 2tr in 1ch. Fasten off.

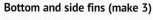

Tail

Lightly stuff body with batting or spare yarn. With dorsal fin to the left, pinch the tail end flat between your fingers. Join yarn.

ROW 1: Inserting hook into next st on front and next st on back of the flattened piece each time, make 1ch in first pair of sts, 1sc in each of next 4 pairs of sts. (5 sts)

ROW 2: 1ch, 1sc in each of next 4 sts.

ROW 3: 6ch, skip 2ch, ss in next ch, (1dtr, 1tr, 1dc) in st below, 1dc in each of next 3 sts, (1dc, 1tr, 1dtr) in 1ch. Fasten off.

Finishing

Sew on faceted sequins for eyes. Sew flat sequins on body.

Yarn: Worsted-weight yarn

Extras: Black and yellow yarn

METHOD

Body and tail

Make 3ch, join with ss into a ring.

ROUND 1: 1sc in each st. (3 sts)

ROUND 2: 2sc in each st. (6 sts)

ROUND 3: [1sc in next st, 2sc in next st] 3 times. (9 sts)

ROUND 4: [2sc in next st, 1sc in each of next 2 sts] 3 times. (12 sts)

ROUNDS 5-6: Sc all.

ROUND 7: 2sc tog over next 2 sts, 10sc. (11 sts)

ROUND 8: 4sc, 2sc tog over next 2 sts, 5sc. (10 sts)

ROUND 9: 2sc tog over next 2 sts, 8sc. (9 sts)

ROUND 10: 3sc, 2sc tog over next 2 sts, 4sc. (8 sts)

ROUND 11: 2sc tog over next 2 sts, 4sc, 2sc tog over next 2 sts. (6 sts)

ROUND 12: 1sc, 2sc tog over next 2 sts, 1sc, 2sc tog over next 2 sts. (4 sts)

To form the tail, turn and continue in rows.

ROW 13: 3sc, 1ch, turn.

ROW 14: 2sc in each st. (6 sts) Fasten off.

Top fin

Make 4ch, ss in 2nd ch from hook, 1sc, 1dc. Fasten off.

Bottom and side fins (make 3)

Make 3ch. Fasten off.

Finishing

Sew on fins. Using black yarn, sew French knots for eyes and embroider along edge of top fin and tail. Sew loops of yellow yarn around the eyes and secure.

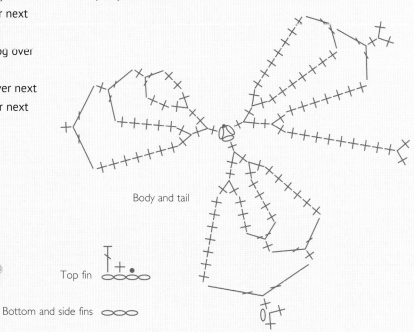

Body and tail

Top fin

Bottom and side fins

124 SARDINE \/

Yarn: Sport-weight metallic yarn

Extras: 2 sequins

METHOD

Head and body

Make a slip ring.

ROW 1: 5ch, 10dtr in ring, pull end to close ring, turn. (11 sts)

ROW 2: 2ch, 1sc in each of next 3 sts, 2sc in next st, 1sc in next st, 2sc in next st, 1sc in each of next 3 sts, 1sc in top ch of 5ch. (13 sts)

ROW 3: 2ch, working into back loop only of each sc, 1sc in each of next 11 sts, 1sc in top ch of 2ch. Resume working into both loops of each st from here onward.

ROW 4: 2ch, 1sc in each of next 4 sts, 2sc in next st, 1sc in next st, 2sc in next st, 1sc in each of next 4 sts, 1sc in top ch of 2ch. (15 sts)

ROW 5: 2ch, 1sc in each st, 1sc in top ch of 2ch.

ROWS 6-10: As row 5.

ROW 11: 2ch, 2sc tog over next 2 sts, 1sc in each of next 9 sts, 2sc tog over next 2 sts, 1sc in top ch of 2ch. (13 sts)

ROWS 12-14: As row 5.

ROW 15: 2ch, 2sc tog over next 2 sts, 1sc in each of next 7 sts, 2sc tog over next 2 sts, 1sc in top ch of 2ch. (11 sts)

ROWS 16-18: As row 5.

ROW 19: 2ch, 2sc tog over next 2 sts, 1sc in each of next 5 sts, 2sc tog over next 2 sts, 1sc in top ch of 2ch. (9 sts)

ROW 20: As row 5.

ROW 21: 2ch, 2sc tog over next 2 sts, 1sc in each of next 3 sts, 2sc tog over next 2 sts, 1sc in top ch of 2ch. (7 sts)

ROW 22: As row 5.

Tail

ROW 23: 5ch, 1tr in st below, 1dc in next st, 2dc in next st, (1tr, 1ch, 1dtr, 1ch, 1tr) in next st, 2dc in next st, 1dc in next st, (1tr, 1dtr) in top ch of 2ch. Fasten off.

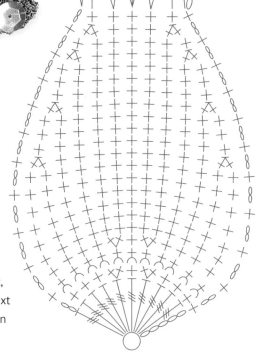

Finishing

RS facing and tail downward, join yarn in first st of row 2, 1ch, working into surface strand only of each stitch, 1sc in each st to end of row. Fasten off. Join ends of tail and seam, stuffing with spare yarn before completing. Sew on sequins for eyes.

125 BLUE DAMSELFISH \/

Yarn: Worsted-weight yarn in bright blue (A) and light blue (B)

Extras: Black yarn; batting

METHOD

NOTE: The body is first worked in rounds. To form the tail, the piece is held flat and 2 sts are worked into at once. The pattern proceeds from then on with rows.

Body

Using A, make a slip ring.

ROUND 1: 3sc in ring, pull end to close ring.

ROUND 2: 2sc in each st. (6 sts)

ROUND 3: [1sc in next st, 2sc in next st] 3 times. (9 sts)

ROUND 4: [1sc in each of next 2 sts, 2sc in next st] 3 times. (12 sts)

ROUND 5: [1sc in each of next 3 sts, 2sc in next st] 3 times. (15 sts)

ROUNDS 6-8: Sc all.

ROUND 9: [1sc in each of next 3 sts, 2sc tog over next 2 sts] 3 times. (12 sts)

ROUND 10: [1sc in each of next 2 sts, 2sc tog over next 2 sts] 3 times. (9 sts)

Stuff the body.

ROUND 11: [1sc in next st, 2sc tog over next 2 sts] 3 times. (6 sts)

To form the tail, pinch the work flat between your fingers.

ROW 12: 1ch, [inserting hook into next st on front and next st on back of the flattened piece, work 1sc] 3 times. (3 sts)

ROW 13: Using B, 2sc in each st. (6 sts)

ROW 14: Sc all.

Fasten off.

Back fins (make 2)

Using B, make 5ch. Starting in 2nd ch from hook, 2ss, 2sc. Fasten off.

Front fins (make 2)

Using B, make 3ch. Starting in 2nd ch from hook, 2sc. Fasten off.

Finishing

Use tails of yarn to attach fins to body. Embroider stripes on the face with black yarn, and sew French knots on top of these. Highlight the eyes by sewing light blue yarn (B) around the French knots.

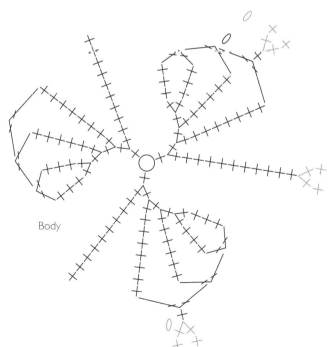

Body

Front fin

Back fin

GOBY

Yarn: Worsted-weight yarn

Extras: White embroidery thread; black felt

METHOD

NOTE: The body is first worked in rounds. To form the tail, the body is held flat and 2 sts are worked at once. The pattern proceeds from then on with rows.

Body

Make a slip ring.

ROUND 1: 6sc in ring, pull end to close ring.

ROUND 2: [1sc in next st, 2sc in next st] 3 times. (9 sts)

ROUND 3: [1sc in next 2 sts, 2sc in next st] 3 times. (12 sts)

ROUND 4: Sc all.

ROUND 5: [1sc in next 3 sts, 2sc in next st] 3 times. (15 sts)

ROUND 6: Sc all.

ROUND 7: [1sc in next 3 sts, 2sc tog over next 2 sts] 3 times. (12 sts)

ROUND 8: Sc all.

ROUND 9: [1sc in each of next 2 sts, 2sc tog over next 2 sts] 3 times. (9 sts)

ROUNDS 10-11: Sc all.

ROUND 12: [1sc in next st, 2sc tog over next 2 sts] 3 times. (6 sts)

To form the tail, pinch the work flat between your fingers.

ROW 13: 1ch, [inserting hook into next st on front and next st on back of the flattened piece, work 1sc] 3 times. (3 sts)

ROW 14: 1ch, 2sc in each st. (6 sts)

ROW 15: 1ch, ss all.

Fasten off.

Dorsal fin

Make 5ch. Starting in 2nd ch from hook, 4ss. Fasten off.

Eye area (make 2)

Make a slip ring, 6sc in ring, pull end to close ring, ss in next st. Fasten off, leaving a long tail of yarn to use to secure to the body.

Side fin (make 2)

Make 3ch.

ROW 1: Starting in 2nd ch from hook, 2sc. (2 sts)

ROW 2: 1ch, 1sc, 2sc in next st. (3 sts)

Fasten off.

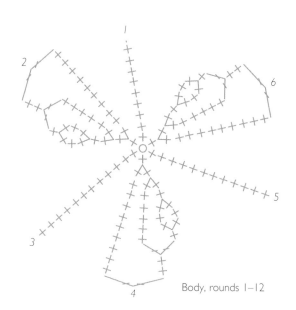

Body, rounds 1–12

Body, rows 13–15

Eye area

Dorsal fin

Side fin

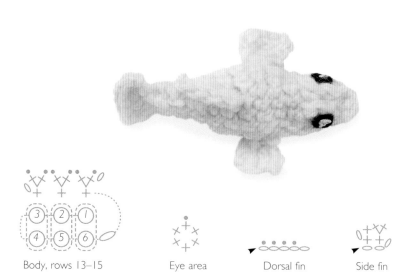

BLUE LINE GROUPER

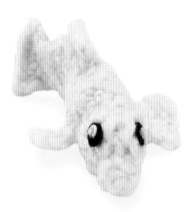

Finishing

Using crochet hook, secure the dorsal and side fins to the body with knots as necessary. Sew the middle and lower edge of the eye area down to the body. Using embroidery thread, sew French knots on top of small circles of felt for eyes, and attach these to the body.

Yarn: Lightweight yarn

Extras: Blue sewing thread; 2 pony beads; blue embroidery thread; blue felt

METHOD
Body
Make a slip ring.

ROUND 1: 6sc in ring, pull end to close ring.

ROUND 2: [2sc in next st, 1sc in next st] 3 times. (9 sts)

ROUND 3: [2sc in next st, 1sc in next st] 4 times, 2sc in next st. (14 sts)

ROUND 4: [2sc in next st, 1sc in each of next 6 sts] twice. (16 sts)

ROUNDS 5-10: Sc all.

ROUND 11: [2sc tog over next 2 sts, 1sc in each of next 6 sts] twice. (14 sts)

ROUND 12: [2sc tog over next 2 sts, 1sc in each of next 5 sts] twice. (12 sts)

ROUND 13: [1sc in each of next 2 sts, 2sc tog over next 2 sts] 3 times. (9 sts)

ROUND 14: [2sc tog over next 2 sts, 1sc in next st] 3 times. (6 sts)

ROUND 15: [1sc in next st, 2sc tog over next 2 sts] twice. (4 sts)

ROUND 16: Ss in next st. Fasten off.

Finishing

Using sewing thread, couch stitch the embroidery thread onto the body in a random design. You can begin and end this process at the tail (round 16) so that the ends of the thread can be hidden by the fins. Cut felt for the dorsal, ventral, tail, and side fins. Using sewing thread, stitch the fins in place and attach pony beads for eyes.

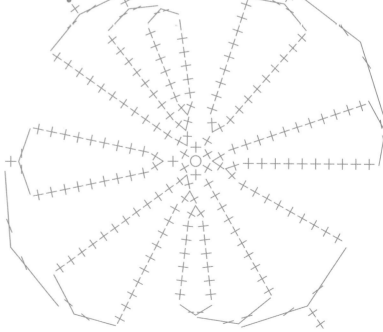

PURPLE GAMMA V

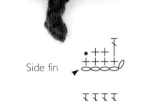

Yarn: Superfine yarn

Extras: White felt; 2 black pony beads; batting

METHOD

Body

Make a slip ring.

ROUND 1: 6sc in ring, pull end to close ring.

ROUND 2: [1sc in next st, 2sc in next st]
3 times. (9 sts)

ROUNDS 3-4: Sc all.

ROUND 5: [1sc in each of next 2 sts, 2sc in
next st] 3 times. (12 sts)

ROUND 6: [1sc in each of next 2 sts, 2sc in
next st] 4 times. (16 sts)

ROUND 7: [2sc in next st, 1sc in each of next
7 sts] twice. (18 sts)

ROUND 8: Sc all.

ROUND 9: [1sc in each of next 5 sts, 2sc in
next st] 3 times. (21 sts)

ROUNDS 10-12: Sc all.

ROUND 13: [1sc in each of next 5 sts, 2sc tog
over next 2 sts] 3 times. (18 sts)

ROUND 14: Sc all.

ROUND 15: [1sc in each of next 4 sts, 2sc tog
over next 2 sts] 3 times. (15 sts)

ROUND 16: Sc all.

ROUND 17: 1sc in each of next 9 sts, 2sc tog
over next 2 sts, 1sc in each of next 4 sts.
(14 sts)

ROUND 18: [2sc tog over next 2 sts, 1sc in
each of next 5 sts] twice. (12 sts)

ROUND 19: Sc all.

ROUND 20: [2sc tog over next 2 sts, 1sc in
each of next 4 sts] twice. (10 sts)

ROUND 21: Sc all.

ROUND 22: [1sc in each of next
3 sts, 2sc tog over next 2 sts]
twice. (8 sts)

ROUND 23: Sc all.

Stuff the fish. To form the tail, pinch the
work flat between your fingers.

ROW 24: 1ch, [inserting hook into next st on
front and next st on back of the flattened
piece, work 1sc] 4 times. (4 sts)

ROW 25: 1ch, 2sc in next st, sc in next
2 sts, 2sc in next. (6 sts)

Side fin

Dorsal fin

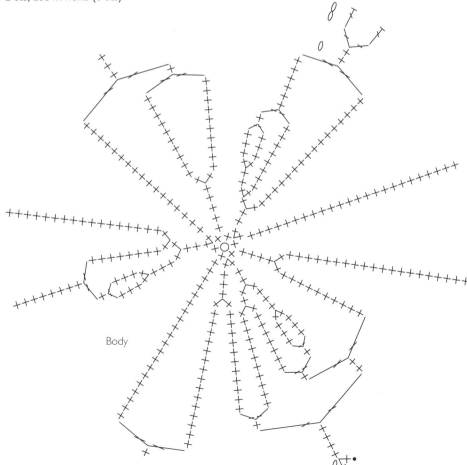

Body

ROW 26: 2ch, 1dc in each of next 2 sts, 1sc in each of next 2 sts, ss in next 2 sts. Fasten off.

Side fin (make 2)

Make 5ch.
ROW 1: Starting from 2nd ch from hook, 1sc in each of next 4ch. (4 sts)
ROW 2: Ss in next st, 1sc in each of next 2 sts, 1dc in next st.
Fasten off.

Dorsal fin

Make 8ch.
ROW 1: Ss in 2nd ch from hook, 1sc in each of next 2ch, 1dc in each of next 4ch. (7 sts)
Fasten off.

Finishing

Attach the side and dorsal fins. Sew the pony beads to small circles of felt for eyes and attach these to the body.

129 PARROTFISH V

Yarn: Worsted-weight yarn

Extras: Batting; 2 safety eyes; red and pink felt; red embroidery thread

METHOD

NOTE: The tail is left unfinished here because it will be covered with pieces of felt after finishing.

Body

Make a slip ring.
ROUND 1: 6sc in ring, pull end to close ring.
ROUND 2: [1sc in next st, 2sc in next st] 3 times. (9 sts)
ROUND 3: [2sc in next st, 1sc in each of next 2 sts] 3 times. (12 sts)
ROUND 4: [2sc in each of next 2 sts, 1sc in next st] 4 times. (20 sts)
ROUNDS 5-6: Sc all.
ROUND 7: [2sc tog over next 2 sts, 1sc in each of next 3 sts] 4 times. (16 sts)
ROUND 8: [2sc tog over next 2 sts, 1sc in each of next 2 sts] 4 times. (12 sts)
Stuff the body lightly (don't force it to be completely round) and add the eyes.
ROUND 9: [2sc tog over next 2 sts] 6 times. (6 sts)
ROUNDS 10-11: Sc all.
ROUND 12: Ss in each of next 2 sts. Fasten off.

Finishing

Cut pieces of red felt for the beak and pink felt for the fins and tail. Sew onto body and then embroider designs on the boundary between body and fins.

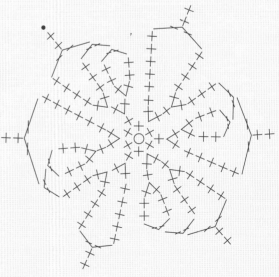

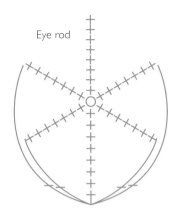

Eye rod

To start body, work 8sc in eye rod tube as indicated by arrow.

Yarn: Worsted-weight yarn

Extras: White and black yarn; batting

METHOD
SPECIFIC ABBREVIATION
Dec = 2sc tog over next 2 sts.

Eye rod
Make a slip ring.
ROUND 1: 6sc in ring, pull end to close ring.
ROUNDS 2-7: Sc all.
ROUND 8: 1sc, 5sc tog over next 5 sts. (2 sts)
Fasten off.

Body
ROUND 1: 8sc in eye rod as shown in diagram. (8 sts)
ROUND 2: [2sc in next st, 1sc in each of next 3 sts] twice. (10 sts)
ROUND 3: [2sc in next st, 1sc in each of next 4 sts] twice. (12 sts)
ROUND 4: [2sc in next st, 1sc in each of next 5 sts] twice. (14 sts)
ROUNDS 5-8: Sc all.
ROUND 9: [Dec, 1sc in each of next 5 sts] twice. (12 sts)
ROUND 10: 1sc in each of next 5 sts, dec, 1sc in each of next 5 sts. (11 sts)
ROUND 11: Dec, 1sc in each of next 9 sts. (10 sts)

ROUND 12: Dec, 1sc in each of next 8 sts. (9 sts)
ROUND 13: Dec, 1sc in each of next 7 sts. (8 sts)
Stuff the body.
ROUND 14: Dec, 1sc in each of next 6 sts. (7 sts)
ROUND 15: Dec, 1sc in each of next 5 sts. (6 sts)
ROUND 16: [Dec] 3 times. (3 sts)
Fasten off.

Fins (make 5)
Make 8ch, 1dc in 4th ch from hook, 1dc in next ch, 1sc in each of next 2ch, ss in next ch. Fasten off.

Finishing
Sew fins to body (1 dorsal fin, 2 side fins, and 2 for the tail). Sew French knots for eyes with black yarn, and wrap loops of white yarn around them.

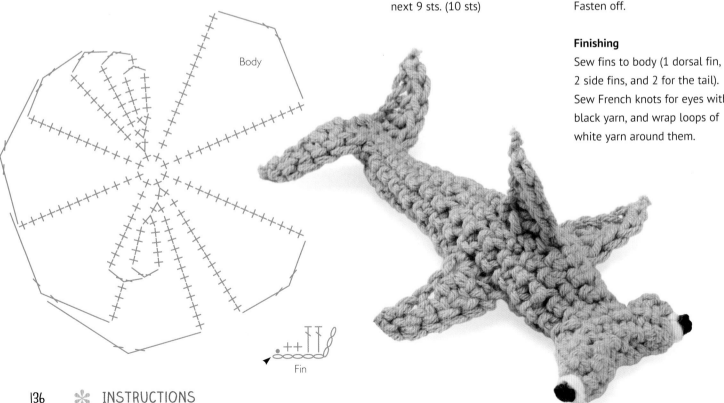

Body

Fin

131 TRIGGERFISH \/

Yarn: Worsted-weight yarn

Extras: 2 safety eyes; batting; black and white felt; seed beads

METHOD

Body

Make a slip ring.

ROUND 1: 6sc in ring, pull end to close ring.

ROUND 2: [1sc in each of next 2 sts, 2sc in next st] twice. (8 sts)

ROUND 3: [2sc in next st, 1sc in each of next 3 sts] twice. (10 sts)

ROUND 4: [1sc in each of next 4 sts, 2sc in next st] twice. (12 sts)

ROUND 5: [2sc in next st, 1sc in each of next 5 sts] twice. (14 sts)

ROUND 6: [2sc in next st, 1sc in each of next 5 sts, 2sc in next st] twice. (18 sts)

ROUND 7: [1sc in each of next 5 sts, 2sc in next st] 3 times. (21 sts)

ROUND 8: [2sc in next st, 1sc in each of next 6 sts] 3 times. (24 sts)

ROUND 9: [1sc in each of next 11 sts, 2sc in next st] twice. (26 sts)

ROUNDS 10-11: Sc all.

ROUND 12: [2sc tog over next 2 sts, 1sc in each of next 2 sts] 6 times, 1sc in each of next 2 sts. (20 sts)

ROUND 13: [1sc in each of next 3 sts, 2sc tog over next 2 sts] 4 times. (16 sts)

Stuff the body and add the eyes.

ROUND 14: [2sc tog over next 2 sts, 1sc in each of next 2 sts] 4 times. (12 sts)

ROUND 15: [1sc in next st, 2sc tog over next 2 sts] 4 times. (8 sts)

To form the tail, pinch the work flat between your fingers.

ROW 16: 1ch, [inserting hook into next st on front and next st on back of the flattened piece, work 1sc] 4 times. (4 sts)

ROW 17: 1ch, 1sc in each of next 4 sts. (4 sts)

ROW 18: Ss in each of next 2 sts, 1sc in next st, 2dc in next st. (5 sts)

Fasten off.

Finishing

Cut a small piece of black felt to decorate the space between the eyes. Cut white felt for the eyespots, side fins, and the dorsal and ventral fins. Sew these to the body and then decorate the back of the fish with seed beads.

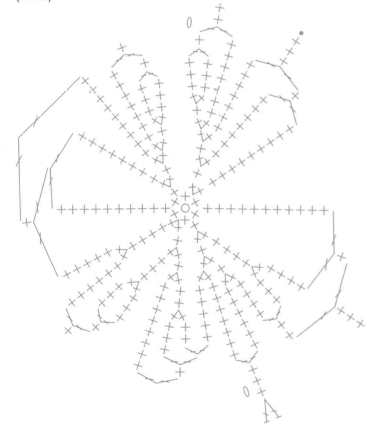

Yarn: Worsted-weight yarn in evergreen (A) and lime (B)

Extras: Black felt; black sewing thread; white lace trim; 2 plastic doll eyes; grocery bag twist tie or appropriately colored pipe cleaner or floral wire

METHOD

Body

Using A, make a slip ring.

ROUND 1: 6sc in ring, pull end to close ring.

ROUND 2: 2sc in each st. (12 sts)

ROUND 3: [2sc in next st, 1sc in next st] 6 times. (18 sts)

ROUND 4: [1sc in next 2 sts, 2sc in next st] 6 times. (24 sts)

ROUND 5: [2sc in next st, 1sc in each of next 3 sts] 6 times. (30 sts)

ROUNDS 6-7: Sc all.

ROUND 8: 15ch, skip 15 sts, 1sc in each of next 15 sts. (30 sts)

ROUND 9: [2sc tog over next 2 sts, 1sc in each of next 3 sts] 6 times. (24 sts)

ROUND 10: [1sc in each of next 2 sts, 2sc tog over next 2 sts] 6 times. (18 sts)

ROUND 11: [2sc tog over next 2 sts, 1sc in next st] 6 times. (12 sts)

ROUND 12: [2sc tog over next 2 sts] 6 times. (6 sts)

ROUND 13: [2sc tog over next 2 sts] 3 times. (3 sts)

Insert the twist tie, leaving ½in (1.5cm) sticking into the body, and crochet around it.

ROUNDS 14-23: Sc all.

ROUND 24: 2sc in each st. (6 sts)

ROUND 25: Ss in next st.

Fasten off.

Tail fin

Using A, make 5ch.

ROW 1: Starting in 2nd ch from hook, 1sc in each ch. (4 sts)

ROW 2: 1ch, 1sc in each sc.

ROW 3: 1ch, 2sc in each sc. (8 sts)

Fasten off.

Side fin (make 2)

Using A, make 3ch.

ROW 1: Starting in 2nd ch from hook, 1sc in each ch. (2 sts)

ROW 2: 1ch, 1sc in each sc.

Fasten off.

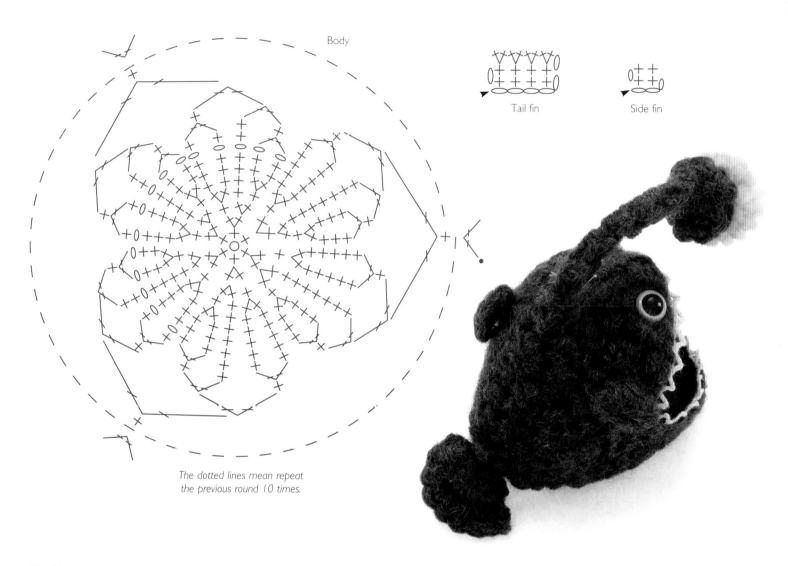

Body

Tail fin

Side fin

The dotted lines mean repeat the previous round 10 times.

Finishing

Using B, make a small pompom by wrapping yarn around your finger approximately 20 times. Thread a piece of the same yarn through the hole and tie off tightly. Trim the pompom to shape and use the ends of the yarn tie to secure the pompom inside the cup at the end of the fish's filament. Use A to sew the fins in place. Attach the eyes according to the package directions. Using black thread, sew lace along the inside edge of the mouth. Cut 2 pieces of black felt about 5½ x 3in (14 x 7.5cm). Position the long edges of the felt along the inside of the mouth and sew in place as you did the lace. You don't need to sew the felt elsewhere; just tuck the remainder into the body of the fish.

Yarn: Worsted-weight yarn

Extras: Black and white yarn

METHOD

Body

Make 3ch, join with ss into a ring.

ROUND 1: 1sc in each ch. (3 sts)

ROUND 2: Sc all.

ROUND 3: [4dc in next st] twice, 1sc in next st. (9 sts)

ROUND 4: [1sc in each of next 2 sts, 2sc in next st] 3 times. (12 sts)

ROUND 5: [1sc in each of next 5 sts, 2sc in next st] twice. (14 sts)

ROUNDS 6-7: Sc all.

ROUND 8: [1sc in each of next 5 sts, 2sc tog over next 2 sts] twice. (12 sts)

ROUND 9: Sc all.

ROUND 10: [1sc in each of next 4 sts, 2sc tog over next 2 sts] twice. (10 sts)

ROUND 11: Sc all.

ROUND 12: [1sc in each of next 3 sts, 2sc tog over next 2 sts] twice. (8 sts)

ROUND 13: Sc all.

ROUND 14: [2sc tog over next 2 sts, 2sc] twice. (6 sts)

ROUND 15: Sc all.

ROUND 16: [2sc tog over next 2 sts, sc] twice. (4 sts)

ROUND 17: Ss in each of next 2 sts. Fasten off.

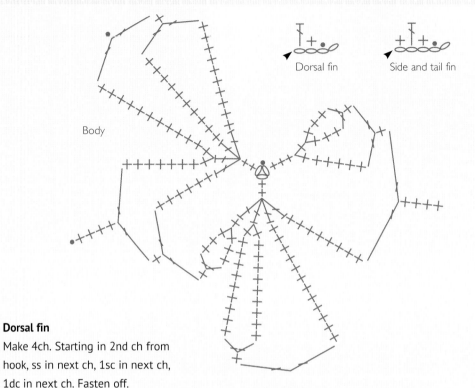

Body

Dorsal fin

Side and tail fin

Dorsal fin

Make 4ch. Starting in 2nd ch from hook, ss in next ch, 1sc in next ch, 1dc in next ch. Fasten off.

Side and tail fins (make 4)

Make 5ch. Starting in 2nd ch from hook, ss in next ch, 1sc in next ch, 1dc in next ch, 1sc in next ch. Fasten off.

Finishing

Sew tail and fins in place. Sew black French knots for eyes and wrap white yarn around them to highlight.

134 SPERM WHALE \/

Yarn: Worsted-weight yarn

Extras: Ivory embroidery thread; batting

METHOD
SPECIFIC ABBREVIATION
Dec = 2sc tog over next 2 sts.

Body
ROUND 1: 5ch, 2sc in 2nd ch from hook, 2sc in next ch, 3sc in next ch. Continuing along other side of chain, 2sc in same ch, 2sc in each of next 2ch, 3sc in each of next 2ch. (19 sts)

ROUNDS 2-7 (RED): Sc all.

ROUND 8: Dec, 1sc in each of next 17 sts. (18 sts)

ROUND 9: 1sc in each of next 16 sts, dec. (17 sts)

ROUND 10: Dec, 1sc in each of next 15 sts. (16 sts)

ROUND 11: Dec, 1sc in each of next 14 sts. (15 sts)

ROUND 12: Dec, 1sc in each of next 13 sts. (14 sts)

ROUND 13: Sc all.

ROUND 14: Dec, 1sc in each of next 12 sts. (13 sts)

ROUND 15: Sc all.

ROUND 16: Dec, 1sc in each of next 11 sts. (12 sts)

ROUND 17: Dec, 1sc in each of next 10 sts. (11 sts)

ROUND 18: Dec, 1sc in each of next 9 sts. (10 sts)

Stuff the body.

ROUND 19: Dec, 1sc in each of next 8 sts. (9 sts)

ROUND 20: Dec, 1sc in each of next 7 sts. (8 sts)

ROUND 21: Dec, 1sc in each of next 6 sts. (7 sts)

ROUND 22: Dec, 1sc in each of next 5 sts. (6 sts)

ROUND 23: [Dec] 3 times. (3 sts) Fasten off.

Fins (make 4)
Make 6ch, 1sc in 2nd ch from hook, 1dc in each of next 2ch, 1sc in next ch, ss in next ch. Fasten off.

Finishing
Sew the fins to the body (2 for the tail and 2 for the side fins). Using white embroidery thread, sew French knots for eyes.

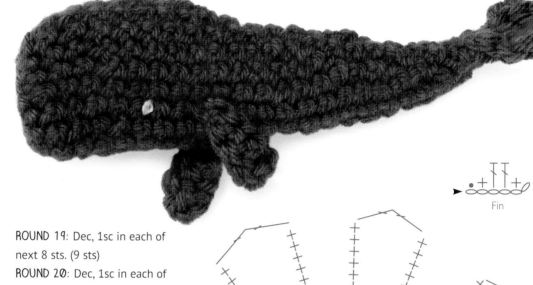

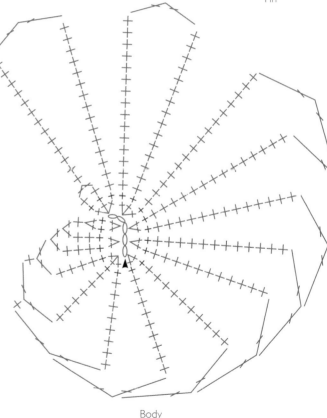

Fin

Body
*Repeat stitches in red 5 more times
(6 rounds in total).*

PYGMY OCTOPUS

Yarn: Worsted-weight acrylic

Extras: Contrasting embroidery trim

METHOD

Make a slip ring.

ROUND 1: 6sc in ring, pull end to close ring. (6 sts)

ROUND 2: 2sc in each st. (12 sts)

ROUND 3: [1sc in next st, 2sc in next st] 6 times. (18 sts)

ROUND 4: [2sc in next st, 1sc in each of next 5 sts] 3 times. (21 sts)

ROUND 5: 1sc in each of next 9 sts, 2sc in next st, 1sc in each of next 10 sts, 2sc in next st. (23 sts)

ROUND 6: 1sc in each of next 11 sts, 2sc tog over next 2sc, 1sc in each of next 10 sts. (22 sts)

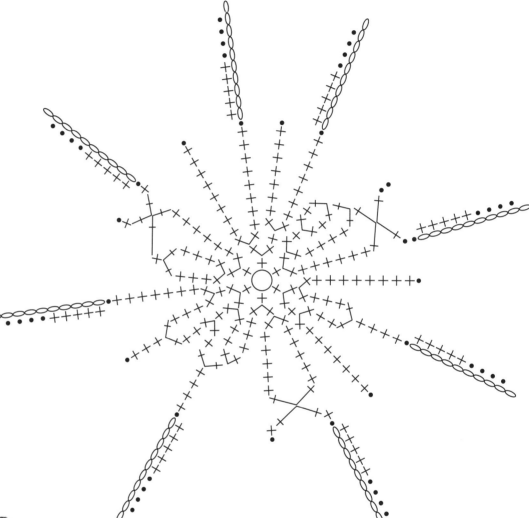

ROUND 7: 1sc in each of next 2 sts, [1sc in each of next 3 sts, 2sc tog over next 2 sts] 4 times. (18 sts)

ROUND 8: [1sc in each of next 7 sts, 2sc tog over next 2 sts] 2 times. (16 sts)

ROUND 9: 1sc in next st, [1sc in each of next 3 sts, 2sc tog over next 2 sts] 3 times. (13 sts)

ROUND 10: 1sc in next st, [1sc in each of next 3 sts, 2sc in next st] 3 times. (16 sts)

Yarn: Worsted-weight yarn

Extras: Ivory and brown embroidery thread

METHOD

Body

Make a slip ring.

ROUND 1: 6sc in ring, pull end to close ring.

ROUND 2: 2sc in each st. (12 sts)

ROUND 3: [1sc in each of next 3 sts, 2sc in next st] 3 times. (15 sts)

ROUNDS 4-5: Sc all.

ROUND 6: [1sc in each of next 2 sts, 2sc in next st] 5 times. (20 sts)

ROUND 7: [1sc in each of next 4 sts, 2sc in next st] 4 times. (24 sts)

ROUND 8: Sc all, then ss in each of next 2 sts.

ROUND 11: 1sc in each of next 14 sts, ss in each of next 2sc. (16 sts)

Arms

ROUND 12: [Ss in next st of round 11, 10ch, starting in 2nd ch from hook, ss in each of next 4ch, 1sc in each of next 5ch, ss in next st of round 11] 8 times.
Fasten off.

Finishing

Using contrasting embroidery thread, sew French knots for eyes between rounds 10 and 11, spaced apart on either side of 2 arms.

Arms

ROUND 9: [3ch, skip 1ch, ss in next 2ch, ss in each of next 3 sts of round 8] 8 times.
Fasten off.

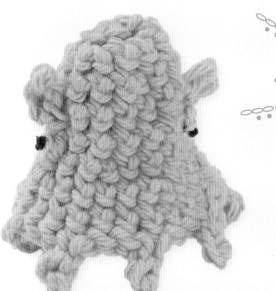

"Ears" (fins)

Picking up a st in round 4, make 7ch and the ss in the same st you picked up. This makes one fin. Repeat in same round, skipping 6 sts to make the 2nd fin.

Finishing

Using yarn, sew French knots as the base of the fins for eyes. Using brown embroidery thread, add French knots on top of these as pupils, then wrap ivory thread around them and secure with a couple of stitches.

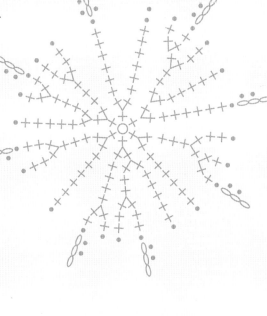

137 SHRIMP \|/

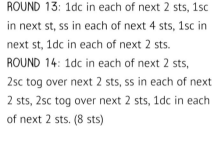

Yarn: Lightweight yarn

Extras: 2 pony beads; batting

METHOD

Make 3ch, join with ss into a ring.

ROUND 1: 1sc in each ch. (3 sts)

ROUND 2: Sc all.

ROUND 3: 2sc in each of next 2 sts, 1sc in next st. (5 sts)

ROUND 4: 2sc in each of next 4 sts, 1sc in next st. (9 sts)

ROUND 5: 1sc in each of next 3 sts, 2sc in each of next 2 sts, 1sc in each of next 4 sts. (11 sts)

ROUND 6: 1sc in each of next 4 sts, 2sc in each of next 2 sts, 1sc in each of next 5 sts. (13 sts)

ROUND 7: 1sc in each of next 5 sts, 2sc in each of next 2 sts, 1sc in each of next 6 sts. (15 sts)

ROUNDS 8-9: Sc all.

ROUND 10: 1dc in next st, 1sc in each of next 3 sts, [2sc tog over next 2 sts] 3 times, 1sc in each of next 3 sts, 1dc in each of next 2 sts. (12 sts)

ROUND 11: 1dc in each of next 2 sts, 2sc tog over next 2 sts, ss in each of next 4 sts, 2sc tog over next 2 sts, 1dc in each of next 2 sts. (10 sts)

Stuff the body.

ROUND 12: 1dc in each of next 2 sts, 1sc in next st, ss in each of next 4 sts, 1sc in next st, 1dc in each of next 2 sts.

ROUND 13: 1dc in each of next 2 sts, 1sc in next st, ss in each of next 4 sts, 1sc in next st, 1dc in each of next 2 sts.

ROUND 14: 1dc in each of next 2 sts, 2sc tog over next 2 sts, ss in each of next 2 sts, 2sc tog over next 2 sts, 1dc in each of next 2 sts. (8 sts)

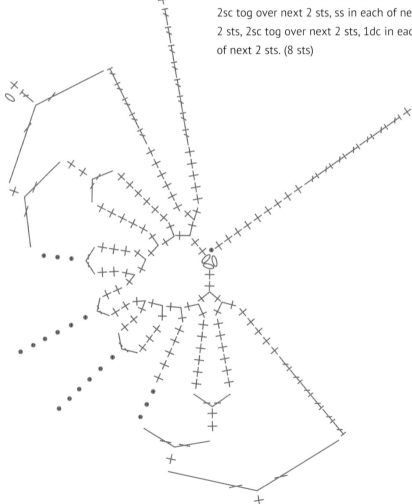

HERMIT CRAB \/

ROUND 15: 1dc in each of next 2 sts, 1sc in next st, ss in each of next 2 sts, 1sc in next st, 1dc in each of next 2 sts.
ROUND 16: 1dc in next st, 2sc tog over next 2 sts, ss in each of next 2 sts, 2sc tog over next 2 sts, 1dc in next st. (6 sts)
ROUND 17: 1dc in each of next 2 sts.
To finish the tail, turn and continue in rows.
ROW 18: 1sc in each of next 4 sts. (4 sts)
Fasten off.

Legs
Cut a 12in (30cm) piece of yarn. Fold in half and attach the midpoint to the belly of the body. Use the tails to make legs by working 6ch with each one, then fasten off. Repeat twice more to make 3 pairs of legs in total.

Finishing
Sew pony beads onto the body for eyes.

Yarn: Superfine yarn in light brown (A) and dark brown (B)

Extras: Seed beads

METHOD
SPECIFIC ABBREVIATION
Dec = 2sc tog over next 2 sts.

Shell
Using A, make 10ch, join with ss into a ring.
ROUND 1: 1sc in each ch. (10 sts)
ROUNDS 2-3: Sc all.
ROUND 4: 1sc in each of next 7 sts, dec, 1sc in next st. (9 sts)
ROUND 5 & EVERY ALT ROUND: Sc all.
ROUND 6: 1sc in next st, dec, 1sc in each of next 6 sts. (8 sts)
ROUND 8: 1sc in each of next 3 sts, dec, 1sc in each of next 3 sts. (7 sts)
ROUND 10: 1sc in each of next 4 sts, dec, 1sc in next st. (6 sts)
ROUND 12: 1sc in next st, dec, 1sc in each of next 3 sts. (5 sts)

ROUND 14: 1sc in each of next 3 sts, dec. (4 sts)
ROUND 16: Dec, 1sc in each of next 2 sts. (3 sts)
ROUND 18: Dec, 1sc in next st. (2 sts)
ROUND 20: Sc all.
Fasten off, leaving a long tail of yarn for sewing in place.

Crab
Using B, make a slip ring.
ROUND 1: 4sc in ring, pull end to close ring. (4 sts)
ROUNDS 2-3: Sc all.
Fasten off.

Claws and legs
Using B, make 8ch for each of 2 claws. Cut 3 pieces of yarn, each 3in (7cm) long, to make 3 pairs of legs.

Finishing
Sew beads in place for eyes. Coil shell up and sew in place with long tail of yarn. Attach claws to last round of the crab's body, and stitch the middle of the pairs of legs to the last round as well. Tie a knot at the end of each leg. Tuck the crab into the cavity of the shell and sew in place.

Shell

Work as a spiral in continuous rounds, starting here.

Crab

139 SEAHORSE \|/

Yarn: Lightweight yarn

Extras: Batting; grocery bag twist tie; 2 pony beads; white felt

METHOD
SPECIFIC ABBREVIATION
Dec = 2sc tog over next 2 sts.

Body
Make 3ch, join with ss into a ring.
ROUND 1: 1sc in each ch. (3 sts)
ROUND 2: Sc all.
ROUND 3: 3sc in each st. (9 sts)
ROUND 4: 2dc in each of next 3 sts, 1sc in each of next 2 sts, ss in each of next 2 sts, 1sc in each of next 2 sts. (12 sts)
ROUND 5: 1dc in each of next 6 sts, dec, ss in next 2 sts, dec. (10 sts)
ROUND 6: 1dc in each of next 4 sts, 1sc in each of next 2 sts, ss in next 2 sts, 1sc in each of next 2 sts. (10 sts)
ROUND 7: 1dc in each of next 4 sts, 1sc in each of next 2 sts, ss in next 2 sts, 1sc in each of next 2 sts. (10 sts)
ROUND 8: 1dc in each of next 4 sts, 1sc in each of next 2 sts, ss in next 2 sts, 1sc in each of next 2 sts. (10 sts)
ROUND 9: 1sc in each of next 5 sts, 2sc in each of next 5 sts. (15 sts)

ROUND 10: 1sc in each of next 9 sts, 2sc in each of next 3 sts, 1sc in each of next 3 sts. (18 sts)
ROUNDS 11-12: Sc all.
ROUND 13: [1sc in each of next 4 sts, dec] 3 times. (15 sts)
ROUND 14: Sc all.
ROUND 15: [1sc in each of next 3 sts, dec] 3 times. (12 sts)
ROUND 16: Sc all.
Stuff the seahorse and insert the twist tie. You will crochet around this to support the tail.
ROUND 17: [1sc in each of next 2 sts, dec] 3 times. (9 sts)
ROUND 18: Sc all.
ROUND 19: [1sc, dec] 3 times. (6 sts)

ROUNDS 20-21: Sc all.
ROUND 22: Dec, 1sc in each of next 4 sts. (5 sts)
ROUND 23: Dec, 1sc in each of next 3 sts. (4 sts)
ROUNDS 24-25: Sc all.

Cut the exposed part of the twist tie or push it into the body so that none sticks out of the end of the tail.
ROUND 26: [Dec] twice. (2 sts)
Fasten off.

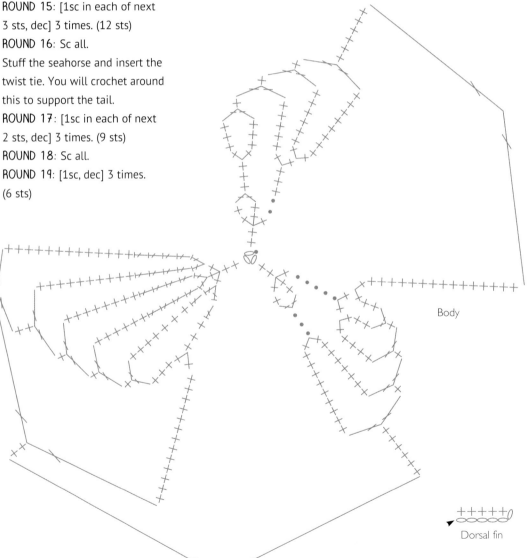

Body

Dorsal fin

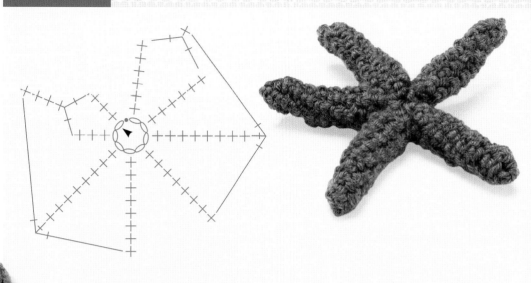

Dorsal fin

Make 6ch, starting
in 2nd ch from hook,
1sc in each ch. (5 sts)
Fasten off.

Finishing

Attach the dorsal fin. Sew pony
beads to small circles of felt,
then sew these onto the body.

Yarn: Worsted-weight acrylic

METHOD

Legs (make 5)

Make 8ch, join with ss into a ring.
ROUND 1. 1sc in each ch. (8 sts)
ROUNDS 2-3: Sc all.

ROUND 4: 2sc tog over next 2 sts,
1sc in each of next 6 sts. (7 sts)
ROUNDS 5-6: Sc all.
ROUND 7: 1sc in each of next 5sc,
2sc tog over next 2 sts. (6 sts)
ROUND 8. Sc all.
ROUND 9: [3sc tog over next 3 sts]
2 times. (2 sts)
Fasten off.

Finishing

Sew legs together by threading yarn
through each leg between chain
ring and round 1, perpendicular to
axis of the leg. Pull yarn tight and
sew up any uneven areas.

ANEMONE   I

Yarn: Worsted-weight yarn in evergreen (A); worsted-weight yarn in lime green and fine yarn in blue, to be worked together (B)

METHOD

Make 30ch, join with ss into a ring.

ROUND 1: 1sc in each ch. (30 sts)

ROUNDS 2-3: Sc all.

ROUND 4: [1sc in each of next 3 sts, 2sc tog over next 2 sts] 6 times. (24 sts)

ROUND 5: Sc all.

ROUND 6: Ss in each of next 2 sts. Splice B colors and continue with both together: 5ch, skip 1ch, ss in each of next 4ch, ss in next st of round 5] 24 times, ss in next st of round 6. Fasten off.

Finishing

Using your crochet hook, loop a tail of yarn A through several stitches on the inside mouth of the anemone. Pull to cinch closed slightly, then tie off and conceal the end.

PHOSPHORESCENT JELLYFISH 1

Yarn: Worsted-weight yarn

Extras: Glow-in-the-dark embroidery thread

METHOD

Make a slip ring.

ROUND 1: 6sc in ring, pull end to close ring. (6 sts)

ROUND 2: 2sc in each st. (12 sts)

ROUND 3: [1sc in next st, 2sc in next st] 6 times. (18 sts)

ROUND 4: [1sc in next st, 2sc in next st] 9 times. (27 sts)

ROUND 5: [1sc in each of next 2 sts, 2sc in next st] 9 times. (36 sts)

ROUNDS 6-7: Sc all.

ROUND 8: Ss in each of next 2 sts.

Fasten off

Finishing

Using embroidery thread, surface crochet 6 rows of chain sts down the cap of the jellyfish. Leave 4–5in (10–13cm) tails of yarn at the edge of the cap, and knot several times to prevent fraying. Cut 6 lengths of thread, each 8–10in (20–25cm) long, and knot these, doubled, to the edge of the cap in the spaces between the embroidered chains. Knot these tails as well to finish forming the tentacles.

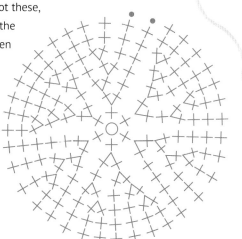

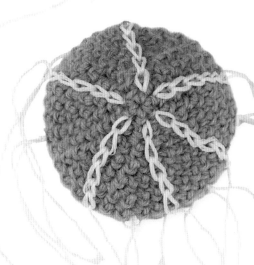

BRANCHING SEAWEED   \/

Yarn: DK yarn

METHOD

NOTE: Fasten off throughout by pulling yarn through last loop without working yo.

Stem and first branch

ROW 1 (RS): Make 5ch, skip 2ch, 1dc in each of next 3ch. (4 sts)

ROW 2 & ALL WS ROWS: 2ch, 1dc in each st.

ROW 3: 2ch, 2dc tog over next 2 sts, 1dc in next st. (3 sts)

ROW 5: As row 2.

ROW 7: 2ch, 1dc in st below, 2dc in each of next 2 sts. (6 sts)

ROW 9: 2ch, 1dc in st below, 2dc in next st, turn. Continue on these 4 sts.

ROW 11: 2ch, 1dc in st below, 1dc in next st. Continue on these 3 sts.

ROW 13: 2ch, 1dc in st below, 5dc popcorn in next st, 2dc in next st. (5 sts)

ROW 14: 1ch, ss in each of next 3 sts. Fasten off.

2nd branch

ROW 1: Rejoin yarn in next st of row 10, 2ch, 2dc in next st. Continue on these 3 sts.

ROWS 2-4: 2ch, 1dc in each of next 2 sts.

ROW 5: 2ch, 1dc in st below, 5dc popcorn in next st, 2dc in next st. (5 sts)

ROW 6: 1ch, 1sc in each of next 2 sts, ss in next st.

Fasten off.

3rd branch

ROW 1: Skip 1 st of row 8, rejoin yarn in next st, 2ch, 2dc in each of next 2 sts. (5 sts)

ROW 2: 2ch, 1dc in each of next 4 sts.

ROW 3: 2ch, 1dc in st below, 1dc in next st, turn. Continue on these 3 sts.

ROW 4: 2ch, 1dc in each of next 2 sts, turn.

ROW 5: 2ch, 1dc in st below, 5dc popcorn in next st, 2dc in next st. (5 sts)

ROW 6: 1ch, 1sc in each of next 2 sts, ss in next st.

Fasten off.

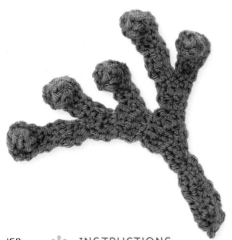

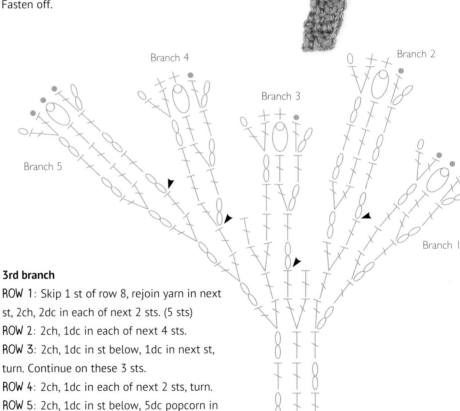

Branch 4

Branch 2

Branch 3

Branch 5

Branch 1

Specific symbol

◯ 5dc popcorn

SEA URCHIN SHELL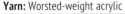

4th branch

ROW 1: In group of 5 sts at base of 3rd branch, skip 1 st, rejoin yarn in next st, 2ch, 1dc in st below, 2dc in next st. (4 sts)

ROW 2: 2ch, 1dc in each of next 3 sts.

ROW 3: 2ch, 1dc in st below, 1dc in next st, turn. Continue on these 3 sts.

ROW 4: 2ch, 1dc in each of next 2 sts.

ROW 5: 2ch, 1dc in st below, 5dc popcorn in next st, 2dc in next st. (5 sts)

ROW 6: 1ch, 1sc in each of next 2 sts, ss in next st.

Fasten off.

5th branch

ROW 1: In group of 4 sts at base of 4th branch, rejoin yarn in next st, 2ch, 2dc in next st. (3 sts)

ROWS 2-4: 2ch, 1dc in each of next 2 sts.

ROW 5: 2ch, 1dc in st below, 5dc popcorn in next st, 2dc in next st. (5 sts)

ROW 6: 1ch, ss in each of next 5 sts.

Fasten off.

Finishing

Press carefully, avoiding popcorns.

Yarn: Worsted-weight acrylic

Extras: Accent color yarn

METHOD

Make 10ch, join with ss into a ring.

ROUND 1: 2sc in each ch. (20 sts)

ROUND 2: [1sc in next st, 2sc in next st] 10 times. (30 sts)

ROUNDS 3-5: Sc all.

ROUND 6: [1sc, 2sc tog over next 2 sts] 10 times. (20 sts)

ROUND 7: [2sc tog over next 2 sts] 10 times. (10 sts)

ROUND 8: Ss in next 2 sts.

Fasten off.

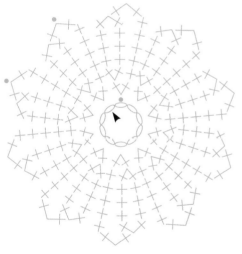

Finishing

Using accent color, sew French knots as shown in the photographs, with 5-fold symmetry around the holes. Use the initial chain ring as the top of the urchin because the hole will look cleaner than the hole made by the last round of decreases.

Yarn: Worsted-weight acrylic in yellow (A) and orange (B)

METHOD

Large polyp (make 3)

Using A, make 10ch, join with ss into a ring.

ROUND 1: 1sc in each ch. (10 sts)

Break off A 2in (5cm) from work and splice to B.

ROUNDS 2-7: Sc all, concealing knot of spliced yarn inside work on round 2.

ROUND 8: Ss in each of first 2sc.

Fasten off, leaving a long tail for finishing (on large polyps only).

Medium polyp (make 2)

As above, skipping rounds 6–7.

Small polyp (make 2)

As above, skipping rounds 4–7.

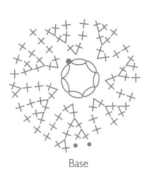

Base

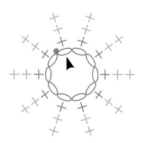

Polyp
Make 7 in varying heights.

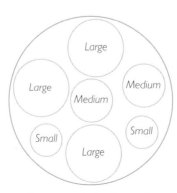

Arrangement of polyps on base.

Base

Using B, make 7ch, join with ss into a ring.

ROUND 1: 2sc in each ch. (14 sts)

ROUND 2: [1sc in next st, 2sc in next st] 7 times. (21 sts)

ROUND 3: [1sc in each of next 2 sts, 2sc in next st] 7 times. (28 sts)

ROUND 4: [1sc in each of next 4 sts, 2sc in next st] twice, ss in each of next 2 sts. (14 sts)

Fasten off.

Finishing

Use long ends of yarn left after completing the large polyps to sew all polyps to base.

146 BULLION CORAL \/

Yarn: Worsted-weight yarn in pumpkin orange (A) and light pink (B)

METHOD

SPECIFIC INSTRUCTION

Bullion st = [yo] 6 times, insert hook in next stitch, yo and pull through all but last loop on hook, yo and pull through both remaining loops.

Module 1

Using A, make 4ch, join with ss into a ring.
ROUND 1: 3ch, 3 bullion sts in each ch of ring, ss in first 2 bullion sts of this round. (12 bullion sts)
Change to B.

ROUND 2: 2sc in each bullion st and in 3rd ch of 3ch at start of round 1, ss in first 2sc of this round. (26 sts)
Fasten off.

Module 2 (make 3)

Using A, make 3ch, join with ss into a ring.
ROUND 1: 3ch, 3 bullion sts in each ch of ring, ss in first 2 bullion sts of this round. (9 bullion sts)
Change to B.
ROUND 2: 2sc in each bullion st and in 3rd ch of 3ch at start of round 1, ss in first 2sc of this round. (20 sts)
Fasten off.

Module 3

Using A, make 2ch, join with ss into a ring.
ROUND 1: 3ch, 3 bullion sts in each ch of ring, ss in first 2 bullion sts of this round. (6 bullion sts)
Change to B.
ROUND 2: 2sc in each bullion st and in 3rd ch of 3ch that started round 1, ss in first 2sc of this round. (14 sts)
Fasten off.

Finishing

Using B, sew together in arrangement shown.

Specific symbol
Bullion stitch

Module 1

Module 2

Module 3

Module 2

Module 2

SEA FIG \/

Yarn: Lightweight yarn in magenta (A), sunshine yellow (B), and leaf green (C)

METHOD

NOTE: The use of short (ss) and tall (dc) stitches in the leaf causes a slight curvature that mimics the form of succulent leaves.

Petals

Using A, make a small pompom by wrapping yarn around two fingers approximately 30 times. Tie a piece of yarn around the middle of the bundle, cut the loops, and trim. The pompom does not need to be full; it should be somewhat two-dimensional.

Blossom center

Using B, make a slip ring.
ROUND 1: 6sc in ring, pull end to close ring. (6 sts)
ROUND 2: Ss in next st.
Fasten off.

Leaf (make 2–3)

Using C, make 4ch, join with ss into a ring.
ROUND 1: 2sc in each ch. (8 sts)
ROUND 2: Ss in each of next 4 sts, 1dc in each of next 4 sts. (8 sts)
ROUND 3: [2sc tog over next 2 sts, 1sc in each of next 2 sts] twice. (6 sts)
ROUND 4: Ss in each of next 3 sts, 1dc in each of next 3 sts. (6 sts)
ROUND 5: [2sc tog over next 2 sts, sc] twice. (4 sts)
ROUND 6: [2sc tog over next 2 sts] twice. (2 sts)
Fasten off.

Short stem

Using C, make 6ch, join with ss into a ring.
ROUND 1: 1sc in each ch. (6 sts)
ROUNDS 2-5: Sc all.
Ss in next st and fasten off.

Long stem

Proceed as for the short stem, but work 10 rounds of sc instead of 5.

Leaf

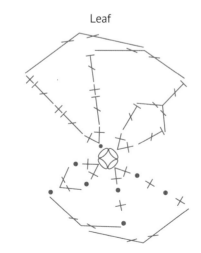

Blossom
center

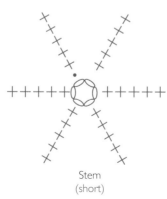

Stem
(short)

Finishing

Loop the tails of yarn left from making the blossom center through its underside so that they protrude out from either edge of the circle as shown. Then use these ends to tie around the petals, perpendicular to the direction in which the petals were originally tied. Pull the ends of yarn from this knot through the tube of the stem, and secure. Then sew the leaves, curved side facing the blossom, to the stem. For sea figs with a long stem, use 3 leaves; for those with a short stem, use 2 leaves.

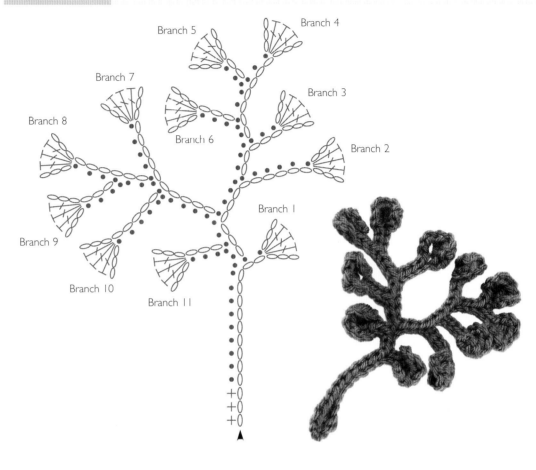

Branch 1
Branch 2
Branch 3
Branch 4
Branch 5
Branch 6
Branch 7
Branch 8
Branch 9
Branch 10
Branch 11

Positioning tails of yarn for blossom center.

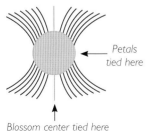

Positioning blossom center over petals.

← Petals tied here

Blossom center tied here

Yarn: Worsted-weight acrylic

Extras: Accent color yarn

METHOD

SPECIAL INSTRUCTION

Leaf = 3dc in 4th ch from hook, 3ch and ss in same place.

BRANCH 1: 17ch, leaf, ss in next ch.
BRANCH 2: 15ch, leaf, ss in next 5ch.
BRANCH 3: 9ch, leaf, ss in next 3ch.
BRANCH 4: 10ch, leaf, ss in next 2ch.
BRANCH 5: 5ch, leaf, ss in next 5ch.
BRANCH 6: 6ch, leaf, ss in next 11ch.
BRANCH 7: 13ch, leaf, ss in next 4ch.
BRANCH 8: 9ch, leaf, ss in next 3ch.
BRANCH 9: 6ch, leaf, ss in next 7ch.
BRANCH 10: 8ch, leaf, ss in next 12ch.
BRANCH 11: 6ch, leaf, ss in next 14ch, sc in next 3ch.
Fasten off.

Yarn: DK yarn in red (A), yellow (B), and beige (C)

METHOD

Using A, make 4ch, join with ss into a ring.

ROUND 1: 4ch, [3tr in ring, 3ch, 1sc in ring, 3ch] twice, 3tr in ring, 3ch, ss in first of 4ch. (3 petals)

Fasten off A. Join B to any sc between petals.

ROUND 2: 6ch, 1dc in same place, [5ch, skip 1 petal, (1dc, 3ch, 1dc) in next sc] twice, 5ch, skip 1 petal, ss in 3rd of 6ch.

ROUND 3: 3ch, *(2dc, 1ch, 2dc) in next 3ch sp, 2ch, 1sc in next dc, 2ch, (3dc, 1ch, 3dc) in 5ch sp, 2ch,# 1sc in next dc, 2ch,* rep from * to * once more, then once again from * to #, ss in first of 3ch. (6 petals: 3 small, 3 large)

Fasten off B. Join C to 1ch sp at center of any small petal.

ROUND 4: 6ch, 1dc in same place, *7ch, 1sc in 1ch sp at center of next (large) petal, 7ch,# (1dc, 3ch, 1dc) in 1ch sp at center of next (small) petal,* rep from * to * once more, then once again from * to #, ss in 3rd of 6ch.

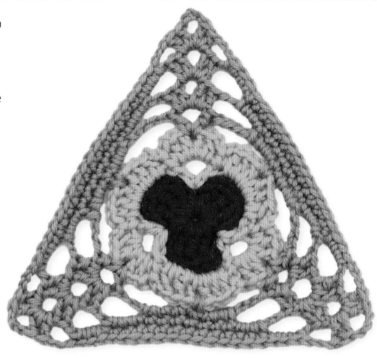

ROUND 5: Ss in 3ch sp, 6ch, 2dc in same place, *5ch, 3sc in next 5ch sp, 1sc in next sc, 3sc in next 5ch sp, 5ch,# (2dc, 3ch, 2dc) in next 3ch sp,* rep from * to * once more, then once again from * to #, 1dc in first ch sp, ss in 3rd of 6ch.

ROUND 6: Ss in 3ch sp, 6ch, 2dc in same place, *5ch, 3sc in next 5ch sp, 1sc in each of 7sc, 3sc in next 5ch sp, 5ch,# (2dc, 3ch, 2dc) in next 3ch sp,* rep from * to * once more, then once again from * to #, 1dc in first ch sp, ss in 3rd of 6ch.

ROUND 7: Ss in 3ch sp, 6ch, 2dc in same place, *3ch, 3sc in 5ch sp, 1sc in each of 13sc, 3sc in 5ch sp, 3ch,# (2dc, 3ch, 2dc) in next 3ch sp,* rep from * to * once more, then once again from * to #, 1dc in first ch sp, ss in 3rd of 6ch.

Fasten off C.

Yarn: DK yarn in purple (A), green (B), and beige (C)

METHOD
SPECIFIC ABBREVIATION
LF = leaf: 2ttr tog in back loop of ss between 2 petals, 5ch, ss in top of 2ttr tog just made.

Using A, make 5ch, join with ss into a ring.
ROUND 1: [3ch, 1tr in ring, 3ch, ss in top of tr just made, 3ch, ss in ring] 4 times, 2ch, (1dc, 2tr) in ring, 3ch, ss in top of tr just made, (1tr, 1dc) in ring, 2ch, ss in ring.
Fasten off A. Join B to 3ch picot at top of large petal.
ROUND 2: 8ch, LF, 5ch, [1sc in 3ch picot at tip of next petal, 4ch] twice, LF, [4ch, 1sc in next picot] twice, 5ch, LF, 7ch, ss in first of 8ch.
ROUND 3: 1ch, 7sc in 7ch sp, (1sc, 3ch, 1sc) in 3ch picot at tip of leaf, 5sc in 5ch sp, [1sc in next sc, 4sc in 4ch sp] twice, (1sc, 3ch, 1sc) in next picot, [4sc in 4ch sp, 1sc in next sc] twice, 5sc in 5ch sp, (1sc, 3ch, 1sc) in next picot, 7sc in 7ch sp, ss in first ch. (17sc on each side)
Fasten off B. Join C to any 3ch sp.
ROUND 4: 8ch, 2dc in same ch sp, *1dc in each of 17sc, (2dc, 5ch, 2dc) in 3ch sp,* rep from * to * once more, 1dc in each of 17sc, 1dc in first ch sp, ss in 3rd of 8ch. (21dc on each side)
ROUND 5: Ss in 5ch sp, 6ch, 2dc in same ch sp, *1dc in each of 21dc, (2dc, 3ch, 2dc) in 5ch sp,* rep from * to * once more, 1dc in each of 21dc, 1dc in first ch sp, ss in 3rd of 6ch. (25dc on each side)
Fasten off C.

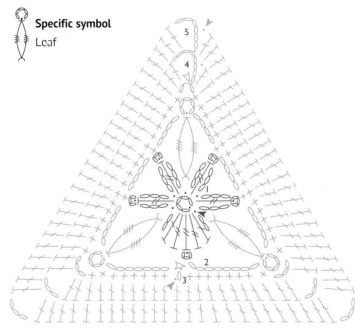

Specific symbol
Leaf

WINDFLOWER TRIANGLE   1

Yarn: DK yarn in cream (A), blue (B), and gray (C)

METHOD

Using A, make 9ch, join with ss into a ring.

ROUND 1: 3ch, 2tr tog in ring, [5ch, 2dc tog in ring, 5ch, 3tr tog in ring] twice, 5ch, 2dc tog in ring, 5ch, ss in 2tr tog at beg of round.

Fasten off A. Join B to 5ch sp before any 3tr tog.

ROUND 2: 4ch, *skip 3tr tog, 6sc in next 5ch sp, 1ch, skip 2dc tog,# 6sc in next 5ch sp, 3ch,* rep from * to * once more, then once again from * to #, 5dc in last 5ch sp, ss in first ch of round.

Fasten off B. Join C to any 3ch sp.

ROUND 3: 6ch, 1dc in same ch sp, 1ch, *[1dc in next sc, 1ch, skip 1sc] 3 times, 1dc in 1ch sp, [1ch, skip 1sc, 1dc in next sc] 3 times,# (1ch, 1dc, 3ch, 1dc, 1ch) in 3ch sp,* rep from * to * once more, then once again from * to #, 1ch, ss in 3rd of 6ch.

ROUND 4: Ss in 3ch sp, 6ch, 1dc in same ch sp, 1ch, *[1dc in next dc, 1ch, skip 1ch] 9 times,# (1dc, 3ch, 1dc) in 3ch sp, 1ch,* rep from * to * once more, then once again from * to #, ss in 3rd of 6ch.

ROUND 5: Ss in 3ch sp, 6ch, 1dc in same ch sp, 1ch, *[1dc in next dc, 1ch, skip 1ch] 11 times,# (1dc, 3ch, 1dc) in 3ch sp, 1ch,* rep from * to * once more, then once again from * to #, ss in 3rd of 6ch. (12 ch sps on each side, plus corner sps)

Fasten off C.

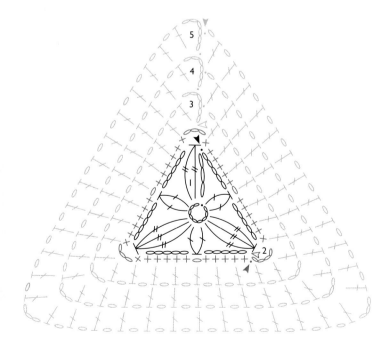

Yarn: DK yarn in blue (A), peach (B), and gray (C)

METHOD

Using A, make 4ch, join with ss into a ring.

ROUND 1: 5ch, [1dc in ring, 2ch] 5 times, ss in 3rd of 5ch. Fasten off A. Join B to any dc.

ROUND 2: 1ch, *5ch, 3dtr tog in next 2ch sp, 5ch, 1FPsc in next dc,* rep from * to * 5 more times, working last FPsc in same place as beg of round. Fasten off B. Join C to any 3dtr tog.

ROUND 3: 8ch, 1dtr in same st, *3ch, 1tr in next FPsc, 3ch, 1sc in next 3dtr tog, 3ch, 1tr in next FPsc, 3ch,# (1dtr, 3ch, 1dtr) in next 3dtr tog,* rep from * to * once more, then once again from * to #, ss in 5th of 8ch.

ROUND 4: Ss in 3ch sp, 6ch, 2dc in same ch sp, *[1dc in next st, 3dc in 3ch sp] 4 times, 1dc in next st,# (2dc, 3ch, 2dc) in 3ch sp at corner,* rep from * to * once more, then once again from * to #, 1dc in first ch sp, ss in 3rd of 6ch. (21dc on each side)

ROUND 5: Ss in 3ch sp, 6ch, 2dc in same ch sp, *1dc in each of 21dc, (2dc, 3ch, 2dc) in 3ch sp,* rep from * to * once more, 1dc in each of 21dc, 1dc in first ch sp, ss in 3rd of 6ch. (25dc on each side) Fasten off C.

Mix and match 151 + 152

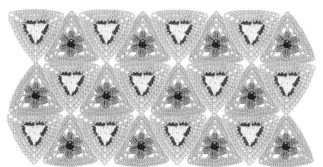

Yarn: DK yarn in pink (A) and green (B)

METHOD

Using A, make a slip ring.

ROUND 1: 3ch, 2tr tog in ring, [10ch, 3tr tog in ring] twice, 10ch, ss in ch closing 2tr tog, pull end to close ring. (3 petals)

ROUND 2: 3ch, (2tr tog, 4ch, 3tr tog, 4ch, 3tr tog, 4ch, 2tr tog) in same place as base of first 3ch, *ss in 10ch sp (first flower made), (2tr tog, 4ch, 3tr tog, 4ch, 3tr tog, 4ch, 3tr tog, 4ch, 2tr tog) in ch closing next petal,* rep from * to * once more, ss in 10ch sp, 2tr tog in center of first flower, 4ch, ss in ch closing first 2tr tog of round.

Fasten off A. Join B to 4ch sp before any corner petal.

ROUND 3: 6ch, ss in 5th ch from hook, *skip 1 petal, 4sc in next 4ch sp, 1ch, skip 1 petal, 4sc in next 4ch sp, skip 1 petal, 1sc in ss between petals, skip 1 petal, 4sc in next ch sp, 1ch, skip 1 petal, 4sc in 4ch sp,# 5ch, ss in 5th ch from hook,* rep from * to * once more, then once again from * to #, ss in first of 6ch.

ROUND 4: Ss in 5ch picot, 6ch, 2dc in same picot, *6ch, skip 4sc, 1sc in 1ch sp, 1ch, skip 4sc, (2dc, 1ch, 2dc) in next sc, 1ch, skip 4sc, 1sc in 1ch sp, 6ch, skip 4sc,# (2dc, 3ch, 2dc) in 5ch picot,* rep from * to * once more, then once again from * to #, 1dc in first ch sp, ss in 3rd of 6ch.

ROUND 5: Ss in 3ch sp, 7ch, ss in 5th ch from hook, 1ch, 1sc in same place, *1sc in each of 2dc, 6sc in 6ch sp, skip 1sc, 1sc in 1ch sp, 1sc in each of 2dc, 1sc in 1ch sp, 3ch, ss in last sc made, 1sc in each of 2dc, 1sc in 1ch sp, skip 1sc, 6sc in 6ch sp, 1sc in each of 2dc,# (1sc, 6ch, ss in 5th ch from hook, 1ch, 1sc) in 3ch sp,* rep from * to * once more, then once again from * to #, ss in first of 7ch.

Fasten off B.

Yarn: DK yarn in peach (A), cream (B), and green (C)

METHOD

Using A, make a slip ring.

ROUND 1: 3ch, [1hdc in ring, 3ch, ss in top of hdc, 1ch] 5 times, ss in 2nd of 3ch, 3ch, ss in same place, pull end to close ring. (6 stamens)

Fasten off A. Join B to ring between any 2hdc.

ROUND 2: Work behind round 1: 3ch, [1hdc over 1ch and into ring, 1ch] 5 times, ss in 2nd of 3ch.

ROUND 3: 3ch, 2dc in 1ch sp, [1dc in next hdc, 3dc in next 1ch sp, 1dc in next hdc, 2dc in next 1ch sp] twice, 1dc in next hdc, 3dc in next 1ch sp, ss in 2nd of 3ch. (21dc)

ROUND 4: 3ch, 3tr tog over next 3dc, *7ch, 5dtr tog over (same place as last insertion and foll 4dc), 7ch,# 4tr tog over (same place as last insertion and foll 3dc),* rep from * to * once more, then once again from * to #, ss in top of 3tr tog. (6 petals: 3 large, 3 small)

Fasten off B. Join C to ch closing any 5dtr tog (top of large petal).

ROUND 5: 3ch, 1sc in same place, *8sc in 7ch sp, 1sc in 4tr tog, 8sc in 7ch sp,# (1sc, 2ch, 1sc) in 5dtr tog,* rep from * to * once more, then once again from * to #, ss in first of 3ch.

ROUND 6: Ss in 2ch sp, 7ch, 2tr in same ch sp, *7ch, skip 6sc, 1sc in next sc, 5ch, skip 5sc, 1sc in next sc, 7ch, skip 6sc,# (2tr, 3ch, 2tr) in next 2ch sp,* rep from * to * once more, then once again from * to #, 1tr in first ch sp, ss in 4th of 7ch.

ROUND 7: Ss in 3ch sp, 7ch, 2tr in same ch sp, *5ch, 3sc in 7ch sp, 1sc in next sc, 5sc in 5ch sp, 1sc in next sc, 3sc in 7ch sp, 5ch,# (2tr, 3ch, 2tr) in next 3ch sp,* rep from * to * once more, then once again from * to #, 1tr in first ch sp, ss in 4th of 7ch.

Fasten off C.

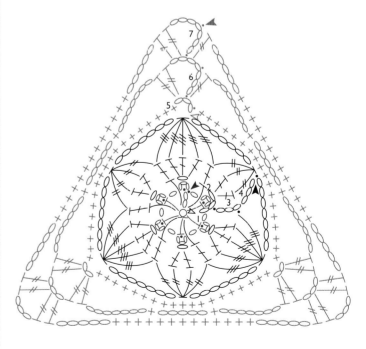

MICHAELMAS DAISY TRIANGLE

Yarn: DK yarn in yellow (A) and purple (B)

METHOD

First daisy

Using A, make 5ch, join with ss into a ring.
ROUND 1: 1ch, 8sc in ring, ss in first ch.
(9 sts)
Fasten off A. Join B to any sc.
ROUND 2: 10ch, ss in 2nd of these 10ch,
1sc in next sc, 9ch, ss in first of these 9ch,
rep from * to * 7 more times, fasten off with
ss in first ch of round. (9 petals)

2nd daisy

Work as for first daisy to last 2 petals of
round 2.
TO JOIN PETALS: *1sc in next sc, 4ch,
inserting hook from back ss in any petal of
first flower, 4ch, ss in first ch of this petal,*
rep from * to * once more, inserting hook in
next petal of first flower to work the joining
ss. Fasten off as round 2 of first daisy.

3rd daisy

Work as for first daisy to last 4 petals of
round 2.
Join next 2 petals to first daisy and last 2
petals to 2nd daisy in same way as above, to
match the arrangement shown on the chart.

Border

Join A to 3rd of 5 unattached petals of
any daisy.
ROUND 3: 4ch, 1sc in next petal, 3ch, 1sc
in next petal, *2ch, 1hdc in join between
next 2 petals, 2ch,# [1sc in next petal, 3ch]
4 times,* rep from * to * once more, then
once again from * to #, [1sc in next petal,
3ch] twice, ss in first of 4ch.
ROUND 4: 3ch, 1sc in same ch, *[3sc in
3ch sp, 1sc in next sc] twice, 2sc in 2ch sp,
1sc in hdc, 2sc in 2ch sp, [1sc in next sc,
3sc in 3ch sp] twice,# (1sc, 2ch, 1sc) in
next sc,* rep from * to * once more, then
once again from * to #, ss in first of 3ch.
(23sc on each side)
ROUND 5: Ss in 2ch sp, 3ch, 1sc in same
ch sp, *1sc in each of 23sc, (1sc, 2ch, 1sc) in
2ch sp,* rep from * to * once more, 1sc in
each of 23sc, ss in first of 3ch. (25sc on
each side)
Fasten off A.

Yarn: DK yarn in orange (A), yellow (B), and green (C)

METHOD
SPECIFIC ABBREVIATIONS
3ch P = 3ch picot: 3ch, ss in top of last st.
5ch P = 5ch picot: 5ch, ss in top of last st.

Using A, make 4ch, join with ss into a ring.
ROUND 1: 1ch, 8sc in ring, ss in first ch.
(9 sts)
Fasten off A. Join B to back loop of any sc.
ROUND 2: 1ch, [2sc in back loop of next sc]
8 times, 1sc in back loop of first sc, ss in first
ch. (18 sts)
ROUND 3: 3ch, *2dc tog over next 2sc, 3ch P,
2ch, 1sc in next sc, 2ch,* rep from * to *
7 more times, 2dc tog over next 2sc, 3ch P,
2ch, ss in first of 3ch. (6 petals)
Fasten off B. Join C to 3ch P at top of
any petal.
ROUND 4: 5ch, 1dc in same 3ch P, *3ch, 1dc
in sc between petals, 3ch, 1sc in next 3ch P,
5ch, 1dc in sc between petals, 5ch,# (1dc,
3ch, 1dc) in next 3ch P,* rep from * to * once
more, then once again from * to #, ss in 3rd
of 5ch.

ROUND 5: Ss in 3ch sp, 5ch, 2dc in same
ch sp, *1ch, 5dc in next dc, 1ch, 1sc in next
sc, 1ch, 5dc in next dc, 1ch,# (2dc, 2ch, 2dc)
in 3ch sp at corner,* rep from * to * once
more, then once again from * to #, 1dc in
first ch sp, ss in 3rd of 5ch.
ROUND 6: Ss in 2ch sp, 8ch, ss in 6th ch from
hook, 3dc in same ch sp, *(3dc, 3ch P, 2dc) in
next 1ch sp, (3dc, 3ch P, 2dc) in next sc, (3dc,
3ch P, 2dc) in next 1ch sp,# (4dc, 5ch P, 3dc)
in 2ch sp at corner,* rep from * to * once
more, then once again from * to #, 3dc in
first ch sp, ss in 3rd of 8ch.
Fasten off C.

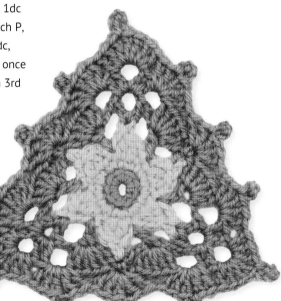

*Blocks may be joined using
the joining with picots method.*

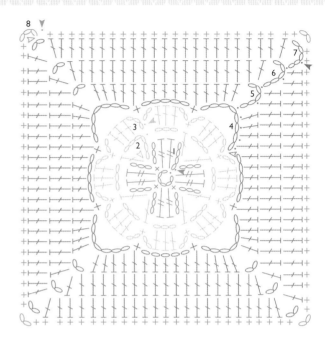

Yarn: DK yarn in orange (A), yellow (B), and beige (C)

METHOD

Using A, make 6ch, join with ss into a ring.

ROUND 1: 1ch, [3ch, 2tr in ring, 3ch, 1sc in ring] 3 times, 3ch, 2tr in ring, 3ch, ss in first ch. (4 petals)

Fasten off A. Join B to sc between any 2 petals.

ROUND 2: 6ch, 1dc in same place, [3ch, skip 1 petal, (1dc, 3ch, 1dc) in next sc] 3 times, 3ch, skip 1 petal, ss in 3rd of 6ch.

ROUND 3: 3ch, [3dc in next 3ch sp, 2ch, 1sc in next dc, 2ch] 7 times, 3dc in next 3ch sp, 2ch, ss in first of 3ch. (8 petals)

Fasten off B. Join C to any sc before 3dc worked in a ch sp.

ROUND 4: 8ch, skip 1 petal, 1sc in next sc, [5ch, skip 1 petal, 1sc in next sc, 7ch, skip 1 petal, 1sc in next sc] 3 times, 5ch, skip 1 petal, ss in first of 8ch. (8 loops)

ROUND 5: Ss in each of next 4ch, 5ch, 4dc in same ch sp, *1dc in next sc, 5dc in 5ch sp, 1dc in next sc,# (4dc, 2ch, 4dc) in 7ch sp,* rep from * to * twice more, then once again from * to #, 3dc in first ch sp, ss in 3rd of 5ch. (15dc on each side)

ROUND 6: Ss in 2ch sp, 5ch, 2dc in same place, *1dc in each of 15dc, (2dc, 2ch, 2dc) in 2ch sp,* rep from * to * twice more, 1dc in each of 15dc, 1dc in first ch sp, ss in 3rd of 5ch. (19dc on each side)

ROUND 7: Ss in 2ch sp, 5ch, 2dc in same place, *1dc in each of 19dc, (2dc, 2ch, 2dc) in 2ch sp,* rep from * to * twice more, 1dc in each of 19dc, 1dc in first ch sp, ss in 3rd of 5ch. (23dc on each side)

Fasten off C. Join A to 2ch sp at any corner.

ROUND 8: 3ch, 1sc in same ch sp, *1sc in each of 23dc, (1sc, 2ch, 1sc) in 2ch sp,* rep from * to * twice more, 1sc in each of 23dc, ss in first of 3ch. (25sc on each side)

Fasten off A.

Yarn: DK yarn in orange (A), yellow (B), and green (C)

METHOD

CENTRAL FLOWER: Using A, make 6ch, ss in 3rd ch from hook, 2ch, skip 2ch, 1sc in first ch made. Do not turn.

SMALL PETALS: [5ch, ss in 3rd ch from hook, 2ch, skip 2ch, 1sc in side edge of sc, do not turn] 8 times.

MEDIUM PETALS: [7ch, ss in 3rd ch from hook, 4ch, skip 4ch, 1sc in side edge of sc, do not turn] 9 times.

LARGE PETALS: [9ch, ss in 3rd ch from hook, 6ch, skip 6ch, 1sc in side edge of sc, do not turn] 9 times. Without turning work and counting along side edge, ss in 8th sc to form a ring. Fasten off A. Turn work over and join B to back loop of any sc in the ring just made.

ROUND 1: 3ch, 2dc in back loop of each of 7 sts, 1dc in base of 3ch, ss in 3rd of 3ch. (16dc)

ROUND 2: 3ch, 2dc in each dc, 1dc in base of 3ch, ss in 3rd of 3ch. (32dc)

ROUND 3: 3ch, [1dc in next dc, 2dc in next dc] 15 times, 1dc in last dc, 1dc in base of 3ch, ss in 3rd of 3ch. (48dc)

ROUND 4: 3ch, [1dc in each of 2dc, 2dc in next dc] 15 times, 1dc in each of 2dc, 1dc in base of 3ch. (64dc) Fasten off B.

ROUND 5: Join C to any dc, 2ch, 3dc tog in same place as base of 2ch, [4ch, skip 3dc, 4dc tog in next dc] 15 times, 4ch, skip 3dc, ss in 3dc tog. (80 sts) Fasten off C.

ROUND 6: Join B to any 4ch sp, 6ch, (2tr, 1dc) in same ch sp, *(2dc, 3hdc) in next 4ch sp, 5sc in next 4ch sp, (3hdc, 2dc) in next 4ch sp, (1dc, 2tr, 2ch, 2tr, 1dc) in next 4ch sp,* rep from * to * 3 more times ending last rep with (1dc, 1tr) in first ch sp, ss in 4th of 6ch. (21 sts on each side)

ROUND 7: Ss in 2ch sp, 5ch, 2dc in same ch sp, *1dc in each of 21 sts, (2dc, 2ch, 2dc) in 2ch sp,* rep from * to * ending last rep with 1dc in first ch sp, ss in 3rd of 5ch. (25 sts on each side) Fasten off B. Coil the free end of the central flower tightly and sew it in place.

Specific symbol
 1sc in side edge of previous sc.

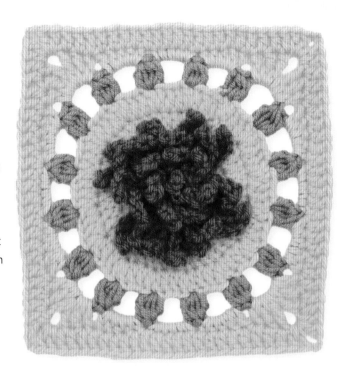

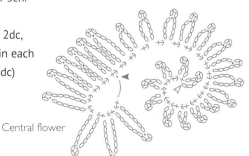
Central flower

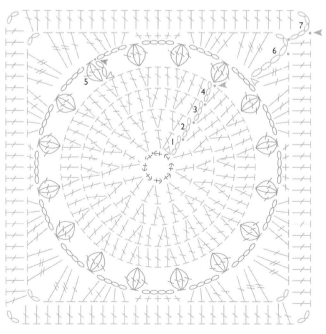

Yarn: DK yarn in pink (A), blue (B), and peach (C)

METHOD

Using A, make 12ch, join with ss into a ring.

ROUND 1: 1ch, 23sc in ring, ss in first ch. (24sc)

ROUND 2: 6ch, 3dtr tog over next 3sc, *7ch, 4dtr tog over (same sc and next 3sc),* rep from * to * 6 more times, ending with last insertion in base of 6ch, 7ch, ss in st closing first petal. (8 petals) Fasten off A. Join B to st closing any petal.

ROUND 3: 1ch, *7sc in 7ch sp, 1sc in st closing next petal,* rep from * to * 7 more times omitting last sc, ss in first ch. (64sc)

ROUND 4: 1ch, *3ch, skip 1sc, 1sc in next sc,* rep from * to * all around omitting last sc, ss in first ch. (32 ch sps)

ROUND 5: Ss in next 2ch, 1ch, *3ch, 1sc in next 3ch sp,* rep from * to * all around omitting last sc, ss in first ch.

ROUND 6: As round 5. Fasten off B. Join C to next 3ch sp.

ROUND 7: 1ch, *[3sc in next 3ch sp] 3 times, 1sc in next 3ch sp, 3ch, skip 1ch sp, (3tr tog, 5ch, 4dtr tog, 3ch, ss in top of 4dtr tog, 5ch, 3tr tog) all in next 3ch sp, 3ch, skip 1ch sp, 1sc in next ch sp,* rep from * to * 3 more times omitting last sc, ss in first ch. Fasten off C.

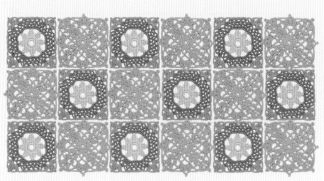

Mix and match 159 + 160

CORAL TRELLIS SQUARE

Yarn: DK yarn

METHOD

SPECIFIC ABBREVIATION

CL = cluster: [yo] twice, insert hook as directed, [yo, pull through 2 loops] twice (2 loops remain on hook), *yo, insert under 2 threads of lowest step of st just made, yo, pull a loop through, yo, pull through 2 loops,* rep from * to * once more, yo, pull through all 4 loops on hook.

Make 8ch, join with ss into a ring.

ROUND 1: 7ch, [CL in ring, 5ch, CL in ring, 2ch, 1dtr in ring, 2ch] 3 times, CL in ring, 5ch, CL in ring, 2ch, ss in 5th of 7ch.

ROUND 2: 7ch, [CL in 2ch sp, 5ch, 1sc in 5ch sp, 5ch, CL in 2ch sp, 2ch, 1dtr in dtr, 2ch] 3 times, CL in 2ch sp, 5ch, 1sc in 5ch sp, 5ch, CL in 2ch sp, 2ch, ss in 5th of 7ch.

ROUND 3: 7ch, *CL in 2ch sp, [5ch, 1sc in 5ch sp] twice, 5ch, CL in 2ch sp, 2ch,# 1dtr in dtr, 2ch,* rep from * to * twice more, then once again from * to #, ss in 5th of 7ch.

ROUND 4: 7ch, *CL in 2ch sp, 5ch, 1sc in 5ch sp, [1ch, CL] 3 times in next 5ch sp, 1ch, 1sc in next 5ch sp, 5ch, CL in 2ch sp, 2ch,# 1dtr in dtr, 2ch,* rep from * to * twice more, then once again from * to #, ss in 5th of 7ch.

ROUND 5: 6ch, ss in 5th ch from hook, *5ch, 1sc in next 5ch sp, 5ch, 1sc in 1ch sp between first and 2nd of 3CL, 6ch, ss in 4th ch from hook, 2ch, 1sc in 1ch sp between 2nd and 3rd of same 3CL, 5ch, 1sc in next 5ch sp, 5ch,# 1sc in dtr, 5ch, ss in top of sc,* rep from * to * twice more, then once again from * to #, ss in first of 6ch. Fasten off.

Specific symbol
Cluster

Blocks may be joined using the joining with picots method.

Yarn: DK yarn in yellow (A), white (B), and green (C)

METHOD

Using A, make 6ch, join with ss into a ring.

ROUND 1: 1ch, 11sc in ring, ss in first ch. (12 sts)

Fasten off A. Join B to back loop of any sc.

ROUND 2: 6ch, 1dtr in back loop of same sc, 1ch, [1dtr, 1ch] twice in back loop of each sc, ss in 5th of 6ch. (24 petals)

Fasten off B. Join C to any 1ch sp.

ROUND 3: 5ch, 1dc in same ch sp, *1ch, 1hdc in next ch sp, [1ch, 1sc in next ch sp] 3 times, 1ch, 1hdc in next ch sp, 1ch,# (1dc, 2ch, 1dc) in next ch sp,* rep from * to * twice more, then once again from * to #, ss in 3rd of 5ch.

ROUND 4: *Ss in 2ch sp, 5ch, ss in same ch sp, 4ch, skip (1dc, 1ch, 1hdc), ss in next ch sp, 4ch, skip (1sc, 1ch), ss in next sc, 4ch, skip (1ch, 1sc), ss in next ch sp, 4ch, skip (1hdc, 1ch, 1dc),* rep from * to * 3 more times, ss in same 2ch sp as beg of round.

ROUND 5: Ss in each of next 2ch, ss under rem 3ch, *5ch, ss in same ch sp, [4ch, ss in next ch sp] 5 times,* rep from * to * 3 more times, ss in same ch sp as beg of round.

ROUND 6: Ss in each of next 2ch, ss under rem 3ch, *5ch, ss in same ch sp, [4ch, ss in next ch sp] 6 times,* rep from * to * 3 more times, ss in same ch sp as beg of round.

ROUND 7: Ss in each of next 2ch, ss under rem 3ch, 6ch, 1dc in same ch sp, *[2ch, 1dc in next ch sp] 7 times, 3ch, 1dc in same ch sp,* rep from * to * twice more, [2ch, 1dc in next ch sp] 6 times, 2ch, ss in 3rd of 6ch.

ROUND 8: Ss in 3ch sp, 6ch, 1dc in same ch sp, 3dc in each 2ch sp and (1dc, 3ch, 1dc) in each corner sp all around, ss in 3rd of 6ch. (23dc on each side)

ROUND 9: Ss in 3ch sp, 3ch, 1sc in same ch sp, 1sc in each dc and (1sc, 2ch, 1sc) in each corner sp all around, ss in 2nd of 3ch. (25sc on each side)

Fasten off C.

Yarn: DK yarn in gold (A), beige (B), and yellow (C)

METHOD
SPECIFIC ABBREVIATION
3ch P = 3ch picot: 3ch, ss in st at base of these 3ch.

Using A, make 5ch, join with ss into a ring.
ROUND 1: 3ch, 15dc in ring, ss in 3rd of 3ch.
Fasten off A. Join B to space between any 2dc.
ROUND 2: 1ch, [2sc in space between next 2dc] 15 times,
1sc in first sp, ss in first ch.
Fasten off B. Join C to back loop of any sc.
ROUND 3: 5ch, 4dtr tog in back loops of next 4sc, *6ch,
5dtr tog over back loops of (same sc as last insertion and
foll 4sc), 7ch, 5dtr tog as before,* rep from * to * twice
more, 6ch, 5dtr tog making last insertion in same place
as base of 5ch, 7ch, ss in top of 4dtr tog. (8 petals made)
Fasten off C. Join B to any 7ch sp.
ROUND 4: 4ch, ss in first of these 4ch, *4sc in same 7ch sp,
1sc in top of petal, 7sc in 6ch sp, 1sc in next petal, 5sc in
7ch sp, 3ch P,* rep from * to * ending 4sc in first 7ch sp,
ss in first of 4ch.
ROUND 5: Ss in 3ch P, 5ch, 1dc in same P, *1dc in each of
17sc, (1dc, 2ch, 1dc) in 3ch P,* rep from * to * twice more,
1dc in each of 17sc, ss in 3rd of 5ch. (19dc on each side)
ROUND 6: Ss in 2ch sp, 5ch, 1dc in same 2ch sp, *1ch,
[1dc in next dc, 1ch, skip 1dc] 9 times, 1dc in next dc, 1ch,#
(1dc, 2ch, 1dc) in 2ch sp,* rep from * to * twice more, then
once again from * to #, ss in 3rd of 5ch.
ROUND 7: Ss in 2ch sp, 3ch, 1sc in same 2ch sp, 1sc in each
dc and 1ch sp, and (1sc, 2ch, 1sc) in 2ch sp at each corner,
ending ss in first of 3ch. (25sc on each side)
Fasten off B.

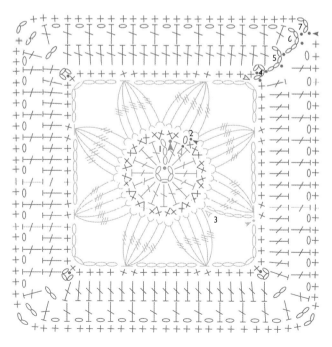

Yarn: DK yarn in purple (A) and chartreuse (B)

METHOD
SPECIFIC ABBREVIATION

PL = picot loop: 4ch, ss in 3rd ch from hook, 4ch, ss in 3rd ch from hook, 1ch.

Using A, make 6ch, join with ss into a ring.

ROUND 1: 5ch, [1dc in ring, 2ch] 7 times, ss in 3rd of 5ch. (8 ch sps)

ROUND 2: Ss in 2ch sp, (1ch, 5dc, 1ch, 1sc) in same ch sp, (1sc, 1ch, 5dc, 1ch, 1sc) in each of seven 2ch sps.

ROUND 3: Work behind round 2: 1BPsc in first dc of round 1, 5ch, [1BPdc in next dc of round 1, 3ch] 7 times, ss in 2nd of 5ch.

ROUND 4: Ss in 3ch sp, 2ch, (7dc, 1ch, 1sc) in same ch sp, (1sc, 1ch, 7dc, 1ch, 1sc) in each of seven 3ch sps, ss in first ch. Fasten off A. Join B from behind, around post of any BPsc of round 3.

ROUND 5: Work behind round 4: 8ch, [1BPdc in next dc, 5ch] 7 times, ss in 3rd of 8ch.

ROUND 6: Ss in each of next 3ch, 1ch, [PL, 1sc in next 5ch sp] 7 times, PL, ss in first ch.

ROUND 7: 9ch, 1dtr in same place as base of these 9ch, *[PL, 1sc at center of next PL] twice, PL, (1dtr, 4ch, 1dtr) in next sc (between 2PL),* rep from * to * twice more, [PL, 1sc in next sc] twice, PL, ss in 5th of 9ch.

ROUND 8: Ss in 4ch sp, 3ch, (4dc, 2ch, 5dc) in same ch sp, *4ch, 1sc at center of next PL, [PL, 1sc at center of next PL] twice, 4ch, (5dc, 2ch, 5dc) in 4ch sp,* rep from * to * twice more, 4ch, 1sc at center of next PL, [PL, 1sc at center of next PL] twice, 2ch, 1hdc in 3rd of 3ch.

ROUND 9: Ss under hdc, 1ch, *5ch, (1sc, 2ch, 1sc) in 2ch sp at corner, 5ch, 1sc in 4ch sp, [2ch, 1sc in next picot] 4 times, 2ch, 1sc in 4ch sp,* rep from * to * 3 more times omitting last sc of final repeat, ss in first ch.

ROUND 10: Ss under 5ch, 1ch, 4sc in 5ch sp, *(1sc, 5ch, ss in last sc made, 1sc) in 2ch sp at corner, 5sc in 5ch sp, 2sc in next 2ch sp, 3sc in next 2ch sp, (1sc, 3ch, ss in last sc made, 1sc) in next 2ch sp, 3sc in next 2ch sp, 2sc in next 2ch sp, 5sc in 5ch sp,* rep from * to * 3 more times omitting last 5sc of final repeat, ss in first ch. Fasten off B.

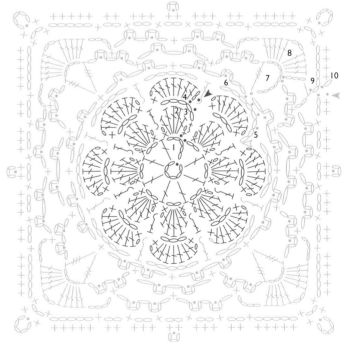

Blocks may be joined using the joining with picots method.

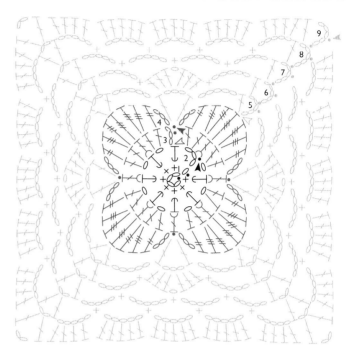

Yarn: DK yarn in burgundy (A), red (B), and yellow (C)

METHOD

Using A, make 4ch, join with ss in first ch.

ROUND 1: 1ch, 7sc in ring, ss in first ch. (8 sts)

ROUND 2: 4ch, [1hdc in front loop of next sc, 1ch] 7 times, ss in 3rd of 4ch.

Fasten off A. Join B to back loop of any hdc.

ROUND 3: 3ch, [2dc in 1ch sp, 1dc in back loop of next hdc] 7 times, 2dc in 1ch sp, ss in 3rd of 3ch.

ROUND 4: [3ch, 1tr in next hdc, 2dtr in next hdc, 1dtr in next hdc, 2dtr in next hdc, 1tr in next hdc, 3ch, ss in next hdc] 4 times, working final ss in same place as base of first 3ch. (4 petals)

Fasten off B. Join C to center tr of any petal.

ROUND 5: 5ch, 1dc in same tr, *5ch, (1dc, 3ch, 1dc) in ss between petals, 5ch,# (1dc, 2ch, 1dc) in center tr of next petal, rep from * to * twice more, then once again from * to #, ss in 3rd of 5ch.

ROUND 6: Ss in 2ch sp, 5ch, 1dc in same ch sp, *5ch, 1sc in 5ch sp, (3dc, 1ch, 3dc) in next 3ch sp, 1sc in next 5ch sp, 5ch,# (1dc, 2ch, 1dc) in next 2ch sp,* rep from * to * twice more, then once again from * to #, ss in 3rd of 5ch.

ROUND 7: Ss in 2ch sp, 5ch, 1dc in same ch sp, *5ch, 1sc in next 5ch sp, 5ch, 1sc in next 1ch sp, 5ch, 1sc in next 5ch sp, 5ch,# (1dc, 2ch, 1dc) in next 2ch sp,* rep from * to *

twice more, then once again from * to #, ss in 3rd of 5ch.

ROUND 8: Ss in 2ch sp, 5ch, 1dc in same ch sp, *[5ch, 1sc in next 5ch sp] 4 times, 5ch,# (1dc, 2ch, 1dc) in next 2ch sp,* rep from * to * twice more, then once again from * to #, ss in 3rd of 5ch.

ROUND 9: Ss in 2ch sp, 5ch, 1dc in same ch sp, *4dc in next 5ch sp, [5dc in next 5ch sp] 3 times, 4dc in next 5ch sp,# (1dc, 2ch, 1dc) in next 2ch sp,* rep from * to * twice more, then once again from * to #, ss in 3rd of 5ch. (25dc on each side)

Fasten off C.

Yarn: DK yarn in dark blue

METHOD

Make 30ch.

ROW 1 (WS): 1dc in 3rd ch from hook, 1dc in each of 26ch. (28dc)

ROW 2: 3ch, skip first dc, 1dc in each of 3dc, *2ch, skip 2dc, 1dc in each of 4dc,* rep from * to * twice more, 2ch, skip 2dc, 1dc in each of 3dc, 1dc in 3rd of 3ch.

ROW 3: 3ch, skip first dc, 1dc in each of 3dc, *2dc in 2ch sp, 1dc in next dc, 2ch, skip 2dc, 1dc in next dc, make flower around edge of mesh space just made:

Working counterclockwise and always inserting the hook from inside the mesh space (as if it were a foundation ring), 3ch, 3dc under post of last dc made (at left side of space), 3ch, ss in corner (that is, top of dc of previous row), 3ch, 1dc in same place, 1dc in top of each of next 2dc of previous row, 3ch, ss in corner, 3ch, 3dc under next dc (at right side of space), 3ch, ss in corner, 3ch, 3dc under 2ch (across top of space), 3ch, then inserting hook from the front ss in top of next dc of main row (4 petals made).

Hold the first petal made to the front and work 2dc in next 2ch sp of previous row,* 1dc in next dc, 2ch, skip 2dc, 1dc in next dc, rep from * to * once more, 1dc in each of 3dc, 1dc in 3rd of 3ch.

ROW 4: When working into 2ch sps, part the petal sts to work the dc between them, over the enclosed ch: 3ch, skip first dc, 1dc in each of 3dc, *2ch, skip 2dc, 1dc in next dc, 2dc in 2ch sp, 1dc in next dc,* rep from * to * twice more, 2ch, skip 2dc, 1dc in each of 3dc, 1dc in 3rd of 3ch.

ROW 5: As row 1.

ROW 6: 3ch, skip first dc, 1dc in each of 3dc, *2ch, skip 2dc, 1dc in next dc, 2dc in 2ch sp, 1dc in next dc,* rep from * to * twice more, 2ch, skip 2dc, 1dc in each of 3dc, 1dc in 3rd of 3ch.

Rep rows 3–6 once more, then rows 3–4 once again.

ROW 13: 3ch, skip first dc, 1dc in each dc and 2dc in each 2ch sp, ending 1dc in 3rd of 3ch.

Fasten off.

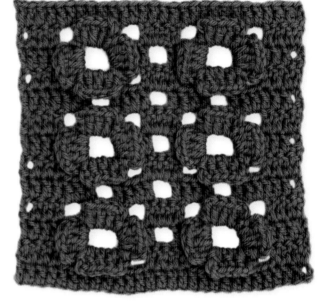

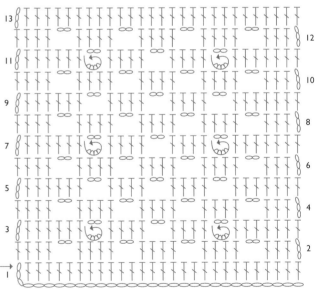

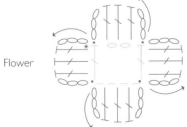

Flower

Specific symbols

Flower worked around hole.

* Start of flower.

Direction of working.

Yarn: DK yarn in blue (A) and white (B)

METHOD

Square

Using A, make 30ch.

ROW 1: 1dc in 4th ch from hook, 1dc in each of 26ch. (28dc)

ROW 2: 3ch, skip first dc, 1dc in each rem dc, 1dc in 3rd of 3ch.

ROW 3: 3ch, skip first dc, 1dc in each of 21dc, 2ch, skip 2dc, 1dc in each of 3dc, 1dc in 3rd of 3ch.

ROW 4: As row 2, working 2dc in 2ch sp.

ROWS 5-6: As row 2.

ROW 7: 3ch, skip first dc, 1dc in each of 12dc, 2ch, skip 2dc, 1dc in each of 12dc, 1dc in 3rd of 3ch.

ROW 8: As row 2, working 2dc in 2ch sp.

ROWS 9-10: As row 2.

ROW 11: 3ch, skip first dc, 1dc in each of 3dc, 2ch, skip 2dc, 1dc in each of 21dc, 1dc in 3rd of 3ch.

ROW 12: As row 2, working 2dc in 2ch sp.

ROW 13: As row 2.

Fasten off A.

Daisies

Work first daisy in the round around a hole.

ROUND 1: RS facing, join B to first of 2 skipped dc on row 2, 1ch, 1sc in next dc, 1sc in corner, 2sc in dc at left edge of hole, 1sc in corner, 1sc in base of each of 2dc at top of hole, 1sc in corner, 2sc in dc at right edge of hole, 1sc in corner, ss in first ch. (12 sts)

ROUND 2: 6ch, [ss in next sc, 6ch] 11 times, ss in last ss of round 1.

Fasten off B.

Make a daisy around each of the remaining holes.

Daisy

Round 1 of daisy around hole in block.

Mix and match 165 + 166

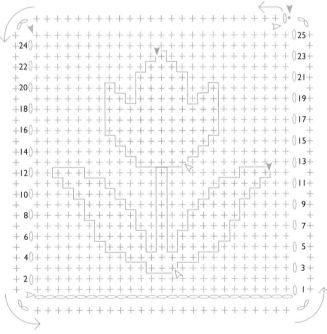

Yarn: DK yarn in pale green (A), mid-green (B), and yellow (C)

METHOD
SPECIFIC ABBREVIATION
Chg to A (or B or C) = changing to A (or B or C) for the final "yo, pull through" of last st worked.

Using A, make 26ch.
ROW 1: 1sc in 2nd ch from hook, 1sc in each of 24ch. (25sc; turning ch does not count as a st in this pattern)
ROW 2: 1ch, 1sc in first sc, 1sc in each sc to end. (25sc)
On rows 3–23, enclose color not in use by working over it until it is required.
ROW 3: Read chart row 3 from right to left: with A, 1ch, 1sc in each of 11sc, chg to B, 1sc in each of 3sc, chg to A, 1sc in each of 11sc.
ROW 4: Read chart row 4 from left to right: with A, 1ch, 1sc in each of 9sc, chg to B, 1sc in each of 7sc, chg to A, 1sc in each of 9sc.
Continue reading from chart rows 5–23 in this way, changing colors as indicated.
ROWS 24-25: Using A, as row 2.
Fasten off A. Join B to last sc of row 25.
EDGING ROUND: 1ch, 1sc in each of 24sc, 2ch, 1sc in side edge of each of 25 rows, 2ch, 1sc in base of each of 25 sts, 2ch, 1sc in side edge of each of 25 rows, 2ch, ss in first ch. (25sc on each side)
Fasten off B.

168 SNEEZEWORT SQUARE \/

Yarn: DK yarn in rust red (A), orange (B), and yellow (C)

METHOD

Using A, make 12ch, join with ss into a ring.

ROUND 1: 1ch, 23sc in ring, ss in first ch. (24 sts)

ROUND 2: 1ch, *1sc in next sc, 3ch, ss in last sc made,# 1sc in next sc,* rep from * to * 10 more times, then once again from * to #, ss in first ch. (12 picots)

Fasten off A. Join B to any sc between 2 picots.

ROUND 3: 6ch, [skip 1 picot, 1sc in next sc, 5ch] 11 times, skip 1 picot, ss in first of 6ch. (12 loops)

ROUND 4: 3ch, *(1hdc, 1sc, 1ch, 1sc, 1hdc) in 5ch loop,# 1dc in next sc,* rep from * to * 10 more times, then once again from * to #, ss in 3rd of 3ch. (12 petals)

Fasten off B. Join C to 1ch sp at center of any petal.

ROUND 5: 6ch, [1sc in next 1ch sp, 5ch] 11 times, ss in first of 6ch. (12 ch sps)

ROUND 6: 5ch, 3dc in same place as base of these 5ch, [1sc in next 5ch sp, 5ch] twice, 1sc in next 5ch sp,# (3dc, 2ch, 3dc) in next sc, * rep from * to * twice more, then once again from * to #, 2dc in same place as base of first 5ch, ss in 3rd of these 5ch.

ROUND 7: Ss in 2ch sp, 5ch, 3dc in same ch sp, *[5ch, 1sc in next 5ch sp] twice, 5ch,# (3dc, 2ch, 3dc) in next 2ch sp,* rep from * to * twice more, then once again from * to #, 2dc in first 2ch sp, ss in 3rd of 5ch.

ROUND 8: Ss in 2ch sp, 5ch, 3dc in same ch sp, *5ch, 1sc in next 5ch sp, (3dc, 1ch, 3dc) in next 5ch sp, 1sc in next 5ch sp, 5ch,# (3dc, 2ch, 3dc) in next 2ch sp,* rep from * to * twice more, then once again from * to #, 2dc in first 2ch sp, ss in 3rd of 5ch.

Fasten off C.

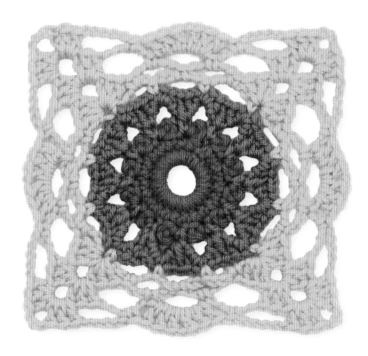

Yarn: DK yarn

METHOD

Make 8ch, join with ss into a ring.

ROUND 1: 1ch, (3sc, 4hdc, 4dc, 4hdc) in ring, ss in first ch. (16 sts)

ROUND 2: 3ch, 3tr tog inserting hook (once in same place as base of these 3ch, twice in next sc), (from now on, insert hook twice in each st of round 1 to work dec), 4ch, 4tr tog over next 2sc, 5ch, 4dtr tog over next 2hdc, 6ch, 4dtr tog over next 2hdc, [7ch, 4ttr tog over next 2dc] twice, 7ch, 4dtr tog over next 2hdc, 6ch, 4dtr tog over next 2hdc, 5ch, ss in ch closing 3tr tog. (8 petals: 2 small, 2 medium, 2 large, 2 medium)

ROUND 3: Work all sc in ch closing a petal: 11ch, 1sc in 2nd petal, 5ch, 1sc in 3rd petal, 10ch, 1sc in 4th petal, 7ch, 1sc in 5th petal, 10ch, 1sc in 6th petal, 7ch, 1sc in 7th petal, 10ch, 1sc in 8th petal, 5ch, ss in first of 11ch.

ROUND 4: Ss in each of 6ch, 3ch, 5sc in same ch sp, 1ch, skip 1sc, 5sc in 5ch sp, 1ch, skip 1sc, (6sc, 2ch, 4sc) in 10ch sp, 1ch, skip 1sc, 7sc in 7ch sp, 1ch, skip 1sc, (5sc, 2ch, 5sc) in 10ch sp, 1ch, skip 1sc, 7sc in 7ch sp, 1ch, skip 1sc, (4sc, 2ch, 6sc) in 10ch sp, 1ch, skip 1sc, 5sc in 5ch sp, 1ch, 4sc in first ch sp, ss in first of 3ch. (18 sts on each side of square)

Fasten off and rejoin to 2ch sp at next corner. Now work in rows on two sides only.

ROW 1: 1ch, 1sc in each sc and 1ch sp to next corner, (1sc, 2ch, 1sc) in 2ch sp, 1sc in each sc and 1ch sp to next corner, 1sc in 2ch sp, turn. (20 sts on each of 2 sides)

ROW 2: 1ch, skip first sc, 1sc in each sc to next corner, (1sc, 2ch, 1sc) in 2ch sp, 1sc in each sc ending 1sc in 1ch, turn. (21sc on each side)

ROW 3: As row 2. (22sc each side)

ROW 4: As row 2. (23sc each side)

Now work all around the block.

FINAL ROUND: 3ch, 2sc in first sc, 1sc in each of 22sc to corner, (1sc, 2ch, 1sc) in 2ch sp, 1sc in each of 22sc, (2sc, 2ch, 1sc) in 1ch, 4sc in side edge of 4 rows, 1sc in 2ch sp, 1sc in each sc and 1ch sp (making 18sc), (1sc, 2ch, 1sc) in 2ch sp, 1sc in each sc and 1ch sp (making 18sc), 1sc in 2ch sp, 4sc in side edge of 4 rows, ss in first of 3ch. (25sc on each of 4 sides)

Fasten off.

final round

170 RUFFLED FLOWER SQUARE \\/

Yarn: DK yarn in peach (A) and green (B)

METHOD

Using A, make 10ch, join with ss into a ring.

ROUND 1: 7ch, [1tr in ring, 3ch] 11 times, ss in 4th of 7ch. (12 ch sps)

ROUND 2: Ss in 3ch sp, 4ch, 3tr in same ch sp, *4tr around post of next tr (working down the post toward the center), 1tr in center ring, 4tr around post of next tr (working up the post away from the center), (3ch sp has been skipped),# 4tr in next 3ch sp,* rep from * to * 4 more times, then once again from * to #, ss in 4th of 4ch.

Fasten off A. Join B to any empty 3ch sp behind round 2.

ROUND 3: 1ch, 2sc in same ch sp, [3ch, 3sc in next empty 3ch sp] 5 times, 3ch, ss in first ch of round.

ROUND 4: 1ch, 2sc in next sc, 1sc in next sc, *4sc in 3ch sp, 1sc in next sc, 2sc in next sc, 1sc in next sc,* rep from * to * 4 more times, 4sc in 3ch sp, ss in first ch.

ROUND 5: 4ch, [skip 2sc, 1sc in next sc, 3ch] 15 times, ss in first of 4ch. (16 ch sps)

ROUND 6: Ss in rem 3ch sp, 5ch, [1sc in next 3ch sp, 4ch] 15 times, ss in first of 5ch.

ROUND 7: Ss in next ch, ss in rem 3ch sp, 6ch, [1sc in next 4ch sp, 5ch] 15 times, ss in first of 6ch.

ROUND 8: Ss in each of 2ch, ss in rem 3ch sp, 6ch, 3tr in same ch sp, *2ch, 1sc in next 5ch sp, [5ch, 1sc in next 5ch sp] twice, 2ch,# (3tr, 2ch, 3tr) in next 5ch sp,* rep from * to * twice more, then once again from * to #, 2tr in first ch sp, ss in 4th of 6ch.

ROUND 9: Ss in 2ch sp, 6ch, 3tr in same ch sp, *1tr in each of 3tr, 2tr in 2ch sp, 2ch, 1sc in next 5ch sp, 5ch, 1sc in next 5ch sp, 2ch, 2tr in 2ch sp, 1tr in each of 3tr,# (3tr, 2ch, 3tr) in 2ch sp,* rep from * to * twice more, then once again from * to #, 2tr in first ch sp, ss in 4th of 6ch. Fasten off B.

Specific symbol
4tr around post.

Yarn: DK yarn in yellow (A) and green (B)

METHOD

Using A, make 27ch.

ROW 1: 4tr tog over (6th, 8th, 11th, and 13th) ch from hook, 4ch, skip 1ch, 1sc in next ch, turn.

ROW 2: [1ch, 1tr] 4 times in ch closing 4tr tog, 1ch, skip (4tr tog, 3ch), 1sc in next ch. (1 flower)

ROW 3: 9ch, 4tr tog over (6th and 8th ch from hook, last 1ch sp of row 2, and foll 1ch sp), 4ch, 1sc in next 1ch sp, 3ch, 4tr tog over (next two 1ch sps, 2nd and 4th unworked base ch), 4ch, skip 1 base ch, 1sc in next ch.

ROW 4: *[1ch, 1tr] 4 times in ch closing 4tr tog, 1ch, skip (4tr tog, 3ch),* ss in next sc, rep from * to * once more, 1sc in next ch. (2 flowers)

ROW 5: 9ch, 4tr tog over (6th and 8th ch from hook, last 1ch sp of row 4, and foll 1ch sp), 4ch, 1sc in next 1ch sp, 3ch, 4tr tog over next four 1ch sps, 4ch, 1sc in next 1ch sp, 3ch, 4tr tog over (next two 1ch sps, 2nd and 4th unworked base ch), 4ch, skip 1 base ch, 1sc in next ch.

ROW 6: *[1ch, 1tr] 4 times in ch closing 4tr tog, 1ch, skip (4tr tog, 3ch),# ss in next sc,* rep from * to * once more, then once again from * to #, 1sc in next ch. (3 flowers)

ROW 7: Ss in each of next 4 sts, 1sc in next 1ch sp, *3ch, 4tr tog over next four 1ch sps, 4ch, 1sc in next 1ch sp,* rep from * to * once more, turn.

ROW 8: *[1ch, 1tr] 4 times in ch closing 4tr tog, 1ch, skip (4tr tog, 3ch), ss in next sc,* rep from * to * once more. (2 flowers)

ROW 9: Ss in each of next 4 sts, 1sc in next 1ch sp, 3ch, 4tr tog over next four 1ch sps, 4ch, 1sc in next 1ch sp, turn.

ROW 10: [1ch, 1tr] 4 times in ch closing 4tr tog, 1ch, skip (4tr tog, 3ch), ss in next sc. (1 flower made) Fasten off A. Join B to center 1ch sp at top of last row.

Continue in rounds for outer edge.

ROUND 1: 3ch, 1sc in same 1ch sp, *16sc along side edge, (1sc, 2ch, 1sc) in same place at corner,* rep from * to * twice more, 16sc along side edge to corner, ss in first of 3ch. (18sc on each side)

ROUND 2: Ss in 2ch sp, 5ch, 2dc in same ch sp, *1dc in each of 18sc, (1dc, 2ch, 1dc) in 2ch sp, 1dc in each of 18sc,* (2dc, 2ch, 2dc) in 2ch sp at lower corner, rep from * to * once more, 1dc in first 2ch sp, ss in 3rd of 5ch. (21dc on each side) Fasten off B.

Yarn: DK yarn in 4 shades of pink (A–D) and gray (E)

METHOD

First flower

Using A, 10ch, 1sc in first ch, [9ch, 1sc in side of last sc]
5 times. (Six 9ch loops)
Fasten off. Sew last sc to first ch.

2nd flower

Using B, work as first flower to last ch loop, 4ch, ss in
9ch loop of first flower, 4ch, 1sc in side of last sc.
Fasten off. Sew last sc to first ch.

3rd and 4th flowers

Make 3rd flower in C, joining to first and 2nd flowers as
shown on chart. Make 4th flower in D, joining to 2nd
and 3rd flowers as shown.

Outer edge

With RS facing, join E to 2nd of 3 empty 9ch loops on
any flower.
ROUND 1: 5ch, 1sc in next 9ch loop, [4ch, 1sc in next
empty 9ch loop] 12 times, 4ch, ss in first of 5ch.
(Fourteen 4ch sps)
ROUND 2: 5ch, 1dc in same place, *[4dc in 4ch sp,
1dc in sc] 3 times, (2dc, 3ch, 2dc) in next 4ch sp,
1dc in next sc, [4dc in 4ch sp, 1dc in sc] twice,
4dc in 4ch sp,* (1dc, 2ch, 1dc) in next sc, rep from
* to * once more, ss in 3rd of 5ch. (18dc on each side)
ROUND 3: Ss in 2ch sp, 3ch, 1sc in same ch sp, *1sc in
each of 18dc, (2sc, 3ch, 2sc) in 3ch sp, 1sc in each of
18dc,* (1sc, 2ch, 1sc) in 2ch sp, rep from * to * once
more, ss in first of 3ch. (21sc on each side)
Fasten off E.

173 KINGCUP DIAMOND

Yarn: DK yarn in yellow (A) and green (B)

METHOD

Using A, make 4ch, join with ss into a ring.

ROUND 1: 5ch, [1dc in ring, 2ch] 7 times, ss in 3rd of 5ch. (24 sts)

ROUND 2: 2ch, 2tr tog in same place as base of these 2ch, [2sc in 2ch sp, 3tr bobble in next dc] 7 times, 2sc in last 2ch sp, ss in top of 2tr tog.

Fasten off A. Turn flower over so bobbles are facing. Join B from behind to post of any dc of round 1. Work round 3 into dc of round 1, leaving round 2 at the front.

ROUND 3: 7ch, 1BPtr in same dc, *3ch, 1BPsc in next dc of round 1, 3ch, (1BPdc, 3ch, 1BPdc) in next dc, 3ch, 1BPsc in next dc, 3ch,* (1BPtr, 3ch, 1BPtr) in next dc, rep from * to * once more, 3ch, ss in 4th of 7ch. (Twelve 3ch sps)

ROUND 4: Ss in 3ch sp, 7ch, 1tr in same ch sp, *5ch, 1sc in next 3ch sp, 3ch, 1sc in next ch sp, 3ch, (1dc, 3ch, 1dc) in next 3ch sp, [3ch, 1sc in next 3ch sp] twice, 5ch,* (1tr, 3ch, 1tr) in next 3ch sp, rep from * to * once more, ss in 4th of 7ch.

ROUND 5: Ss in 3ch sp, 7ch, 1tr in same ch sp, *5ch, 1sc in 5ch sp, 5dc in next 3ch sp, 1sc in next 3ch sp, 3ch, (1dc, 3ch, 1dc) in next 3ch sp, 3ch, 1sc in next 3ch sp, 5dc in next 3ch sp, 1sc in 5ch sp, 5ch,* (1tr, 3ch, 1tr) in next 3ch sp, rep from * to * once more, ss in 4th of 7ch.

ROUND 6: Ss in 3ch sp, 7ch, 1tr in same sp, *5ch, 1sc in next 5ch sp, 5ch, 1sc in 3rd of 5dc, 5ch, 1sc in next 3ch sp, 3ch, (1dc, 3ch, 1dc) in next 3ch sp, 3ch, 1sc in next 3ch sp, 5ch, 1sc in 3rd of 5dc, 5ch, 1sc in next 5ch sp, 5ch,* (1tr, 3ch, 1tr) in next 3ch sp, rep from * to * once more, ss in 4th of 7ch.

ROUND 7: Ss in 3ch sp, 4ch, 2sc in same sp, *[5sc in 5ch sp] 3 times, 3sc in 3ch sp, (1sc, 2ch, 1sc) in next 3ch sp, 3sc in next 3ch sp, [5sc in 5ch sp] 3 times,* (2sc, 3ch, 2sc) in next 3ch sp, rep from * to * once more, 1sc in first ch sp of round, ss in first of 4ch. (21sc on each side)

Fasten off B.

Specific symbol
Turn over.

Yarn: DK yarn

METHOD

Make a slip ring.

ROUND 1: 1ch, 15sc in ring, ss in first ch, pull end to close ring.

ROUND 2: 1ch, *8ch, skip 3sc, 1sc in next sc,* rep from * to * twice more, 8ch, skip 3sc, ss in first ch of round. (4 petals)

ROUND 3: 1ch, *13sc in 8ch loop, 1sc in same place as next sc,* rep from * to * 3 more times.

ROUND 4: 1ch, ss in first of 13sc, *[1sc in next sc, 2ch] 10 times, 1sc in next sc, 2sc tog over (next and foll alt sc),* rep from * to * 3 more times, working last 2sc tog over (next sc and ss at beg of round).

ROUND 5: 1ch, *7ch, skip 9 sts, 1sc in next sc, 7ch, skip 11 sts, 1sc in next sc, 7ch, skip 9 sts, 1sc in 2sc tog,* rep from * to * 3 more times omitting last sc of final repeat, ss in first ch of round. (12 loops)

ROUND 6: Ss in each of next 4ch, *7ch, (1sc, 11ch, 1sc) In next loop (at end of petal), [7ch, 1sc in next loop] 5 times,* rep from * to * once more, ending in same loop as beg of round. (14 loops)

ROUND 7: Ss in each of next 4ch, *7ch, (1sc, 11ch, 1sc) in 11ch loop, [7ch, 1sc in next loop] 6 times,* rep from * to * once more, ending in same loop as beg of round. (16 loops)

ROUND 8: Ss in each of next 4ch, *7ch, 1sc in 11ch loop, 7ch, ss in last sc (large picot made), [7ch, 1sc in next loop] twice, 3ch, ss in last sc (small picot made), [7ch, 1sc in next loop] twice, 5ch, ss in last sc (medium picot made), [7ch, 1sc in next loop] twice, 3ch, ss in last sc, 7ch, 1sc in next loop,* rep from * to * once more, ending in same loop as beg of round.
Fasten off.

Blocks may be joined using the joining with picots method.

Yarn: DK yarn in yellow (A), pink (B), and blue (C)

METHOD

Using A, make 4ch, join with ss into a ring.

ROUND 1: 1ch, 7sc in ring, ss in first ch. (8 sts)

Fasten off A. Join B to back loop of any sc.

ROUND 2: 1ch, *1sc in back loop of next sc, 10ch, ss in 10th ch from hook, 1sc in back loop of next sc,* rep from * to * 3 more times omitting last sc of final repeat, ss in first ch of round. (4 petals)

ROUND 3: 1ch, *(2sc, 2hdc, 2dc, 1tr, 2dc, 2hdc, 2sc) in 10ch loop, skip 1sc, 1sc in next sc,* rep from * to * 3 more times omitting final sc, ss in first ch of round.

Fasten off B. Join C to back loop of tr at tip of any petal.

ROUND 4: 6ch, 1sc in same place, *3ch, (1tr, 1ch, 1tr, 1ch, 1tr) in next sc between petals, 3ch,# (1sc, 5ch, 1sc) in back loop of tr at tip of next petal,* rep from * to * twice more, then once again from * to #, ss in first of 6ch.

ROUND 5: Ss in each of next 2ch, ss in rem 3ch loop, 6ch, 1sc in same place, *5ch, 1sc in next 3ch sp, 5ch, skip (1tr, 1ch, 1tr, 1ch, 1tr), 1sc in next 3ch sp, 5ch,* 1sc in 5ch loop at tip of 2nd petal, rep from * to * once more, (1sc, 5ch, 1sc) in 5ch loop at tip of 3rd petal, rep from * to * once more, 1sc in 5ch loop at tip of 4th petal, rep from * to * once more, ss in first of 6ch.

ROUND 6: Ss in each of next 2ch, ss in rem 3ch loop, 6ch, 2dc in same place, *[5dc in 5ch sp] 3 times, (1dc, 2ch, 1dc) in next sc (at tip of next petal), [5dc in 5ch sp] 3 times,* (2dc, 3ch, 2dc) in next 5ch loop (at tip of 3rd petal), rep from * to * once more, 1dc in first loop of round 5, ss in 3rd of 6ch.

ROUND 7: Ss in 3ch sp, 6ch, 2dc in same place, *1dc in each of 18dc, (1dc, 2ch, 1dc) in 2ch sp, 1dc in each of 18dc,* (2dc, 3ch, 2dc) in 3ch sp, rep from * to * once more, 1dc in first ch sp, ss in 3rd of 6ch. (21 sts on each side)

Fasten off C.

Yarn: DK yarn in bright blue (A) and 4 pastel colors (B–E)

METHOD

Diamond

Using A, make 23ch.

ROW 1: 2dc tog over 4th and 5th ch from hook, 1dc in each of 16ch, 2dc in next ch, 1dc in last ch. (21 sts)

ROW 2: 3ch, skip 1dc, 2dc in next dc, 1dc in each dc to last 3 sts, 2dc tog over next 2 sts, 1dc in 3rd of 3ch.

ROW 3: 3ch, skip 1dc, 2dc tog over next 2 sts, 1dc in each of 2dc, 2ch, skip 2dc, 1dc in each of 8dc, 2ch, skip 2dc, 1dc in each of 2dc, 2dc in next dc, 1dc in 3rd of 3ch.

ROW 4: As row 2, working 2dc in each 2ch sp.

ROW 5: 3ch, skip 1dc, 2dc tog over next 2 sts, 1dc in each dc to last 2 sts, 2dc in last dc, 1dc in 3rd of 3ch.

ROW 6: As row 2.

ROW 7: As row 5.

ROW 8: 3ch, skip 1dc, 2dc in next dc, 1dc in each of 2dc, 2ch, skip 2dc, 1dc in each of 8dc, 2ch, skip 2dc, 1dc in each of 2dc, 2dc tog over next 2 sts, 1dc in 3rd of 3ch.

ROW 9: As row 5, working 2dc in each 2ch sp.

ROW 10: As row 2.

Fasten off A.

Daisies

Using colors B, C, D, and E, work 1 daisy around each hole.

ROUND 1: RS facing, join yarn to first of 2 skipped dc at lower edge of hole, 1ch, 1sc in next dc, 1sc in corner, 2sc in dc at left edge of hole, 1sc in corner, 1sc in base of each of 2dc at top of hole, 1sc in corner, 2sc in dc at right edge of hole, 1sc in corner, ss in first ch. (12 sts)

ROUND 2: 6ch, [ss in next sc, 6ch] 11 times, ss in last ss of round 1.

Fasten off.

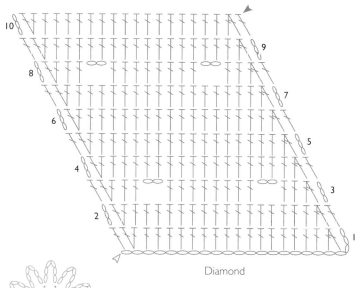

Diamond

Daisy

Yarn: DK yarn

METHOD

Make 6ch, join with ss into a ring.

ROUND 1: 1ch, 11sc in ring. (12 sts)

ROUND 2: 1ch, [7ch, skip 1sc, 1sc in next sc] 5 times, 2ch, 1dtr in first ch of round. (6 petals)

ROUND 3: 3ch, 4dc under dtr, [3ch, 5dc in 7ch sp] 5 times, 3ch, ss in 3rd of 3ch.

ROUND 4: 3ch, 1dc in each of 4dc, [3ch, 1sc in 3ch sp, 3ch, 1dc in each of 5dc] 5 times, 3ch, 1sc in 3ch sp, 3ch, ss in 3rd of 3ch.

ROUND 5: 2ch, 4dc tog over next 4dc, *[5ch, 1sc in next 3ch sp] twice,# 5ch, 5dc tog over next 5dc,* rep from * to * 4 more times, then once again from * to #, 2ch, 1dc in 4dc tog.

ROUND 6: 1ch, [5ch, 1sc in next ch sp] 17 times, 2ch, 1dc in first ch. (18 ch sps)

ROUND 7: 1ch, *1ch, (4sc, 3ch, 4sc) in next 5ch sp, 1ch, 1sc in next 5ch sp, 5ch,# 1sc in next 5ch sp,* rep from * to * 4 more times, then once again from * to #, ss in first ch. Fasten off.

Mix and match 177 + 178

Yarn: DK yarn in bright yellow (A), pale yellow (B), and green (C)

METHOD

SPECIFIC ABBREVIATION

3ch P = 3ch picot: 3ch, ss in top of previous st.

Using A, make 5ch, join with ss into a ring.

ROUND 1: 1ch, 11sc in ring, ss in first ch. (12 sts)

ROUND 2: 1ch, [2sc in front loop of next sc, 1sc in front loop of next sc] 5 times, 2sc in front loop of last sc, ss in first ch. (18 sts)

Fasten off A. Join B to back loop of any sc of round 1 that contains 2sc.

ROUND 3: Work in back loops of round 1: *5ch, 3dtr tog over (same loop and next 2 back loops), 3ch P, 4ch, ss in same back loop,* rep from * to * 5 more times ending in same loop as beg of round. (6 petals) Fasten off B. Join C to any 3ch P.

ROUND 4: 1ch, *4ch, 1dtr in ss between two petals, 4ch, 1sc in next 3ch P,* rep from * to * 5 more times omitting final sc, ss in first ch. (12 ch sps)

ROUND 5: 5ch, 1dc in same place, *4dc in 4ch sp, 1dc in dtr, 4dc in 4ch sp, (1dc, 2ch, 1dc) in sc,* rep from * to * 4 more times, 4dc in 4ch sp, 1dc in dtr, 4dc in 4ch sp, ss in 3rd of 5ch. (11dc on each side)

ROUND 6: Ss in 2ch sp, 5ch, 1dc in same ch sp, *[1ch, skip 1dc, 1dc in next dc] 5 times, 1ch, skip 1dc,# (1dc, 2ch, 1dc) in 2ch sp,* rep from * to * 4 more times, then once again from * to #, ss in 3rd of 5ch.

ROUND 7: Ss in 2ch sp, 5ch, 1dc in same ch sp, *1dc in each dc and ch sp to next corner, (1dc, 2ch, 1dc) in 2ch sp,* rep from * to * 4 more times, 1dc in each dc and ch sp, ss in 3rd of 5ch. (15dc on each side) Fasten off C.

Specific symbol
3dtr tog in back loops of round 1.

Yarn: DK yarn in red (A), orange (B), and beige (C)

METHOD

Using A, make 6ch, join with ss into a ring.

ROUND 1: 1ch, 17sc in ring, ss in first ch. (18 sts)

ROUND 2: 1ch, 1sc in same place, [1sc in each of 2sc, 2sc in next sc] 5 times, 1sc in each of 2sc, ss in first ch. (24 sts)

ROUND 3: 1ch, 1sc in same place, [1sc in each of 3sc, 2sc in next sc] 5 times, 1sc in each of 3sc, ss in first ch. (30 sts) Fasten off A. Join B to any sc that is the first of 2sc in same place.

ROUND 4: 10ch, [skip 4sc, 1sc in next sc, 9ch] 5 times, skip 4sc, ss in first of 10ch. (6ch loops)

ROUND 5: Ss in 9ch sp, 1ch, *5sc in 9ch loop, 3sc in 5th of these 9ch, 5sc in same ch loop,# 3sc tog over (same ch loop, next sc, and foll ch loop),* rep from * to * 4 more times, then once again from * to #, 2sc tog over same ch loop and next sc, ss in first ch. (84 sts)

Blocks may be joined using the joining with picots method.

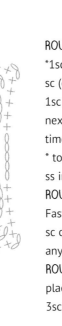

ROUND 6: 1ch, skip first sc, *1sc in each of 5sc, 3sc in next sc (center sc of 3 in same place), 1sc in each of 5sc,# 3sc tog over next 3sc,* rep from * to * 4 more times, then once again from * to #, 2sc tog over last 2 sts, ss in first ch. (84 sts)

ROUND 7: As round 6. (6 petals) Fasten off B. Join C to center sc of 3 in same place at tip of any petal.

ROUND 8: 3ch, 1sc in same place, *6ch, skip 6sc, 1sc in 3sc tog, 6ch, skip 6sc,# (1sc, 2ch, 1sc) in next sc (center sc of 3 in same place),* rep from * to * 4 more times, then once again from * to #, ss in first of 3ch. (12 ch loops)

ROUND 9: Ss in 2ch sp, 3ch, 1sc in same place, *1sc in next sc, 3sc in 6ch loop, 5ch, 3sc in next 6ch loop,# 1sc in next sc, (1sc, 2ch, 1sc) in 2ch loop,* rep from * to * 4 more times, then once again from * to #, 1sc in st closing previous round, ss in first of 3ch. Fasten off C.

SPINNING DAHLIA HEXAGON V

Yarn: DK yarn in yellow (A) and orange (B)

METHOD

Using A, make 17ch, join into a ring with ss in
10th ch from hook, then continue along rem 7ch.
ROW 1: 1sc in next st, 1hdc in next st, 1dc in next
st, 2dc in next st, 1tr in next st, 2tr in next st, 2dtr
in next st, turn. (10 sts)
ROW 2: 2ch, 1sc in space between first and 2nd sts,
[1sc in next sp between 2 sts] 8 times, ss in sc at
beg of row 1, ss in ring, turn. (First petal made)
ROW 3: Skip 1ss, beg in back loop of next ss work
as row 1 into back loops of 7 sts.
ROW 4: As row 2. (2nd petal made)
Rep rows 3–4 ten more times. (12 petals made)
Fasten off leaving a long tail. Run the tail through
the ss worked into the ring and pull up firmly,
then slip stitch the chain edge behind the top
of the last row.
Join B to the tip of any petal.
ROUND 1: 1ch, *(1dtr, 4ch, 1dtr) in base of dtr at end
of same petal, 1sc in tip of next petal,* rep from * to
* ending ss in first ch
ROUND 2: 5ch, 1dc in same place, *4ch, 1sc in next
4ch sp, 1sc in dtr, 1sc in sc, 1sc in dtr, 1sc in next
4ch sp, 4ch, (1dc, 2ch, 1dc) in next sc,* rep from
* to * 4 more times, 4ch, 1sc in next 4ch sp,
1sc in dtr, 1sc in sc, 1sc in dtr, 1sc in next 4ch sp,
4ch, ss in 3rd of 5ch.
Fasten off B.

SNOWDROP HEXAGON   \/

Yarn: DK yarn in green (A) and cream (B)

METHOD

Using A, make a slip ring.

ROUND 1: 4ch, [2dc in ring, 1ch, 1dc in ring, 1ch] 5 times, 2dc in ring, 1ch, ss in 3rd of 4ch, pull end to close ring. (24 sts)

ROUND 2: 6ch, [1tr in each of 2dc, 2ch, 1tr in next dc, 2ch] 5 times, 1tr in each of 2dc, 2ch, ss in 4th of 6ch. (42 sts)

ROUND 3: 7ch, [1FPtr in each of 2tr, 4ch, 1dc in next tr, 4ch] 5 times, 1FPtr in each of 2tr, 4ch, ss in 3rd of 7ch. (66 sts)

Fasten off A. Join B to 2nd of 4ch following any 2FPtr.

ROUND 4: 3ch, 5tr tog inserting hook (once in same place as base of 3ch, twice in next dc, twice in foll 3rd ch), *13ch, skip 2FPtr, 6tr tog inserting hook (twice in 2nd of 4ch, twice in next dc, twice in foll 3rd ch),* rep from * to * 4 more times, 13ch, ss in ch closing first 5tr tog.

Fasten off B. Join A to ch closing any 6tr tog.

ROUND 5: 1ch, 3hdc tog in same ch, *1ch, 7sc in 13ch sp, 2FPtr tog over 2FPtr of round 3 below, 7sc in same ch sp, 1ch,# 3hdc tog in ch closing next group,* rep from * to * 4 more times, then once again from * to #, ss in first 3hdc tog. (15 sts on each side, 3 sts at each corner)

Fasten off A.

SPIRAL WINDFLOWER HEXAGON ।

Yarn: DK yarn in orange (A), white (B), and blue (C)

METHOD

NOTE: It is easy to adjust the size of this hexagon by repeating round 6 to any size required.

Using A, make 6ch, join with ss into a ring.

ROUND 1: 1ch, 11sc in ring, ss in first ch. (12 sts)

Fasten off A. Join B to any sc.

ROUND 2: 1ch, *3ch, (1tr, 1ch, 1tr) in next sc, 3ch, 1sc in next sc,* rep from * to * 5 more times omitting last sc of final repeat, ss in first ch of round. (6 petals)

Fasten off B. Join C to 1ch sp at top of any petal.

ROUND 3: 1ch, *6ch, 1sc in 1ch sp at top of next petal,* rep from * to * 4 more times, 6ch, ss in first ch of round.

ROUND 4: *4ch, 3sc in 6ch sp, 1sc in sc,* rep from * to * 5 more times working last sc in first ch.

ROUND 5: *4ch, 2sc in 4ch sp, 1sc in each of 3sc, skip 1sc,* rep from * to * 5 more times.

ROUND 6: *4ch, 2sc in 4ch sp, 1sc in each sc to last sc of group, skip 1sc,* rep from * to * 5 more times.

Rep round 6 six more times, until there are 4ch and 12sc on each side of hexagon, ss in next sc.

Fasten off C.

Yarn: DK yarn in pale pink (A), dark pink (B), and gray (C)

METHOD

Using A, make a slip ring.

ROUND 1: 2ch, 8hdc in ring, ss in 2nd of 2ch, pull end to close ring. (9 sts)

Join in B, leaving A at back of work.

ROUND 2: Using B, 1ch, 2sc in each hdc, 1sc in same place as first ch of round, ss in first ch. (18 sts)

Change to A, leaving B at back of work.

ROUND 3: Using A, *3ch, [2tr in next sc] twice, 3ch, ss in next sc,* rep from * to * 5 more times, ending in same sc as beg of round.
Fasten off A.

ROUND 4: Using B, 3ch, *ss in 3rd of 3ch of round 3, [2ch, ss in next tr] 4 times, 2ch, ss in next ch, 1dc in same place as ss of round 3 below,* rep from * to * omitting last dc of final repeat, ss in 3rd of 3ch at beg of round.
Fasten off B. Join C to any dc.

ROUND 5: 1ch, *5ch, skip (ss, 2ch, ss, 2ch, ss), ss in back loop of next ch, 5ch, skip (1ch, ss, 2ch, ss, 2ch, ss), 1sc in next dc, * rep from * to * 5 more times omitting last sc of final repeat, ss in first ch of round.

ROUND 6: 6ch, 1sc in next 5ch loop, *5ch, 1sc in next 5ch loop, 3ch, 1dc in next sc, 3ch, 1sc in next 5ch loop,* rep from * to * 4 more times, 5ch, 1sc in next 5ch loop, 3ch, ss in 3rd of 6ch.

ROUND 7: 6ch, 1sc in next loop, *[5ch, 1sc in next loop] twice, 3ch, 1dc in next dc, 3ch, 1sc in next loop,* rep from * to * 4 more times, [5ch, 1sc in next loop] twice, 3ch, ss in 3rd of 6ch.

ROUND 8: 6ch, ss in 4th ch from hook (3ch picot made), *3ch, 1sc in next loop, [5ch, 1sc in next loop] 3 times, 3ch, 1dc in next dc, 3ch, ss in top of dc just made,* rep from * to * omitting last dc and picot of final repeat, ss in same ch as base of first picot.
Fasten off C.

Blocks may be joined using the joining with picots method.

Yarn: DK yarn in pink (A) and gray (B)

METHOD

Using A, make 9ch, join into a ring with 1 ss in first ch.

ROUND 1: 1ch, 17sc in ring, ss in first ch. (18 sts)

ROUND 2: 4ch, [skip 2sc, 1sc in next sc, 3ch,] 5 times, skip 2sc, ss in first of 4ch. (6 ch sps)

ROUND 3: (1sc, 3ch, 5dc, 3ch, 1sc) in each of 6 ch sps, ss in first sc.

ROUND 4: Work behind round 3: 1ch, [5ch, 1sc between next 2sc where petals adjoin] 5 times, 5ch, ss in first ch of round.

ROUND 5: (1sc, 3ch, 7dc, 3ch, 1sc) in each of 6 ch sps, ss in first sc. Fasten off A. Join B between any 2 petals, between 2sc.

ROUND 6: Work behind round 5: 1ch, [6ch, 1sc between next 2sc where petals adjoin] 5 times, 6ch, ss in first ch of round.

ROUND 7: 5ch, 1dc in same place as base of these 5ch, *7dc in 7ch sp, (1dc, 2ch, 1dc) in next sc,* rep from * to * 4 more times, 7dc in 7ch sp, ss in 3rd of 5ch.

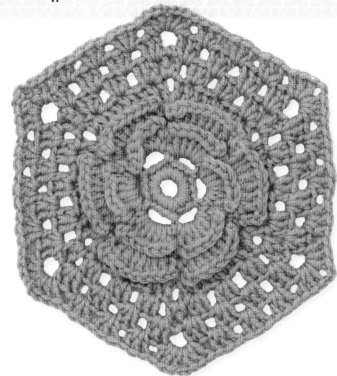

ROUND 8: Ss in 2ch sp, 5ch, 1dc in same ch sp, *skip 1dc, 3dc in next dc, [skip 2dc, 3dc in next dc] twice, skip 1dc,# (1dc, 2ch, 1dc) in 2ch sp,* rep from * to * 4 more times, then once again from * to #, ss in 3rd of 5ch.

ROUND 9: Ss back between previous dc and 3ch, 5ch, *skip 1dc, 3dc in sp between 2 groups, [skip 3dc, 3dc in space between 2 groups] 3 times,# 2ch, skip (1dc, 2ch, 1dc),* rep from * to * 4 more times, then once again from * to # omitting final dc of last repeat, ss in 3rd of 5ch.

ROUND 10: Ss in 3ch sp, 5ch, 3dc in same ch sp, *[skip 3dc, 3dc in space between 2 groups] 3 times,# skip 3dc, (3dc, 2ch, 3dc) in 2ch sp,* rep from * to * 4 more times, then once again from * to #, skip last group, 2dc in first ch sp, ss in 3rd of 5ch. Fasten off B.

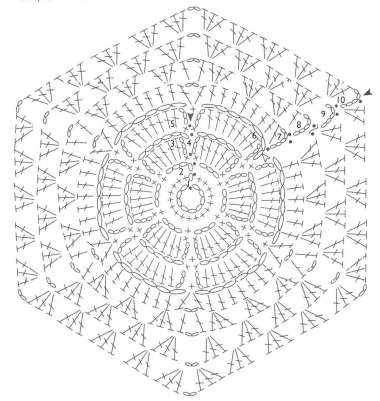

185 CORNFLOWER HEXAGON \/

Yarn: DK yarn in purple (A), blue (B), and gray (C)

METHOD
SPECIFIC ABBREVIATION

Petal = 1dtr in position as given, [1tr in side of this dtr, inserting hook under 2 threads of 2nd wrap from base] twice.

Using A, make 6ch, join with ss into a ring.

ROUND 1: 3ch, [1sc in ring, 2ch] 11 times, 2ch, ss in first of 3ch. Fasten off A. Join B to any 2ch sp.

ROUND 2: 5ch, 2tr in 4th ch from hook, [1ch, 1 petal in next 2ch sp] 11 times, 1ch, ss in 5th of 5ch.

Fasten off B. Join C to any 1ch sp.

ROUND 3: 3ch, 1sc in same ch sp, *[1sc between next 2 sts] twice, 1sc in next 1ch sp, [1sc between next 2 sts] twice,# (1sc, 2ch, 1sc) in next 1ch sp,* rep from * to * 4 more times, then once again from * to #, ss in first of 3ch.

ROUND 4: Ss in 2ch sp, 5ch, 1dc in same ch sp, *5ch, skip 3sc, 1sc in next sc, 5ch, skip 3sc,# (1dc, 2ch, 1dc) in 2ch sp,* rep from * to * 4 more times, then once again from * to #, ss in 3rd of 5ch.

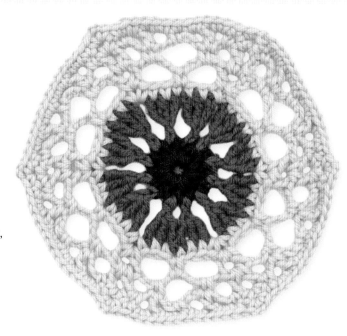

ROUND 5: Ss in 2ch sp, 5ch, 1dc in same ch sp, *3ch, 1sc in next 5ch sp, 6ch, 1sc in next 5ch sp, 3ch,# (1dc, 2ch, 1dc) in 2ch sp,* rep from * to * 4 more times, then once again from * to #, ss in 3rd of 5ch.

ROUND 6: Ss in 2ch sp, 3ch, 1sc in same ch sp, *1sc in 3ch sp, 2ch, 1dc in next sc, 2ch, 1sc in 6ch sp, 2ch, 1dc in next sc, 2ch, 1sc in 3ch sp,# (1sc, 2ch, 1sc) in 2ch sp,* rep from * to * 4 more times, then once again from * to #, ss in first of 3ch.

ROUND 7: Ss in 2ch sp, 3ch, 1sc in same ch sp, *skip 1sc, 1sc in next sc, [2sc in next 2ch sp, 1sc in next st] 4 times, skip 1sc,# (1sc, 2ch, 1sc) in corner 2ch sp,* rep from * to * 4 more times, then once again from * to #, ss in first of 3ch. (15sc on each side)

Fasten off C.

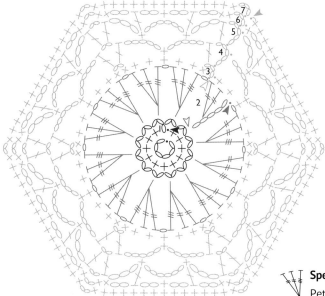

Specific symbol
Petal

186 LARGE FLOWER HEXAGON ∨

Yarn: DK yarn in mid-blue (A) and dark blue (B)

METHOD

Using A, make 8ch, join with ss into a ring.

ROUND 1: 3ch, 1tr in ring, [2ch, 2tr tog in ring] 11 times, 2ch, ss in first tr of round.

ROUND 2: Ss in 2ch sp, 1ch, [5ch, 1sc in next 2ch sp] 11 times, 5ch, ss in first ch of round.

ROUND 3: Ss in each of 2ch, 1ch, *10ch, 1sc in same 5ch sp, [5ch, 1sc in next 5ch sp]# twice,* rep from * to * 4 more times, then once again from * to #, 2ch, 1dc in first ch of round.

ROUND 4: *(5dc, 3ch, 5dc) in 10ch loop, 1sc in next 5ch sp, (2dc, 1ch, 2dc) in next sc, 1sc in next 5ch sp,* rep from * to * 5 more times omitting last sc of final repeat, ss in first dc of round.
Fasten off A. Join B to 3ch sp at tip of any petal.

ROUND 5: 1ch, *5ch, (1tr, 3ch, 1tr) in next 1ch sp, 5ch, 1sc in next 3ch sp,* rep from * to * 5 more times omitting last sc of final repeat, ss in first ch of round.

ROUND 6: Ss in 5ch sp, 1ch, 4sc in same sp, *1sc in tr, 3sc in 3ch sp, 1sc in tr, 5sc in 5ch sp, 2ch, skip 1sc,# 5sc in 5ch sp,* rep from * to * 4 more times, then once again from * to #, ss in first ch of round. (15 sts on each side)
Fasten off B.

Mix and match 185 + 186

Yarn: DK yarn in orange (A), pink (B), and beige (C)

METHOD

Using A, make a slip ring.

ROUND 1: 3ch, 2tr tog in ring, [5ch, 3tr tog in ring] 5 times, 5ch, ss in top of 2tr tog, pull end to close ring. (6 petals) Fasten off A. Join B to any 3tr tog.

ROUND 2: 3ch, (2tr tog, 7ch, 3tr tog) in same place as base of first 3ch, *(3tr tog, 7ch, 3tr tog) in top of next 3tr tog,* rep from * to * 4 more times, ss in top of first 2tr tog. (6 pairs of petals)

ROUND 3: 3ch, (2tr tog, 5ch, 2tr tog) in same place as base of first 3ch, *ss in 7ch sp, skip 3tr tog, (2tr tog, 5ch, 3tr tog, 5ch, 2tr tog) in top of next 3tr tog,* rep from * to * 4 more times, ss in 7ch sp, 2tr tog in same place as base of first 3ch of round, 5ch, ss in first 2tr tog. (6 flowers completed) Fasten off B. Join C to ch closing 3tr tog at top of any flower.

ROUND 4: 3ch, 1sc in same place, *5sc in 5ch sp, 2sc tog over next two 2tr tog (omitting ss between petals), 5sc in 5ch sp,# (1sc, 2ch, 1sc) in ch closing next 3tr tog,* rep from * to * 4 more times, then once again from * to #, ss in first of 3ch. (13sc on each side)

ROUND 5: Ss in 2ch sp, 3ch, 1sc in same ch sp, *1sc in each of 13 sts, (1sc, 2ch, 1sc) in 2ch sp,* rep from * to * 4 more times, 1sc in each of 13 sts, ss in first of 3ch. (15sc on each side)

Fasten off C.

GARLAND HEXAGON \/

Yarn: DK yarn in mid-pink (A), dark pink (B), and gray (C)

METHOD

First flower
Using A, make a slip ring.
ROUND 1: 4ch, [1dc in ring, 1ch] 9 times, ss in 3rd of 4ch, pull end to close ring. (20 sts)
ROUND 2: 4ch, [1sc in next dc, 3ch, skip 1ch] 9 times, ss in first of 4ch. (Ten 3ch loops)
Fasten off.

2nd flower
Using B, work as first flower to end of round 1.
ROUND 2: 4ch, [1sc in next dc, 3ch, skip 1ch] 7 times, [1sc in next dc, 1ch, ss in 3ch loop of first flower, 1ch, skip 1ch] twice, ss in first of 4ch.
Fasten off.

Remaining flowers
Make 3rd flower in A, 4th flower in B, and 5th flower in A, joining each to previous flower at two loops as shown on chart. Make 6th flower in B, joining to 5th and first flowers as shown, to form a circle.

Center
With RS facing, join C to any empty 3ch loop inside circle, 5ch, 5dtr tog over next 5 empty 3ch loops. Fasten off.

Outer edge
With RS facing, join C to 3rd of 5 empty 3ch loops on any flower.
ROUND 1: 6ch, 1dc in same 3ch loop, *1ch, 1sc in next 3ch loop, 3ch, 2tr tog over (next 3ch loop and first empty 3ch loop of next flower), 3ch, 1sc in next 3ch loop, 1ch,# (1dc, 3ch, 1dc) in next 3ch loop*, rep from * to * 4 more times, then once again from * to #, ss in 3rd of 6ch.
ROUND 2: Ss in 3ch sp, 3ch, 1sc in same ch sp, *1sc in next dc, 1sc in 1ch sp, 1sc in sc, 3sc in 3ch sp, 1sc in 2tr tog, 3sc in 3ch sp, 1sc in sc, 1sc in 1ch sp, 1sc in dc,# (1sc, 2ch, 1sc) in 3ch sp at corner,* rep from * to * 4 more times, then once again from * to #, ss in first of 3ch. (15sc on each side)
Fasten off C.

Specific symbol
5dtr tog

189 SWIRLING HEXAGON \/

Yarn: DK yarn in yellow (A), cream (B), and green (C)

METHOD

Using A, make 12ch, join with ss into a ring.

ROUND 1: 1ch, 23sc in ring, ss in first ch. (24 sts)
Fasten off A. Join B to any sc.

ROUND 2: 9ch, *skip first sc, 1sc in next sc, turn, 1ch, 5sc
in ch sp, turn, 1ch, skip 1sc, 1sc in each of 4sc, 1sc in 1ch
(petal made), skip 1sc of round 1,# 1dc in next sc, 6ch,*
rep from * to * 4 more times, then once again from * to #,
ss in 3rd of 9ch. (6 petals)

Fasten off B. Join C to 6ch sp at end of any petal.

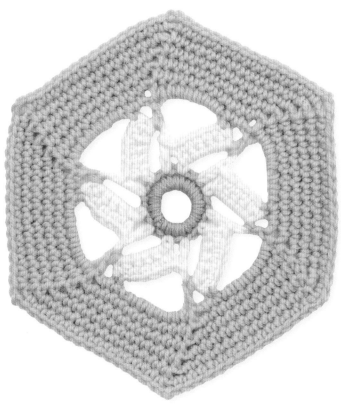

ROUND 3: 5ch, [1sc in 1ch at tip of same petal, 7ch, 1dc in
6ch sp at end of next petal, 2ch] 5 times, 1sc in 1ch at tip
of same petal, 7ch, ss in 3rd of 5ch.

ROUND 4: 3ch, *1sc in 2ch sp, 1sc in next sc, 7sc in 7ch sp,#
1sc in dc, 2ch,* rep from * to * 4 more times, then once
again from * to #, ss in first of 3ch. (10sc on each side)

ROUND 5: 3ch, *1sc in 2ch sp, 1sc in each sc to next 2ch sp,
2ch,* rep from * to * 4 more times, 1sc in 2ch sp, 1sc in
each sc, ss in first of 3ch. (11sc on each side)

Repeat round 5 four more times. (15sc on each side)
Fasten off C.

Yarn: DK yarn in yellow (A), green (B), and cream (C)

METHOD
SPECIFIC ABBREVIATIONS

SPC = starting popcorn made of 3ch, 3dc.
PC = 4dc popcorn.

Using A, make 6ch, join with ss into a ring.
ROUND 1: SPC in ring, [3ch, PC in ring] 5 times, 3ch, ss in top of SPC.
Fasten off A. Join B to any 3ch sp.
ROUND 2: 5ch, [5dc in next ch sp, 2ch] 5 times, 4dc in next ch sp, ss in 3rd of 5ch.
ROUND 3: Ss in 2ch sp, 5ch, 1dc in same ch sp, *1dc in each of 2dc, 1ch, skip 1dc, 1dc in each of 2dc,# (1dc, 2ch, 1dc) in next 2ch sp,* rep from * to * 4 more times, then once again from * to #, ss in 3rd of 5ch.
Fasten off B. Join C to any 2ch sp.
ROUND 4: (SPC, 3ch, PC) in 2ch sp, *3ch, PC in next 1ch sp, 3ch,# (PC, 3ch, PC) in next 2ch sp,* rep from * to * 4 more times, then once again from * to #, ss in top of SPC.
Fasten off C. Join B to any corner 3ch sp between 2 PC in same place.

ROUND 5: 5ch, 2dc in same ch sp, *[1ch, 3dc in next 3ch sp] twice, 1ch,# (2dc, 2ch, 2dc) in corner 3ch sp,* rep from * to * 4 more times, then once again from * to #, 1dc in next ch sp, ss in 3rd of 5ch.
ROUND 6: Ss in 2ch sp, 5ch, 1dc in same ch sp, *(1dc, 1ch, 1dc) in each of three 1ch sps,# (1dc, 2ch, 1dc) in next 2ch sp,* rep from * to * 4 more times, then once again from * to #, ss in 3rd of 5ch.

ROUND 7: Ss in 2ch sp, 5ch, 1dc in same ch sp, *[1dc between next and foll dc, 3dc in 1ch sp] 3 times, 1dc between next and foll dc,# (1dc, 2ch, 1dc) in 2ch sp,* rep from * to * 4 more times, then once again from * to #, ss in 3rd of 5ch. (15dc on each side)
Fasten off C.

191 THISTLE CIRCLE \/

Yarn: DK yarn in green (A), crimson (B), and gray (C)

METHOD
SPECIFIC ABBREVIATION
PS = 4hdc puff stitch.

Using A, make a slip ring.
ROUND 1: 4ch, [1dc in ring, 1ch] 15 times, ss in 3rd of 4ch, pull end to close ring. (32 sts)
ROUND 2: 5ch, [1FPtr in next dc, 2ch, 1dc in next dc, 2ch] 7 times, 1FPtr in next dc, 2ch, ss in 3rd of 5ch. (48 sts)
ROUND 3: 3ch, *[2dc tog, 2ch, 1FPtr, 2ch, 2dc tog] in next FPtr,# 1dc in next dc, * rep from * to * 6 more times, then once again from * to #, ss in 3rd of 3ch.

ROUND 4: Ss in sp before next 2dc tog, 7ch, *skip (2dc tog, 2ch), PS in next FPtr, 5ch,# 2dc tog inserting hook between next 2dc tog and 1dc, then between same dc and foll 2dc tog; 4ch,* rep from * to * 6 more times, then once again from * to #, 1dc between 2dc tog and 7ch, ss in 3rd of 7ch.
Fasten off A. Join B to any 2dc tog.
ROUND 5: 2ch, *7tr in next PS, 1ch,# 1sc in next 2dc tog, 1ch,* rep from * to * 6 more times, then once again from * to #, ss in first ch. (80 sts)

Fasten off B. Join C to 1ch sp to right of any sc.
ROUND 6: 2ch, skip 1sc, 1dc in next 1ch sp, *5ch, 1sc in center tr of 7, 5ch,# 2dc tog over (next 1ch sp and foll 1ch sp),* rep from * to * 6 more times, then once again from * to #, ss in first dc. (96 sts)
ROUND 7: 1ch, *5sc in 5ch sp, 1sc in next sc, 5sc in 5ch sp,# 1sc in 2dc tog,* rep from * to * 6 more times, then once again from * to #, ss in first ch. (96 sts)
Fasten off C.

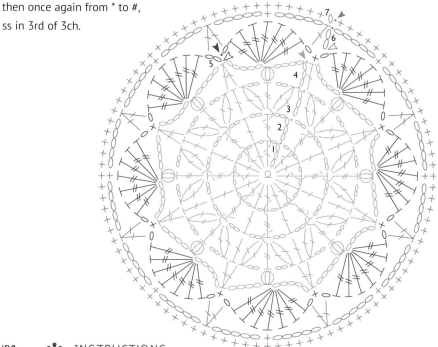

Yarn: DK yarn in navy (A), pink (B), and beige (C)

METHOD

Using A, make 8ch, join with ss into a ring.

ROUND 1: 1ch, 15sc in ring, ss in first ch. (16 sts)

ROUND 2: 2ch, 1dc in same place as base of 2ch, [5ch, skip 1sc, 2dc tog in next sc] 7 times, 5ch, skip last sc, ss in first dc. (Eight 5ch sps)

Fasten off A. Join B to any 5ch sp.

ROUND 3: 1ch, (1hdc, 1dc, 2tr, 1ch, 2tr, 1dc, 1hdc, 1sc) in same ch sp, (1sc, 1hdc, 1dc, 2tr, 1ch, 2tr, 1dc, 1hdc, 1sc) in each of 7 rem ch sps, ss in first ch. (8 petals)

Fasten off B. Join C to 1ch sp at tip of any petal.

ROUND 4: 5ch, [1tr between next 2sc where petals join, 4ch, 1sc in next 1ch sp, 4ch] 7 times, 1tr between 2sc, 4ch, ss in first of 5ch.

ROUND 5: 5ch, 1dc in same place as base of these 5ch, *2ch, (1dc, 2ch, 1dc) in next tr, 2ch,# (1dc, 2ch, 1dc) in next sc,* rep from * to * 6 more times, then once again from * to #, ss in 3rd of 5ch.

ROUND 6: Ss in 2ch sp, 3ch, 2dc in same ch sp, 3dc in each 2ch sp, ss in 3rd of 3ch. (96 sts)

Fasten off C.

Yarn: DK yarn

METHOD
SPECIFIC ABBREVIATION
PC = 4dc popcorn.

Make 4ch, join with ss into a ring.

ROUND 1: 3ch, 15dc in ring, ss in 3rd of 3 ch.

ROUND 2: 6ch, 1dc in st at base of these ch, 1ch, *PC in next dc, 1ch, (1dc, 3ch, 1dc) in next dc, 1ch,* rep from * to * 6 more times, PC in last dc, 1ch, ss in 3rd of 6ch.

ROUND 3: Ss in next ch sp, 8ch, 1dc in same ch sp, *1ch, PC in next dc, 1ch, skip 1PC, PC in next dc, 1ch,# (1dc, 5ch, 1dc) in next 3ch sp,* rep from * to * 6 more times, then once again from * to #, ss in 3rd of 8ch.

Round 4: Ss in next ch sp, 10ch, 1dc in same ch sp, *1ch, PC in next dc, 1ch, skip 2PC, PC in next dc, 1ch,# (1dc, 7ch, 1dc) in next 5ch sp,* rep from * to * 6 more times, then once again from * to #, ss in 3rd of 10ch.

ROUND 5: Ss in each of next 4ch, 6ch, *PC in 1ch sp between next 2PC, 5ch, 1sc in next 7ch sp, 5ch,* rep from * to * 7 more times, ss in first of 6ch.

ROUND 6: Ss in next ch sp, 1ch, 5sc in same ch sp, 6sc in each ch sp, ending ss in first ch of round. (96 sts)

Fasten off.

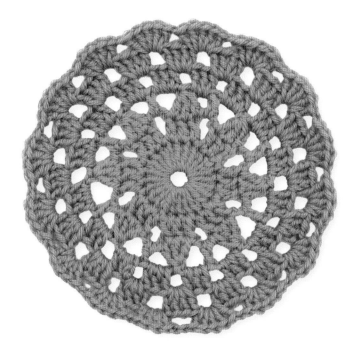

Mix and match 193 + 194

Yarn: DK yarn in orange (A) and blue (B)

METHOD

Using A, make a slip ring.

ROUND 1: 3ch, 23dc in ring, ss in 3rd of 3ch, pull end to close ring.

ROUND 2: 3ch, 1dc in each of 2dc, 3ch, [1dc in each of 3dc, 3ch] 7 times, ss in 3rd of 3ch.

ROUND 3: 2ch, 2dc tog over next 2dc, [3ch, 1dc in 3ch sp, 3ch, 3dc tog over next 3dc] 7 times, 3ch, 1dc in 3ch sp, 3ch, ss in first 2dc tog of round.

Fasten off A. Join B to any 3ch sp before a single dc.

ROUND 4: 4ch, [3dc in next 3ch sp, 1ch] 15 times, 2dc in same ch sp as beg of round, ss in 3rd of 4ch.

ROUND 5: Ss in 1ch sp, 4ch, [4dc in next 1ch sp, 1ch] 15 times, 3dc in same ch sp as beg of round, ss in 3rd of 4ch.

ROUND 6: Ss in 1ch sp, 4ch, [5dc in next 1ch sp, 1ch] 15 times, 4dc in same ch sp as beg of round, ss in 3rd of 4ch. (96 sts) Fasten off B.

BUTTERFLY CIRCLE

Yarn: DK yarn in green (A), orange (B), and navy (C)

METHOD

Using A, make 7ch, join with ss into a ring.

ROUND 1: 3ch, 15dc in ring, ss in 3rd of 3ch. (16dc)

ROUND 2: 6ch, skip 1dc, 1sc in next dc, [5ch, skip 1dc, 1sc in next dc] 6 times, 2ch, skip 1dc, 1dc in first of 6ch. (8 loops)

ROUND 3: 4ch, *(1sc, 5ch, 1sc) in next 5ch sp, 3ch,* rep from * to * 6 more times, 1sc, 5ch, ss in first of 4ch.

Fasten off A. Join B to any 5ch loop.

ROUND 4: 3ch, 2tr tog in same ch loop, *skip 3ch loop, (3tr tog, 11ch, 3tr tog) in next 5ch loop,* rep from * to * 6 more times, 3tr tog in first ch loop, 5ch, 1ttr in 2tr tog at beg of round. (16 groups = 8 pairs of wings)

Blocks may be joined using the joining with picots method.

ROUND 5: *(2dtr tog, 3ch, 1 loose hdc, 3ch, 2dtr tog) in st closing next group, ss in 6th of 11ch,* rep from * to * 7 more times, working final ss in top of ttr.

Fasten off B. Join C to any 3ch sp before a loose hdc.

ROUND 6: 1ch, 3sc in same ch sp, *1sc down through center of loose hdc, 4sc in next 3ch sp, 1ch, 1sc between next 2 groups, 3ch, ss in last sc, 1ch, 4sc in next 3ch sp,* rep from * to * 6 more times, 1ch, 1sc between 2 groups, 3ch, ss in last sc, 1ch, ss in first ch of round. (96 sts)

Fasten off C.

Specific symbol

$+$ 1sc through center
of stitch below.

Yarn: DK yarn in yellow (A), orange (B), pink (C), and beige (D)

METHOD

SPECIFIC ABBREVIATIONS

BS = bullion stitch: [yo] 5 times, insert hook as directed, yo, pull through all 6 loops on hook.

PC = 5tr popcorn.

Using A, make a slip ring.

ROUND 1: 4ch, 15tr in ring, ss in 4th of 4ch, pull end to close ring. (16 sts) Fasten off A. Join B to any tr.

ROUND 2: 4ch, [BS in next tr, 1ch] 15 times, BS in same place as base of 4ch, ss in 3rd of 4ch. (32 sts) Fasten off B. Join C to any 1ch sp.

ROUND 3: 3ch, [skip BS, 1sc in next 1ch sp, 2ch] 15 times, ss in first of 3ch. (48 sts)

ROUND 4: Ss in 2ch sp, 4ch, 4tr in same ch sp, remove hook from working loop and insert through 4th of 4ch, catch working loop and pull it through (starting PC made), [4ch, skip 1sc, PC in next 2ch sp] 15 times, 4ch, ss in top of starting PC. (16PC, 80 sts) Fasten off C. Join D to any 4ch sp.

ROUND 5: 1ch, 4sc in same ch sp, [1ch, skip PC, 5sc in next ch sp] 15 times, 1ch, skip PC, ss in first ch. (96 sts)

ROUND 6: 4ch, skip 1sc, *BS in next sc, 1ch, skip 1sc, 1dc in next sc, 1dc in 1ch sp,# 1dc in next sc, 1ch, skip 1sc,* rep from * to * 14 more times, then once again from * to #, ss in 3rd of 4ch.

ROUND 7: 1ch, 1sc in each st and 1ch sp all around, ending ss in first ch. (96 sts) Fasten off D.

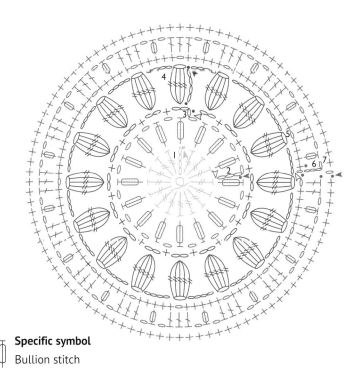

Specific symbol
Bullion stitch

Yarn: DK yarn in purple (A), orange (B), and beige (C)

METHOD
SPECIFIC ABBREVIATION
PC = 4tr popcorn.

Using A, make a slip ring.
ROUND 1: 3ch, 15dc in ring, ss in 3rd of 3ch, pull end to close ring. (16 sts)
ROUND 2: 4ch, (1dc, 1ch) in each of 15dc, ss in 3rd of 4ch. Fasten off A. Join B to any 1ch sp.
ROUND 3: 4ch, 3tr in same ch sp, remove hook from working loop and insert through 4th of 4ch, catch working loop and pull it through, [3ch, PC in next ch sp] 15 times, 3ch, ss in 4th of 4ch at beg of round.
Fasten off B. Join C to any 3ch sp.
ROUND 4: 1ch, 3sc in same ch sp, [5ch, 4sc in next ch sp] 15 times, 2ch, 1dc in first ch of round.
ROUND 5: 1ch, [4ch, 1sc in next 5ch loop] 15 times, 4ch, ss in first ch of round.
ROUND 6: Ss in next 4ch sp, 1ch, 4sc in same ch sp, [5ch, 5sc in next ch sp] 15 times, 5ch, ss in first ch of round.
Fasten off C.

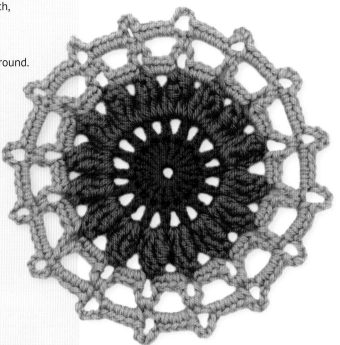

Yarn: DK yarn in blue (A) and green (B)

METHOD
SPECIFIC ABBREVIATION
BO = 4dc bobble.

Using A, make 4ch, join with ss into a ring.

ROUND 1: 4ch, [1dc in ring, 1ch] 7 times, ss in 3rd of 4ch. (16 sts)

ROUND 2: 1ch, [BO in next 1ch sp, 1ch, 1sc in next dc] 7 times, BO in next 1ch sp, 1ch, ss in first ch. (8 bobbles)

ROUND 3: 4ch, 1dc in same place as base of these ch, *1ch, skip BO and foll ch, (1dc, 1ch, 1dc) in next sc,* rep from * to * 6 more times, 1ch, skip BO and foll ch, ss in 3rd of 4ch.

ROUND 4: 1ch, 1sc in same place, [BO in next 1ch sp, 1ch, 2sc in next dc] 15 times, BO in next 1ch sp, ss in first ch. (16 bobbles)
Fasten off A. Turn work over and join B to first of any 2sc. Right side is now facing.

ROUND 5: 4ch, 1dc in same place as base of these ch, [1ch, skip BO and foll ch, 1dc in next sc, 1ch, 1dc in next sc] 15 times, 1ch, skip BO and foll ch, ss in 3rd of 4ch. (64 sts)

ROUND 6: Ss in 1ch sp, 4ch, 1dc in same sp, *2ch, skip (1dc, 1ch, 1dc), (1dc, 1ch, 1dc) in next 1ch sp, * rep from * to * 14 more times, 2ch, skip (1dc, 1ch, 1dc), ss in 3rd of 4ch. (80 sts)

ROUND 7: Ss in 1ch sp, 4ch, 1dc in same sp, *3ch, skip (1dc, 2ch, 1dc), (1dc, 1ch, 1dc) in 1ch sp,* rep from * to * 14 more times, 3ch, skip (1dc, 2ch, 1dc), ss in 3rd of 4ch. (96 sts)

ROUND 8: 1ch, [1sc in 1ch sp, 1sc in next dc, 3sc in 3ch sp, 1sc in next sc] 15 times, 1sc in 1ch sp, 1sc in next dc, 3sc in 3ch sp, ss in first ch. (96 sts)
Fasten off B.

Specific symbol
↶ Turn over work.

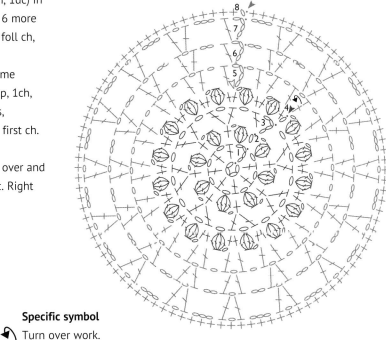

DANDELION CIRCLE \/

Yarn: DK yarn in orange (A) and green (B)

METHOD

Using A, make a slip ring.

ROUND 1: 5ch, [1tr in ring, 1ch] 14 times, ss in 3rd of 4ch, pull end to close ring. (30 sts) Fasten off A. Join B to any tr.

ROUND 2: 1ch, 1sc in each ch sp and tr all around, ss in first ch. (30 sts)

ROUND 3: 1ch, 1sc in each of 2sc, [9ch, skip 2sc, 1sc in each of 3sc] 5 times, 9ch, skip 2sc, ss in first ch. (Six 9ch loops) Fasten off B. Join A to center sc of any 3sc.

ROUND 4: 3ch, 2tr tog over first and 3rd ch of 9ch loop, *9ch, 5tr tog over [7th and 9th ch of same 9ch loop, center sc of 3sc, first and 3rd ch of next 9ch loop],* rep from * to * 4 more times, 9ch, 2tr tog over [7th and 9th ch of same 9ch loop], ss in 2tr tog.

Specific symbol

Slip stitch in space below

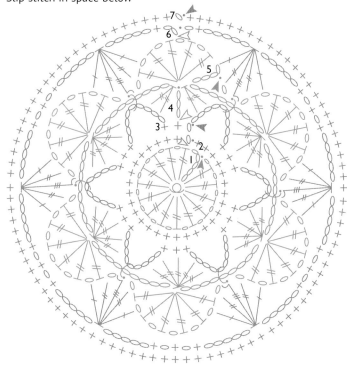

ROUND 5: 4ch, [1tr, 1ch] 5 times in ch closing first 2tr tog of round 4, ss in 9ch loop of round 3 (enclosing ch of round 4), *1ch, [1tr, 1ch] 6 times in ch closing next 5tr tog, ss in 9ch loop of round 3 (enclosing ch of round 4),* rep from * to * 4 more times, 1ch, ss in 3rd of 4ch. (6 flowers complete) Fasten off A. Join B to center 1ch sp at top of any flower.

ROUND 6: 2ch, skip 1tr, 1sc in 1ch sp, *5ch, work 5 sts tog: (1dc in next 1ch sp, 1tr in foll 1ch sp, 1dtr in sp below ss of round 5 [enclosing chs of rounds 4 and 5], 1tr in next 1ch sp, 1dc in foll 1ch sp), 5ch,# [1sc in next 1ch sp, 1ch, skip 1tr] twice, 1sc in next ch sp,* rep from * to * 4 more times, then once again from * to #, 1sc in next 1ch sp, 1ch, skip 1tr, ss in first of 2ch. (96 sts)

ROUND 7: 1ch, 1sc in 1ch sp, 1sc in next sc, *5sc in 5ch sp, 1sc in 5 sts tog, 5sc in 5ch sp,# [1sc in next sc, 1sc in 1ch sp] twice, 1sc in next sc,* rep from * to * 4 more times, then once again from * to #, 1sc in next sc, 1sc in 1ch sp, ss in first ch. (96sc) Fasten off B.

Yarn: DK yarn in yellow (A) and beige (B)

METHOD

Using A, make 6ch, join with ss into a ring.

ROUND 1: 1ch, [3ch, 2tr in ring, 3ch, 1sc in ring]
3 times, 3ch, 2tr in ring, 3ch, ss in first ch of round.
(4 petals)

Fasten off A. Join B to sc between any 2 petals.

ROUND 2: 6ch, 1dc in same place, [3ch, skip 1 petal,
(1dc, 3ch, 1dc) in next sc] 3 times, 3ch, skip 1 petal,
ss in 3rd of 6ch. (8 loops)

ROUND 3: 4ch, [3dc in next 3ch sp, 3ch, 1sc in next
dc, 3ch] 7 times, 3dc in next 3ch sp, 3ch, ss in first
of 4ch. (8 petals)

Fasten off B. Join C to any sc before 3dc worked in a
ch sp over a petal.

ROUND 4: Work behind round 3: 1ch, [4ch, skip
1 petal, 1sc in next sc] 7 times, 4ch, ss in first ch.

ROUND 5: 6ch, [6tr in next 4ch sp, 2ch] 7 times,
5tr in last 4ch sp, ss in 4th of 6ch.

ROUND 6: Ss in 2ch sp, 8ch, ss in 4th ch from hook,
1tr in same ch sp, *1tr in each of 6tr, (1tr, 4ch, ss in
4th ch from hook, 1tr) in next 2ch sp,* rep from * to
* 6 more times, 1tr in each of 6tr, ss in 4th of 8ch.
Fasten off C.

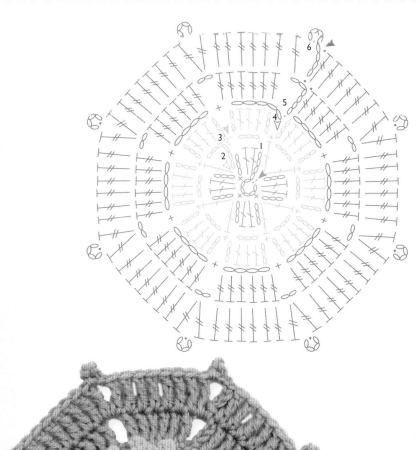

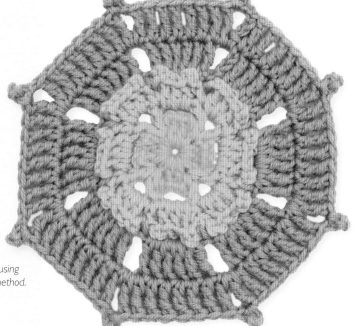

*Blocks may be joined using
the joining with picots method.*

TECHNIQUES

This chapter provides useful information about yarns, hooks, abbreviations, and chart symbols. There are also some notes to help you brush up on your crochet skills, as well as advice on assembling and finishing off your work for the best results.

TOOLS AND MATERIALS

Few materials and minimal equipment are needed to make the designs in this book.

YARN

Yarns are available in a range of weights, from lace weight to super bulky. Because yarns may vary from one manufacturer to another and certainly change from one fiber to another, generic yarn types are used in this book. You should be aware of the characteristics of different fibers, however, from the fullness of cotton to the elasticity of wool. Because the construction of a yarn will affect its behavior, this will also influence the end result. Try using as many different yarns as possible until you are confident.

The weight of yarn you choose together with the hook size will dictate the finished size of the item you make. If the finished size is important to you, such as for the floral blocks, always make a test swatch to check the size and feel of the crocheted fabric.

Most yarns have a paper band or tag attached with vital information such as the weight of the ball or skein, fiber composition, length of yarn on each ball, and how to look after your finished item. Keep this for future reference.

You can combine different types of yarn in many of the projects. The Moulin Rouge sunflower combines worsted-weight cotton and wool with lightweight fringed synthetic yarn. The stem and leaves are made from pure wool for felting.

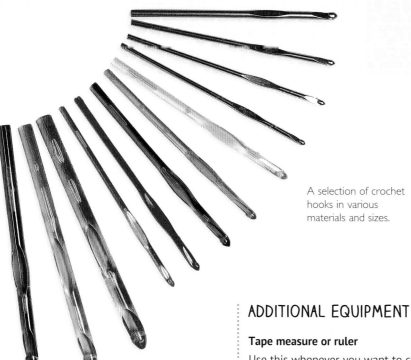

A selection of crochet hooks in various materials and sizes.

Hook sizes

Hook sizes are not specified in this book, and the size of hook you choose will vary depending on the type of yarn you are using. Check the ball band of the yarn for the recommended size. If a metric knitting needle size is given, choose a crochet hook of a similar metric size. For a tighter fabric on small items, use the smallest size recommended or a size smaller than usual for all of the designs in this book except for the blocks. If particularly small hooks are required, this is indicated in the instructions. If in doubt, use a smaller hook size than usual.

CROCHET HOOKS

Crochet hooks are the most important tools in your collection. Good quality crochet hooks are smooth and free of snags, and feel comfortable in your hand.

Crochet hooks are available in a range of materials, such as aluminum, bamboo, plastic, and resin. Aluminum hooks work well with woolly and fuzzy yarns, whereas bamboo hooks can help to control smooth, slippery yarns. Hooks are also made in different styles, such as with a flattened thumb rest, or (for small metal hooks) a wider wooden or plastic handle. Try out the different styles to see which suits you best.

ADDITIONAL EQUIPMENT

Tape measure or ruler
Use this whenever you want to check the size of your crochet.

Markers
Use these to indicate a repeat, to help count stitches, or to mark the beginning of rounds. Alternatively, use a short length of yarn in a contrasting color.

Scissors
Choose a small, sharp-pointed pair of scissors to cut yarn and trim ends neatly.

Pins
Use long, large-headed pins for pressing, blocking, and holding pieces together for sewing up.

Yarn needles
For sewing seams and weaving in yarn ends, you need a blunt-tipped sewing needle with a large eye.

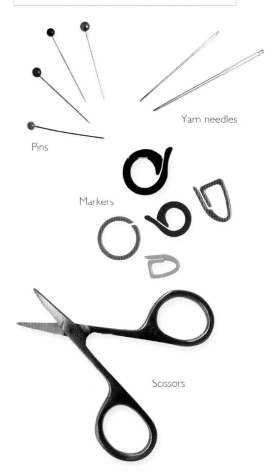

Pins

Yarn needles

Markers

Scissors

CROCHET TECHNIQUES

This section is not a lesson in crochet. It is simply a reminder of a few basics, together with some suggestions and techniques that might be new to an inexperienced crocheter.

SLIPKNOT

Wrap the yarn into a loop, insert the hook into the loop, catch the yarn with the hook, and pull it through. Tighten the loop to form a slipknot; this secures the yarn to the hook.

FOUNDATION CHAIN (CH)

Wrap the yarn over the hook and pull it through the slipknot to form a new loop on the hook. This is the first chain stitch. Make the number of chain stitches specified in the pattern. Each V-shaped loop on the front is one chain stitch. The loop on the hook (the working loop) is not counted as a stitch.

WORKING IN ROWS

Crochet may be worked back and forth in rows.

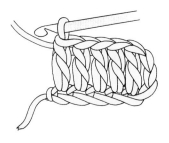

1 Using a foundation chain as the base, with the specified number of chains nearest the hook forming the first stitch, work a stitch into each subsequent chain from right to left. The illustration shows a first row of double crochet, with three chains forming the first stitch.

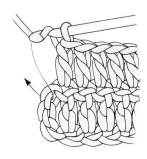

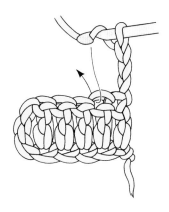

2 Turn the work and make the specified number of chains to form the first stitch of the next row (here, three chains). Be careful to work the second stitch in the right place, as instructed in the pattern. In this example, the second stitch is worked into the second stitch on the previous row. However, if the second stitch was worked into the stitch immediately below (that is, into the first stitch on the previous row), this would be the equivalent of making two stitches in the same place and would result in an increase.

3 The last stitch of this row is worked into the top chain of the three chains that formed the first stitch on the previous row. When you have completed the crochet, cut the yarn about 6in (15cm) from the last stitch. Wrap the yarn over the hook and pull the yarn end through the loop on the hook. Gently pull the yarn to tighten the last stitch.

WORKING IN ROUNDS

When working in rounds, you can start with a ring of chain stitches or with a loop of yarn called a slip ring. You then work counterclockwise around the ring to form a circular or tubular piece of crochet.

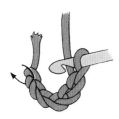

Chain ring

1 Make a short length of foundation chain as specified in the pattern. Join the chain into a ring with a slip stitch by inserting the hook into the first chain, catching the yarn, and pulling it through the chain and the loop on the hook.

2 Work the first round of crochet stitches into the center of the ring, not into the chains, unless specified otherwise. At the end of the round, the final stitch is usually joined to the first stitch with a slip stitch.

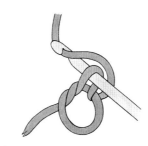

Slip ring

Coil the yarn around two fingers to form a ring and use the hook to catch the yarn and pull it through. Make a chain stitch to anchor the ring (shown above). Work the first round of stitches into the ring, then pull the starting yarn end to close the center.

Fastening off invisibly

Instead of using a slip stitch to join the final round, fasten off the yarn after the last stitch. Thread the end onto a yarn needle and pass it under the top loops of the first stitch of the round and back through the center of the last stitch.

Concentric rounds or a spiral

When crocheting in the round, you can either work in concentric rounds or in a spiral. For concentric rounds, join the last stitch of each round to the first stitch of the round with a slip stitch. For a spiral, omit the final slip stitch and work continuously so that the lines of stitches spiral outward. The pattern will tell you which method to use. In both cases, you may find it helpful to use a marker to indicate the start of each round.

SWITCHING FROM ROUNDS TO ROWS

This technique is used to form the tails of some of the fish in this book. There should be an even number of stitches in the round. Pinch the work flat between your fingers and make one chain. Then insert the hook into the next stitch on the front and the next stitch on the back of the flattened piece and work a single crochet. Repeat for the next pair stitches and so on.

BASIC STITCHES

All crochet stitches are based on a loop pulled through another loop by a hook. There are only a few stitches to master, each of a different length. Here is a concise guide to the basic crochet stitches used to make the projects in this book.

Slip stitch (ss)
Insert the hook into the specified stitch, wrap the yarn over the hook, and pull it through the stitch and the loop on the hook.

Single crochet (sc)
Insert the hook into the specified stitch, wrap the yarn over the hook, and pull it through the stitch (2 loops on hook). Yarn over hook and pull it through both loops.

Half double crochet (hdc)
Yarn over hook, insert the hook into the specified stitch, yarn over hook, and pull it through the stitch (3 loops on hook). Yarn over hook and pull it through all three loops.

Double crochet (dc)
Yarn over hook, insert the hook into the specified stitch, yarn over hook, and pull it through the stitch (3 loops on hook). *Yarn over hook and pull it through two loops; repeat from * once more.

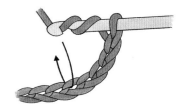

Treble crochet (tr)
Yarn over hook twice, insert the hook into the specified stitch, yarn over hook, and pull it through the stitch (4 loops on hook). *Yarn over hook and pull it through two loops; repeat from * twice more.

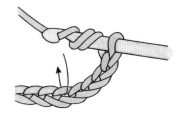

Double treble crochet (dtr)
Yarn over hook three times, insert the hook into the specified stitch, yarn over hook, and pull it through the stitch (5 loops on hook). *Yarn over hook and pull it through two loops; repeat from * three times more.

Triple treble crochet (ttr)
Yarn over hook four times, insert the hook into the specified stitch, yarn over hook, and pull it through the stitch (6 loops on hook). *Yarn over hook and pull it through two loops; repeat from * four times more.

SIMPLE VARIATIONS

Basic stitches may be varied in many ways to achieve different effects. Crochet stitches are usually worked by inserting the hook under the two strands of yarn at the top of the stitch, but simple variations can be made by inserting the hook in different places.

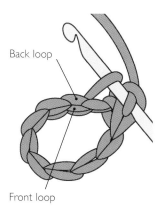

Back loop

Front loop

Front and back loops

Each crochet stitch has two strands of yarn that form the top of the chain or other crochet stitch—these are usually referred to as the front and back loops or strands. Work under one of these loops only when specified. Note that the front loop is the one nearest you, not necessarily at the front (right side) of the work.

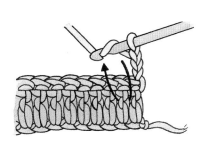

Around the front post (FP)

Work around the stem of the stitch, inserting the hook through the work from front to back, around the post, and to the front again.

Into a chain space (ch sp)

Insert the hook into the space below a chain or chains. Here, a treble crochet is being worked into a chain space.

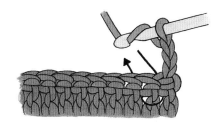

Around the back post (BP)

Work around the stem of the stitch, inserting the hook through the work from back to front, around the post, and to the back again.

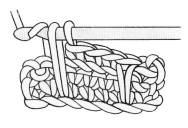

Into a row below (spike stitch)

Spike stitches are made by inserting the hook one or more rows below the previous row. To work a single crochet spike stitch, for example, insert the hook as directed by the pattern, wrap the yarn over the hook, and pull it through. Lengthen the loop to the height of the working row, then complete the stitch.

Flexible fabric

Working in the back loops creates a thinner, more pliant fabric, with a row of loops remaining unworked on one side. These loops can come in handy when securing loose ends or other structural pieces. Working only in the back loops also makes it easier to generate curves in the fabric. For the fish and other small three-dimensional creatures, you may achieve a better result by working in the back loops only—make some test pieces and experiment until you get a result you are happy with.

SPECIAL STITCHES

By working multiple stitches in the same place or working several stitches together at the top, or a combination of both, you can create interesting shapes, patterns, and textures.

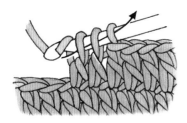

Decrease (e.g. 2sc tog, 3dc tog)

Work the specified number of stitches in the place or places indicated in the pattern, but omit the final stage (the last yarn over) of each stitch so that the last loop of each stitch remains on the hook. Wrap the yarn over the hook and pull it through all of the loops on the hook. The method is the same for all the basic crochet stitches.

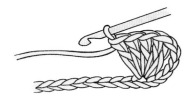

Increase (e.g. 5dc in next ch)

This technique is used to increase the total number of stitches when shaping an item, or to create a decorative effect such as a shell. Simply work the required number of stitches in the same place.

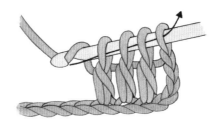

Cluster

A cluster is a decorative group of stitches joined together at the top by using exactly the same technique as a decrease.

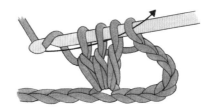

Bobble

A bobble is a group of double crochet or longer stitches worked in the same place and joined together at the top by using the same technique as a decrease. Sometimes a chain stitch is worked after completing the decrease to close the bobble.

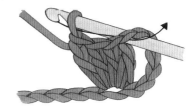

Popcorn

A popcorn is a group of double crochet or longer stitches worked in the same place, and then folded and closed at the top so that the popcorn is raised from the background. Work the specified number of stitches in the same place. Take the hook out of the working loop and insert it under both top loops of the first stitch of the popcorn. Pick up the working loop with the hook and pull it through to fold the group of stitches and close the popcorn at the top.

Puff stitch

A puff stitch is a group of half double crochet stitches worked in the same place and joined together at the top by using the same technique as a decrease.

CHANGING COLORS

There are several methods you can use to join in a new yarn or color.

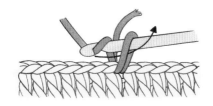

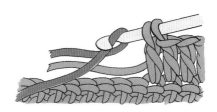

Changing color on a row

1 Using the old color, omit the final stage (the last yarn over) of the final stitch of the row, so that there are two loops on the hook. Wrap the new color over the hook and pull it through the loops on the hook to complete the stitch.

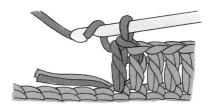

2 Continue working with the new color. You may find it easier to knot the two loose ends together before you cut the yarn no longer in use, leaving ends of about 4in (10cm). Always undo the knot before weaving in the yarn ends.

Changing color on a round

METHOD 1 (ABOVE): Insert the hook where required and pull up a loop of the new color, leaving a 4in (10cm) tail. Make one chain, then continue with the new yarn.

METHOD 2: When joining the last stitch of the round to the first stitch using a slip stitch, work the joining slip stitch with the new color.

Tip

When a pattern tells you to join a new yarn to any stitch on the previous row or round, it is a good idea to join the new yarn to a stitch well away from the yarn end of the previous color. This avoids having a bunch of yarn ends all in the same place, and makes it easier to enclose the ends neatly on the next row or round, or to weave them in later.

ROUND CORDS

These are two methods of making nice round cords by slip stitching into chain, each with a slightly different character.

METHOD 1: With the flat, V-shaped front of the chain toward you, skip one chain, then slip stitch under two strands of each chain.

METHOD 2: Ignore the V-shaped strands, on the front of the chain, skip one chain, then slip stitch into the single looped strand at the back of each chain.

The Sweet Pea stems are made by slip stitching into a length of chain stitches. Whether you slip stitch into the front or back of the chains is up to you.

FINISHING TECHNIQUES

All of the designs in this book are easy to assemble using just a few standard finishing techniques. Here are some tips and suggestions.

Floral block designs made with picots on the last round can be pressed or blocked after joining them together using the picot method.

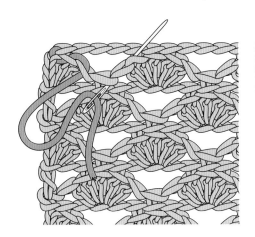

WEAVING IN YARN ENDS

When ends of yarn will not be used for seaming, you may be able to enclose some of them while working the piece. If not, the ends should be woven in on the wrong side after completion. When making any project, read through the pattern first and think ahead, leaving a long end of yarn where it will be useful for sewing a seam.

Use a yarn needle to weave in ends, and always weave in for at least 2in (5cm) to prevent the end from slipping out again. For smooth, slippery yarns, reverse the direction and weave back again for a few stitches. Trim off the excess. On lacy pieces, change direction to suit the pattern so that the tail will not show on the right side.

PRESSING OR BLOCKING

Pressing or blocking can be used to improve the neatness of the stitches and to help the finished crochet fabric hold its shape. Both techniques involve pinning the fabric into the correct size or shape. Depending on the fiber content of the yarn and whether the stitch pattern is textured or not, you can either press with an iron or, in the case of blocking, apply water or steam to help set the stitches.

Pressing

You can press any yarns labeled on the ball band with a recommended ironing temperature (usually natural fibers). Pin out the piece into the required shape or size on a well-padded surface, such as an ironing board or folded blanket. Pin the piece wrong side uppermost if it is textured. Lightly press the crochet, taking care to lift and replace the iron rather than moving it around on the surface. Avoid pressing raised areas of stitches. Some yarns recommend pressing under a damp cloth for steam. If so, allow to dry before unpinning.

Blocking

Ease and pin the piece into shape on a well-padded surface, then either steam with an iron or spray with cold water, depending on the fiber content of the yarn. Alternatively, the piece can be hand-washed in lukewarm water before pinning out. Always be guided by the ball band of the yarn. When in doubt, choose a cold-water method for blocking synthetic fibers. Allow the piece to dry completely before unpinning.

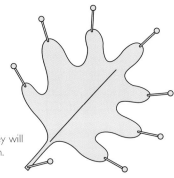

Glass-headed pins are ideal because they will withstand the heat and steam of an iron.

SEAMS

Yarn ends are immensely useful for sewing seams, but if a new length of yarn needs to be joined, start with a backstitch rather than a knot. Unless stated otherwise, mattress stitch on the right side is recommended for most projects. When assembling blocks, consider using a crochet seam.

Overcasting

Using a yarn needle, insert the needle into the back loops of corresponding stitches. For extra strength, work two stitches into the end loops.

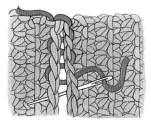

Mattress stitch

Lay the pieces with the edges touching and wrong sides facing upward. Using a yarn needle, weave back and forth around the centers of the stitches, without pulling the stitches too tight.

Backstitch

Hold the pieces with right sides together. Using a yarn needle, work a line of backstitches along the edge.

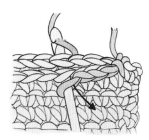

Crochet seams

Join the pieces with wrong sides together for a visible seam, or with right sides together for an invisible one. Work a row of slip stitch (shown above) or single crochet through both top loops of each piece. When working this method along the side edges of blocks worked in rows, work enough evenly spaced stitches so that the seam is not too tight.

JOINING BLOCKS WITH PICOTS

Some of the floral blocks are worked with picots on the outer edges and are designed to be joined together as work progresses. The blocks are joined where corresponding picots meet, giving an open, lacy effect.

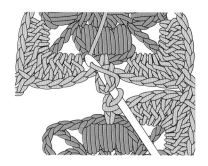

Work the first block as instructed. Then work the second block as far as the first picot to be joined, and work to the central chain of the picot—for example, on a 5ch picot, work 2ch.

With the right side of the first block facing up, insert the hook from below, through the center of the corresponding picot, and work a slip stitch, which counts as 1ch (shown above). Complete the picot, then continue the final round of the second block to the next picot to be joined.

Continue in this way as required, then complete the final round of the second block and fasten off. Where several blocks meet together, insert the hook into the picot diagonally opposite.

The Monarch Butterfly has yarn antennae and its body is lightly stuffed with leftover yarn.

STUFFING

Some of the projects in this book are shaped by stuffing. Leftover matching yarn makes ideal stuffing because there will be no show-through. Either stuff with cut-up pieces of yarn or wind off short lengths of yarn and push these in, one coil at a time.

Alternatively, you can use batting or synthetic toy stuffing, such as polyester fiberfill. Push the stuffing in firmly, one wisp at a time, using it to shape the item without distorting it. Too much stuffing will pack down, whereas too little will never plump up. Don't push the batting in with a pointed implement, but use something like the eraser end of a pencil.

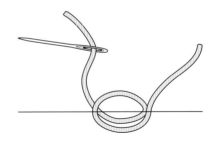

ANTENNAE

A couple of the small critters in this book require yarn antennae. Insert the yarn needle at the position of the first antenna, leaving a yarn end. Bring the needle out at the position of the second antenna, backstitch between the two, then bring the yarn out again at the second antenna position. Trim both ends.

If desired, you can stiffen the antennae by pinning out straight and spraying with a fabric stiffener or strong hairspray. Allow to dry. Bobby pins can also be bent into the shape of antennae (or insect legs) and inserted through the knitting.

WIRING

Some items need a little help to stay in shape, and wiring is the solution. Wire is also used to create the features of some of the small critters in this book. You may also wish to wire petals and leaves to make them easier to bend and sculpt.

You can use craft, jewelry, or florist wire, all of which come in a wide range of colors and gauges (thicknesses). Choose a fine wire, such as 24 gauge (0.5mm), and simply pass the wire through the stitches (around the outer edges of a petal or leaf, for example); you may find it easier to thread the wire into a yarn needle to do this.

Where stronger wire is needed, be careful not to leave a burr when snipping the wire because this will make it difficult to insert. A small file, even an old nail file, can be used to smooth away a burr. Use pliers to twist and tuck the ends of wire safely away.

You can also thread wire through a flower stem to make it bendable, but for adding stronger support to stems for holding them upright in a vase, try inserting clear vinyl tubing (available at hardware and plumbing supply stores) with a couple of pieces of thick wire threaded through.

Caution

Remember that you should never wire an item that is intended for use by children.

The Snail is stuffed with batting. Fine wire is inserted into the horns to make them bendable, and small beads sewn onto the ends to finish them.

EMBROIDERY, BEADS, AND SEQUINS

Although the designs in this book are perfectly fine left undecorated, it can be fun to add extra special details, such as embroidery, beads, and sequins. There is a huge variety of decorative embroidery stitches to choose from. To make the stitches really stand out, use a double strand of yarn or thread to work them.

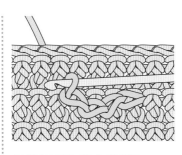

The spots on the Flying Ladybug's wings are made with French knots. Bobby pins are used to form the legs.

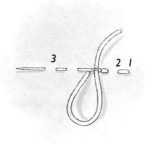

Running stitch

To work a line of running stitch, bring the needle up at 1, down at 2, and up again at 3. Continue in this way for length required.

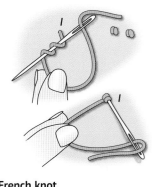

French knot

Bring the needle up at 1 and wind the thread twice (or number of times specified) around the needle tip (top). Holding the thread, insert the needle very close to—but not exactly at—1 and pull through gently (bottom).

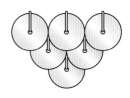

Sequins and beads

Use "invisible" nylon thread to sew on sequins and matching sewing thread for beads. If the holes are too small for a regular sewing needle, use a beading needle to sew them on.

Beads are best anchored with a backstitch. To sew on sequins for fishscales, start at the tail end and, alternating sequins on each row, overlap them as you stitch. Overlapping them more closely will give a truly scaly effect but will add weight.

The Goldfish has shimmering fishscales made from flat sequins, and larger faceted sequins for eyes.

SURFACE CROCHET

Holding the yarn at the back of the work, insert the hook from front to back through the fabric in a space between two stitches. Pull through a loop. Insert the hook between the next two stitches and pull another loop through both the fabric and the first loop on the hook (like working a chain or slip stitch). Work around the posts of stitches, through gaps between stitches, or as specified in the pattern.

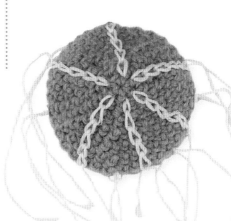

The pattern on the Phosphorescent Jellyfish's cap is made using the surface crochet technique.

ABBREVIATIONS AND CHARTS

The main abbreviations and symbols are listed here for easy reference. Additional ones are explained alongside the patterns.

Abbreviations

alt	alternate
beg	begin(ning)
BO	bobble
BP	back post
ch	chain
ch sp	chain space
dc	double crochet
dec	decrease
dtr	double treble crochet
foll	following
FP	front post
hdc	half double crochet
inc	increase
rem	remain(ing)
rep	repeat
RS	right side of work
sc	single crochet
sp	space
ss	slip stitch
st(s)	stitch(es)
tog	together
tr	treble crochet
ttr	triple treble crochet
WS	wrong side of work
yo	yarn over
* #	asterisks and hash symbols mark a set of instructions to be repeated
( )	round brackets indicate a group of stitches to be worked together or a stitch count
[ ]	work instructions in square brackets the number of times stated after the brackets

Chart symbols

○ ◯	slip ring
⬭	chain
•	slip stitch
+	single crochet
T	half double crochet
⊤ (double crochet)	double crochet
(treble crochet)	treble crochet
(double treble crochet)	double treble crochet
(triple treble crochet)	triple treble crochet
	cluster (e.g. cluster of 4dc)
	bobble (e.g. bobble of 5dc)
	popcorn (e.g. popcorn of 5dc)
(puff stitch)	puff stitch (e.g. puff of 5hdc)
⋈	through back loop (e.g. sc)
⋈	through front loop (e.g. sc)
⌇	front post (e.g. FPdc)
⌇	back post (e.g. BPdc)
→	direction of work
◁	For sunflowers and floral blocks: starting point/join new color
◀	For sunflowers and floral blocks: fasten off
◀	For all other patterns: start of row or round when it is not immediately apparent

Arrangement of symbols

JOINED AT TOP
A group of symbols joined at the top indicates that these stitches should be worked together at the top, as in cluster stitches, and for decreasing the number of stitches (e.g. 3dc tog or 4dc cluster).

JOINED AT BASE
Symbols joined at the base should all be worked into the same place below (e.g. 2sc in same stitch or 5dc shell).

JOINED AT TOP AND BASE
Sometimes a group of stitches are joined at both top and base, making a bobble, popcorn, or puff.

ON AN ANGLE
Symbols may be drawn at an angle, depending on the construction of the stitch pattern.

DISTORTED SYMBOLS
Some symbols may be lengthened, curved, or spiked, to indicate where the hook is inserted below (e.g. 1BPsc or 1FPtr).

READING CHARTS

Most of the designs in this book are accompanied by a chart, which should be read together with the written instructions. The chart represents the right side of the work.

Charts in rows

Each chart should be read from the lower edge upward, progressing in the same way as the work. All right-side rows are read from right to left, and all wrong-side rows are read from left to right. In most cases but not always, the first and all odd-numbered rows are right-side rows and start on the right.

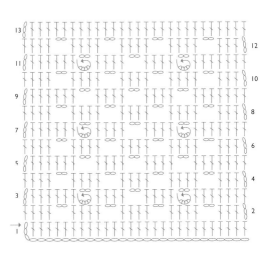

The Embossed Flower Square is an example of a chart where the beginning row starts at the bottom left, making it a wrong-side row.

Charts in rounds

Charts for working in the round begin at the center and are read counterclockwise (in the same direction as working) unless stated otherwise.

Read each round of the Little Gem sunflower chart in a counterclockwise direction.

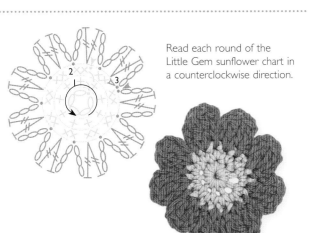

The charts for the center disks of large sunflowers such as Tweed Giant are split into two, one for the front and one for the back.

Charts for 3D sunflowers

Some of the sunflowers have center disks that can be stuffed to make a 3D flower. These disks are worked as a single piece, increasing outward from the center front and then decreasing inward to the center back. Where possible, these disks are shown in the form of a single chart. However, for reasons of clarity and space, a few of the larger ones have been drawn as two separate charts—front and back.

Read the front chart counterclockwise in the usual way, but read the back chart clockwise (to visualize why this is the case, hold an apple with the stalk at center front and draw a counterclockwise spiral around it; continue the spiral around to the back of the apple, where you will see that it runs clockwise). The outer round of the front chart is repeated (in a paler color) as the outer round of the back chart. This is so that you can see clearly where the stitches of the subsequent round should be worked. Do not work this round twice.

INDEX

CREDITS

All photographs and illustrations are the copyright of Quarto Publishing plc. While every effort has been made to credit contributors, Quarto would like to apologise should there have been any omissions or errors – and would be pleased to make the appropriate correction for future editions of the book.

Yarn suppliers

DEBBIE BLISS
www.designeryarns.uk.com
www.knittingfever.com

DMC CREATIVE WORLD
www.dmc.com

LION BRAND YARN
www.lionbrand.com

ROWAN AND JAEGER YARNS
www.westminsterfibers.com

SUBLIME
www.sublimeyarns.com